Politics and Cinema

POLITICS AND CINEMA

ANDREW SARRIS

NEW YORK
COLUMBIA UNIVERSITY PRESS
1978

Library of Congress Cataloging in Publication Data

Sarris, Andrew.
  Politics and cinema.

  Includes index.
  1. Moving-pictures—Political aspects—Addresses,
essays, lectures. 2. Moving-pictures—Reviews.
I. Title.
PN1995.9.P6S2   791.43'7   78-16334
ISBN 0-231-04034-2

The article entitled "Politics and Cinema" originally appeared under the title "My
Criticism, My Politics" in the February 1978 issue of *American Film*. Reprinted with
permission from *American Film*, American Film Institute, John F. Kennedy Center,
Washington, DC 20566.

"Marilyn, by Norman Mailer" first appeared as a book review in *The Washington
Post* (August 1973). Copyright © 1973 *The Washington Post.*

"Sixties Cinema: Zoomshots, Jumpcuts, Freeze Frames, and Girls, Girls, Girls!" first
appeared in *Rolling Stone*, issue no. 148, November 22, 1973. Copyright © 1973
Straight Arrow Publishers, Inc. All rights reserved. Reprinted by permission.

All others reprinted by permission of *The Village Voice*. Copyright © 1971, 1972,
1973, 1974, 1975, 1976, 1978 *The Village Voice*, Inc.

Columbia University Press
New York—Guildford, Surrey

Contents

1

CONTENTS

Politics and Cinema

Dreiser and James: with that juxtaposition we are immediately at the dark and bloody crossroads where literature and politics meet.

—Lionel Trilling, *Reality in America*

The sin of nearly all left-wingers from 1933 onwards is that they have wanted to be anti-Fascist without being anti-totalitarian.

—George Orwell, 1944

Introduction

AS I LOOK BACK ON my critical ruminations I am surprised to discover that the political animal in me persisted long after I started walking on the yellow brick road beyond the silver screen. My late father had brought me up to believe that politics and business were manly activities whereas the arts were strictly for sissies and empty-headed womanizers. My earliest fantasies and "ideas" were therefore political rather than artistic. I wish neither to exaggerate my father's influence nor to suggest that it was at all unusual in American experience. Although my father was a Greek immigrant his notions of what was serious and what was frivolous fitted in very snugly with the Puritan tradition. His attitude toward movies was appropriately utilitarian. The theme, the moral, the message, if you will, were all-important. The style? If my father ever thought of *that* slithery word it would have been in connection with women's fashions. That I would one day become a certified scholar of cinematic style never entered his mind or mine back in the supposedly formative years when one imagines that one's destiny can be freely and logically determined. Growing up as I did in the heady atmosphere of political debate at the kitchen table I had no way of anticipating the long, discouraging years in which I scrounged for a living as a scribbler. Thus when I gladly settled for becoming a chronicler of shadows I was still haunted by memories of more substantial concerns.

I generally date myself as a movie reviewer by noting that my first pieces were published in 1955, the year in which the essayistic voices of James Agee and Robert Warshow were stilled forever. By citing this odd coincidence I do not mean to imply that my criticism rushed in to fill a cultural vacuum caused by the loss of two legendary figures in the field. Film criticism was not taken all that seriously in the mid-fifties, and even Agee and Warshow were insufficiently appreciated until their collected writings were published posthumously. Since then their influence has been enormous, of course, and in many ways they have proved to be irreplaceable. I certainly do not claim to be their direct descendant either stylistically or ideologically. This kind of kinship must be conferred upon a critic by critics of critics. What I did inherit from Agee and Warshow—and from many of their predecessors and contemporaries as well—was a skeptical attitude toward the claims of politics on the cinema.

For the past half century these political claims have been mostly liberal, leftist, anarchistic, and even methodically Marxist. Rightists, by and large, have preferred to express their opposition to the alleged redness of movies with the blue pencil of censorship. Religious people have tended to mistrust the medium itself as the work of the devil rather than turn it to their own uses. This is not to say that a classically reactionary cinema has not always existed, particularly in Hollywood. But the terms in which even this cinema was discussed presupposed a generally leftward orientation in both the writer and the reader. Hence, the critical debate has raged not so much between left and right as between politics and aesthetics. After all, even workaday reviewers have to take a stand eventually against bad movies with good intentions. Otherwise they will find themselves marked for moral blackmail. What? You don't want to reelect Roosevelt? You don't want to stop Hitler? You don't want to prevent World War III? You don't want to end the Vietnam War? You don't want to help the poor? You don't want to end racial discrimination? To this litany of leading questions the allegedly apolitical critic can invoke the sacred abstraction of Art above all other considerations. And if D. W. Griffith be deemed a racist and a bigot, so was Shakespeare. As for social significance it is quite clear that *Uncle Tom's Cabin* changed more hearts and minds than *Moby Dick*, but Harriet Beecher Stowe does not therefore rise above Herman Melville in our literary estimations. Jean Renoir once remarked ruefully that he had made *La Grande Illusion* in 1936 as his statement against war, and in 1939 Europe went to war.

Actually, one seldom encounters in the seventies the resounding rhetoric of social consciousness and socialist realism so common in the thirties and the forties. Absurdism, alienation, anomie have become so much the order of the day in high art that the Old Left's evangelical exhortations to the common man and the little people now seem naive and sentimental. The very subtle anti-Stalinism of Agee and Warshow in the forties and the fifties is difficult to appreciate in the rather easily cynical seventies atmosphere in which all forms of authority are suspect. The God that Failed some time between the slaying of Trotsky and the subjugation of Czechoslovakia has never been resurrected as a monolithic object of faith. The encrusted solidarity of the Old Left has been replaced by the jagged fragmentation of the New Left. There is less talk of One World and more talk of the Third World. One hardly ever hears *The Internationale* even being hummed anymore as a common anthem of the Left. One hears instead a never ending concert of individualistic folk songs. Hence, the subordination of personal expression to social communication is no longer the article of faith it once was. The artist has been joined in the ivory tower by the terrorist. The once supposedly subversive workers have been transformed by their middle-class values into a counterrevolutionary force called labor. The Okies who fled to California in *The Grapes of Wrath* have become the staunchest supporters of Ronald Reagan.

I am constantly reminded by my academic experiences of the widening generation gap between the world in which I grew up and the world in which I am growing old. When I first started teaching film history in the mid-sixties the mention of the name McCarthy to my students meant only Gene, and not Joe. By the mid-seventies my students had forgotten Gene as well. Hence, I have had to assign readings in Eisenstein and Pudovkin and Rotha and Kracauer and Spottiswoode and Reisz and Lindgren and Balasz and Manvell and Sadoul and Grierson and Wright and Arnheim so that all these forgotten Marxist film historians and aestheticians could provide a frame of reference for my own revisionist theories on the cinema. But is that enough? Or does all history, and not just film history, have to come back to life for old ideas to make sense? I would like to be able to slide back into the past with a casualness born of confidence in my readers. Too often, however, I am accused of pedantry and obscurantism for my efforts.

Why then do I persist in perceiving both myself and the film medium in the Heraclitian flux of history? I suppose because I am a revisionist in the most restless sense of constantly revising myself. Consequently, every movie I have ever seen keeps swirling and shifting in ever changing contexts. On the whole, most movies tend to be more complex than profound, but this makes them all the more difficult to pin down, describe, and categorize for all time. What is particularly fascinating is how the same movie can keep changing its ideological coloration over the years. In our own time, for example, many movies once dismissed as shopgirl fantasies have been rediscovered as feminist parables. In the seventies perspective of *From Reverence to Rape: The Treatment of Women in the Movies*, Molly Haskell challenged the thirties left-wing sexism of the late John Grierson in his review of Anthony Asquith's *Dance, Pretty Lady*:

Grierson, admitting the film was a "delight to the eye," nonetheless deplored its subject: "This is it, bless you. Claptrap about a virginity. Why the entire sentiment that makes a plot like that possible went into discard with the good, prosperous, complacent Victoria. It was, relatively, an important matter then. But it is mere infant fodder now when you consider the new problems we carry in our bellies, and think of the new emphases we must in mercy to ourselves create out of our different world." Apparently the way to a socially conscious critic's heart is through his stomach. A woman's virginity (infant fodder, indeed!), and where and how she lost it, is at least as important as the high and mighty manly themes of the films Grierson approved of.

Similarly, Lotte Eisner has reappraised the cinema of Weimar Germany virtually in opposition to the invidious treatment of the same subject by the late Siegfried Kracauer in *From Caligari to Hitler*, perhaps the most famous single book ever written on film content. I began my own film studies by being profoundly influenced by Grierson and Kracauer and even the very socially conscious Bosley Crowther of *The New York Times*. But by the time I began writing my own criticism I had drifted away from their social gospel toward a more romantic approach to movies. Simply by looking at movies again and again I began to see them in terms of recurring myths and fables deep within our psyches rather than as transient impressions of the surface of our society. Also, I began to realize that the cinema did not faithfully record all the realities of politics. The intricacies of economics, for example, did not lend themselves to cinema any more than they do now to television. (Note the boredom on an anchorman's face when he has to discuss a capital budget.) The bureaucratic tedium of political organization is similarly less accessible to the camera than the visual pyrotechnics of a bloody revolution. And few so-called political movies have utilized rhetoric more analytical or more ambiguous than the lyrics of the *Marseillaise*. It is almost invariably the People Yes against Them. Class hatred is disguised as egalitarianism, and nationalism as populism. Up to now, however, very few political movies have been genuinely subversive. The enormous expense of production, and the publicity attendant on exhibition make it mandatory for films to be in tune either with their society or with at least a sympathetic subculture within that society. Hence, the cinema of the left in most Western countries is largely the product of bourgeois self-hatred. It is also often a question of cosmopolitanism at war with provincialism, xenophilia at war with xenophobia, the alienated artist at war with the pious philistine.

As a New York-based critic I have been aware from the beginning that most of my reading constituency constituted a disaffected part of America. One could cater to this constituency or defy it. Out of some innate perversity in my temperament I chose to defy it. I cannot fully explain why. It just seemed the thing to do at the time. The rest is rationalization. If I might speculate on my motives and tactics, however, I could begin with the atmosphere of cranky individualism around *Film Culture* and *The Village Voice*, the publications in which my pieces first appeared. The readership at first seemed to be remote and unfathomable. Consequently, there was no ideological accountability. Since I was not getting paid for my reviews my editors could hardly demand a craven conformity. From a professional standpoint I was on skid row, but as far as freedom and even licence were concerned I had stumbled into a writer's Eden. I was free to indulge both my ethnic emotionalism and my Morningside Heights reflectiveness. My criticism became my autobiography. But even as I began to write my criticism the medium was steadily losing its social relevance. As the sociologists deserted the cinema for television, the aestheticians replaced them. The ultilitarian criteria for movies became obsolete as individual cans of films were perceived more and more as art objects. As old movies became increasingly accessible the "timeliness" of new movies was more clearly perceived as a trivial factor.

In the past two decades, therefore, a critic has not required much courage to pooh-pooh the political intentions of films. Yet politics never entirely disappeared as a cause of concern for even the most aesthetically minded commentator. For one thing there were political struggles among the aestheticians themselves. My espousal of the *auteur* theory in film history has aroused passions as fierce as any in more substantively political debates. For another, I managed to write a great deal about the gap between the political content of cinema and the political content of reality. Indeed, much of the critical discourse of the past half century has been involved with the sometimes fruitful and sometimes frightful tensions between fact and fiction, reality and truth, sincerity and authenticity. Film itself can best be understood in terms of its unresolved dialectics. From the very beginning the literalness of the medium contradicted the fancies of the art form. The documentary nature of the image strained against the dramatic and narrative conceits of the continuity. Painterly composition warred with the illusion of kinesis. Purely formal strategies became the stuff of polemics.

Thus, the late Andre Bazin revolutionized film aesthetics by suggesting that deep focus was more "democratic" than cross-cutting. A whole generation of film critics grew up with the revisionist credo that montage was manipulative. Consequently, a filmmaker could preach liberation in his content, and yet practice repression in his form. Jean-Luc Godard once stated that there could be a moral issue in the choice between a cut and a camera movement. In 1970 I came as close as I ever have to combining my aesthetical politics with my political politics in a single confessional statement:

> It would seem that my strongest instincts are Christian rather than Marxist and that I believe more in personal redemption than social revolution, and therefore I am more moved by the majestic camera movements of Mizoguchi and Ophuls than by the meteoric montage of Eisenstein and Resnais. The ascending and descending staircases of Hitchcock are more meaningful than all the Odessa Steps.

Of course, a preoccupation with form for its own sake involves a political decision of sorts in that one can hardly regard such a preoccupation as urgently revolutionary. Indeed, it can be argued that all films are ultimately political either as statements or as evasions. When one looks back on the cinema of the sixties one is startled by the infrequency with which Vietnam was mentioned. Yet this infrequency is in itself significant in that it reflects a society emotionally detached from that particular war. I suppose that there is an active and passive way to interpret this information. The active way is to scold the film industry for not making more movies about Vietnam. The passive way is to report the reluctance of the studios as a symptom of the public's lack of interest in the war. My way has always tended to be the passive way. I have never believed that it is the critic's function to dictate the subject matter of the creator. If I want a certain movie to be made I should make it myself, and not hector someone else into making it. This is to say that if I wish to partake of creation I must cease being a critic and become a creator or at least the collaborator of a creator.

Jean-Luc Godard and other radical filmmakers of the sixties proposed a choice between art and revolution. One could not have both. Tom Stoppard has made much the same point in *Travesties* by counterposing Joyce and Lenin. Again, this either/or attitude of the sixties has tended to reduce the political obligations of film. Of course, many people brought up in the thirties and forties when the artist was supposed to take up his place at the barricades with his art can never accept the apparent frivolity of purely formal criticism. A disdain for formal distinctions can be the mark of a political activist. It can be the mark also of a philistine. The result is the same. The cinema becomes merely a pretext for political discussion on the most superficial level.

I would be less than candid, however, if I did not concede that my aesthetics were more deeply rooted in my politics than I had at first imagined. Whether I regard myself as a Christian, a liberal, a skeptic, a centrist, or a dedicated democrat, I tend to prefer tinkering with society to smashing it to smithereens. I choose to live with the injustices and inequalities of bourgeois capitalism for fear of losing the music of individual voices. Marxism, as the professed inheritor of historical forces, threatens the integrity of historical scholarship. When I look at the cinema that has been produced by the capitalistic system, and compare it with the cinema that has been produced under the aegis of Marxism, I conclude that the status quo is not only more pleasurable than what is likely to follow it after the revolution, but that the very flawed system in which I matured turns out to be essential to my continued existence. This very essay, filled with doubts, hesitations, and digressions, would be inconceivable in a society with more logical priorities.

I am driven therefore by the imperatives of my politics toward a relatively pluralistic aesthetic in which the very diversity of artistic styles is counted a blessing. As I gaze upon the cinematic configurations of Max Ophuls, Kenji Mizoguchi, Jean Renoir, Charles Chaplin, John Ford, Alfred Hitchcock, Orson Welles, Luis Bunuel, Robert Bresson, Carl Dreyer, Roberto Rossellini, Michelangelo Antonioni, Ingmar Bergman, Howard Hawks, Fritz Lang, Buster Keaton, Jean Vigo, D. W. Griffith, F. W. Murnau, Ernst Lubitsch, and hundreds of other immortals in my chosen medium, I find that no one of these artists sums up or towers above the others, and that each achieves full articulation only in company with all the others. The cinema as I understand it depends for its survival upon a civilization that possesses the largeness of spirit to preserve its past, warts and all. It is therefore not surprising that I have achieved a certain notoriety over the years for deflating the apocalyptic fantasies of the left. I have created unpleasant scenes at convocations of structuralists by arguing that individual artists are not slaves of the structures through which they burrow for beauty and truth. Yet there is no doubt that the debate with structuralism and, for that matter, within structuralism, is closer to the beginning than to the end. In the years to come we shall be forced to consider how narrative forms have conditioned our political perceptions. For me as a believer in individual destiny there has been relatively little conflict between my politics and aesthetics. I am only now beginning to understand the implications of this apparent harmony. My aesthetics have been my politics all along.

Politics and Cinema

SOCIOLOGICALLY inclined critics, mostly of the left, have long argued that even the most escapist movies manage to make statements about their society and its ideology. Hence the old *King Kong* was presumed to be the unconscious product of Freud's *Civilization and Its Discontents*, whereas the new *King Kong* has been reportedly programmed to illustrate Fanon's *Wretched of the Earth*. *The Graduate* was considered "significant" precisely because it evaded the ills of Vietnam, and poor *Caligari* was blamed by Kracauer for helping bring on Hitler through sheer morbidity. Back in 1935, William de Mille concluded whimsically: "So the Mickey Mousians of today will be the New Dealers of tomorrow, whereas the Popeyesians will breed a race of fascists."

Through the years most Hollywood movies have been castigated by the left for crimes of omission, for not treating the problems of *real* people, for not fighting the good fight against fascism, militarism, capitalism, and imperialism. For their part, the old Hollywood moguls squelched their critics with the stock answer: If you have a message, send it by Western Union. (Little did they know that Western Union's service was destined to go the way of the dodo.) Many movies were thus caught in a tug of war between edification and entertainment, between problem raising and happy endings. Under these conditions, relatively few movies turned out to be overtly political.

Of late, however, there has been a settling of old accounts on film and in print, with history being written and rewritten by its various witnesses. *The Front* opened up the Pandora's Box of McCarthyism in the fifties; *The Memory of Justice* attempted to relate the Nuremberg Trials to the later moral decline of the West; the blacklisting of Diana Trilling by Lillian Hellman's publishing house reopened the old wounds incurred by Trotskyists and Stalinists in their travails of decades past.

My own political position—rabidly centrist, liberal, populist, more Christian than Marxist, libertarian to the point of licentious-

9

ness—has been made abundantly clear in these confessional columns. From my vantage point in the muddled middle, I do not expect to convert many of the fans of the more flamboyant extremes on the left and the right. History can play strange and dirty tricks, and memories can differ dramatically and dialectically. Consequently, I can vouch only for my own reactions to the passing parade of partisanship, and I can fall back ultimately only on my own memories.

For some reason, *Our Leading Citizen*, a 1939 Bob Burns vehicle for Paramount, has lingered in my mind as a clue to the political language of its time. I remember seeing the movie with my parents and nodding along with them sympathetically as the homespun do-gooder Burns (the role he always played) ticked off the legitimate grievances of the lovable workers in their labor dispute with a callous, stuffed-shirt industrialist. (Capitalists still wore stuffed shirts in those days.) In the midst of all the boss-worker brouhaha there suddenly appeared a mysterious outsider who went around calling everyone "comrade" and urging more violent action to promote the strike. To this day I can recall my father and mother stiffening with resentment toward the intruder. In my innocence I thought that the comrade-caller was one of the good guys, and I was looking forward to the violence against the bad boss. But, obviously, something was wrong. I turned to my father for guidance. "He's a communist," he whispered. And, sure enough, this character turned out to be the vilest of villains in a movie that reflected Hollywood's traditional sympathy for workers as long as they didn't stay out on strike too long and otherwise make a fuss.

Many years later I read Meyer Levin's politically sophisticated review of *Our Leading Citizen* in an *Esquire* of 1939. Levin assumed that the outside agitator must have been an *agent provocateur* hired by the factory owner. Why? Simply because no labor organizer, communist or not, went around calling everybody "comrade." It just wasn't done. Hence, *Our Leading Citizen* was really a *right*-wing film. But what of the American left in movies? If you analyze the Clifford Odets scripts for *The General Died at Dawn* and *None But the Lonely Heart*, the contributions of the Hollywood Ten, and such non-Hollywoodian movies of the left as *Native Land* and *Salt of the Earth*, you will find no mention of the Communist Party, of Marx or Engels or Lenin or Stalin, of class struggles, of the proletariat, of dialectics and surplus value. In each instance, revolutionary language has been sanitized into populist puerilities. The precisely defined proletariat and peasantry become the vaguely felt "people" and "folk" or even just plain "folks." Similarly, the Americans who went off to fight in Spain on the Loyalist side formed not the Joe Hill Brigade or the Eugene Debs Brigade or the Bill Haywood Brigade or the Marx, Lenin, or Stalin Brigade, but the Abraham Lincoln Brigade and the George Washington Battalion. The enemy could be designated by the left as "fascism," but the alternative was never designated as "communism" or even "Marxism." Rather, it was the People Yes as they sought justice, liberty, freedom, equality, and true democracy, which had little to do with electoral processes.

Curiously, *The Front* establishes a more obscure definition for "front" than was in force during the McCarthy era, when "Communist Fronts" were "exposed" as either reputable organizations infiltrated by communists and their "sympathizers" or disreputable organizations with reputable titles as, for invented example, the Thomas Jefferson Society for the Preservation of Civil Liberties. Thus, the Popular Front rhetoric, which had flourished in the thirties and forties was made to sound sinister and devious in the fifties. McCarthy and the far more malignant McCarran had a field day as they flushed out alleged "subversives" from nobly named organizations. There was also more than a touch of anti-Semitism in the repeated suggestion that Jewish entertainers had an ulterior motive in changing their names when they broke into show business.

Having evolved from a rightist childhood to a centrist adulthood in the late forties, I became a fervent enemy of McCarthyism as a deadly menace to the Democratic Party and its liberal, populist traditions. Most Marxist recollections of the period seem to gloss over the dynamics of party politics in America. In this context, elections are merely bourgeois illusions of free choice, not nearly as thrilling as the monster rallies in Moscow, Peking, Havana, and Hanoi, where unruly pluralism has been sublimated into historical necessity. To this day an "After Hitler, Us" mentality pervades the American left, as made evident in the Hayden-Hayakawa axis in California against Tunney, and the mischief-making maverick candidacy of Gene McCarthy.

It is almost forgotten that Joe McCarthy was a Republican senator from Wisconsin, elected in 1946 after a close primary victory over La Follette with the help of the Communist Party, which was out to get La Follette for his legislative investigation of Communist infiltration into labor unions. Thus, in a marginal sense, McCarthy was a golem who turned with a vengeance on those who chose to use him for their own cynical purposes.

It is also almost forgotten that the right wing of the Republican Party and the right wing of the Democratic Party were united in the late forties and early fifties in an unholy coalition to destroy the last vestiges of the New Deal. To the Marxist revisionists, such leaders as Truman, Stevenson, Kennedy, Johnson, Humphrey, and now Carter were and are as bad or worse than Eisenhower, Nixon, Goldwater, and Ford, since the Democrats have resisted Soviet foreign policy even more strongly than have the Republicans. The more liberal and egalitarian domestic policies of the Democrats have counted for little with the left in this equation. Yet, if there had been no capital punishment in America in the twenties, maybe Sacco and Vanzetti would not have been executed. For that matter, if there had been no capital punishment in Germany in the thirties and forties, the Holocaust might have been averted. Thanks to the election of Nixon over Humphrey in 1968 and of Nixon over McGovern in 1972 and of the appointment of Nixon judges to the Supreme Court, capital punishment is about to return to America after a long hiatus.

My concern over this issue may strike the more oceanic of Marxist revisionists as a small ripple of reform. To my knowledge, no Marxist regime has dispensed with capital punishment and, at last reports, Madame Mao has joined Trotsky and Beria in the Inferno of the Revolution, if I may mix Dante with dialectics. George Orwell once criticized the communists for sawing off the limb they were sitting on when they disdained libertarian safeguards for those with whom they disagreed. Only a few years ago Marcuse was preaching a form of McCarthyism against "fascist" types, and I wonder how much difference there is between rightists of the fifties calling some people communist subversives and leftists of the seventies calling some people war criminals.

In this respect, Marcel Ophuls's *The Memory of Justice* might have been subtitled *We Are All War Criminals*. As history, it strikes me as even more dubious than *The Front*, which at least accepts the responsibiltiy for its distortions in the name of a very personal bitterness. Ophuls's tone is loftier and more knowing, but his theme is too large for his relatively loose treatment. Also, he makes the mistake of assuming that the Holocaust is a given in his moral propositions.

Quite the contrary. Anti-Semitism fourishes among many sectors of the New Left and the Third World as if there had been no Holocaust. I have met young people who regard the Holocaust as one of Daddy's tired World War II stories.

Somehow, Marcel Ophuls never interviews any of the people who have been persecuting and killing Jews for the past 30 years since the Holocaust, but instead scolds the British for Dresden, the French for Algeria, and the Americans for Vietnam, and somehow the Americans come out much worse than the Germans. In his interview about the film, Ophuls has declared that he fought against his producer's bias in favor of the Germans and against the Americans. Nonetheless, Marcel Ophuls's America seems to be a mixture of vulgar superpatriotism (Barbara Keating and the tacky American flags on her front lawn) and morbidly self-serving self-flagellation (Daniel Ellsberg fantasizing about presiding over Robert MacNamara's War Crimes Trial). By contrast, Speer—and even Goering—emerge as civilized renaissance men. At one point Ophuls asks pointedly why Speer keeps talking and writing about the Holocaust. The answer would seem to be simple. The more Speer talks about the Holocaust, the more he implicates us in it for somehow having let it happen. Perhaps Ophuls has been undone by his overfamiliarity with the subject. The idiot left likes nothing better than to brand its current enemies as exact replicas of Hitler, and I think that Ophuls has fallen unwittingly into the trap. Thus, whereas *The Sorrow and the Pity* soared into inspiring self-examination, *The Memory of Justice* sinks into debilitating self-pity. Perhaps the French have a special flair for dramatizing the moral dimensions of their existence. Perhaps the subject of collaboration challenges our preconceptions with factual surprises whereas the subject of justice merely dredges up our deepest prejudices and paranoid delusions. It would never occur to Ophuls (nor to me either) to ask Russian citizens why they tolerated Stalin and the Gulag Archipelago for so long. Even to ask a Russian about the Gulag Archipelago is to risk having him sent there.

My own skepticism about political films was accidentally fortified a few years ago when I discovered myself on the screen with a wine glass in hand in a Marcel Ophuls film about America in the late sixties and early seventies. This film, never released commercially in America, took as its opening premise Marcel Ophuls's return to America to discover what had happened to his forties classmates from Hollywood High. Specifically, a letter from the late Max Ophuls to his son Marcel was reproduced on the screen, and in it Marcel was advised to revisit America so as to understand his own identity. O-phuls tracked down his fellow alumni around America; some had become conformists, some noncomformists. And in the background were the violent demonstrations for peace, intergenerational under-standing, and racial justice. America seemed to be burning. Suddenly the camera shifted to an elegant West Side apartment where, among other Manhattanites, my wife and I were chattering frivolously be-tween sips of wine.

As I recall the occasion, Jules Feiffer had been kind enough to invite me to the party at Harold Hayes's apartment to meet Marcel Ophuls, the son of Max Ophuls, whose work I had toasted in the pages of *The Village Voice*. We arrived to find ourselves in the midst of a German television crew engaged in some undisclosed project. We were never quite sure where the party ended and the production began, and the scene became one of self-conscious confusion. My own reading of the party grouping was that it was more into radical chic than anything else. But that wasn't the impression given in the Marcel Ophuls film. Intercut with sequences of funky street riots, our relative placidity marked us as smug, self-pitying plutocrats, if not the exact American equivalents of the Good Germans of the Nazi era.

I do not believe that any undue malice was involved in this casual misrepresentation. There was simply not enough footage on the screen, nor enough words on the sound track, to describe the political, social, and psychological structure of our gathering more accurately. I mention this incident not out of any sense of personal grievance, but merely to mark one of the rare occasions on which I was on the inside looking out rather than on the outside looking in.

Yet Marcel Ophuls at least asks questions. By contrast, Lillian Hellman professes to know all the answers. She has transformed the art of self-deprecation into a form of self-glorification as she tries to make history itself conform to the pompous polemics of *The Chil-dren's Hour, The Little Foxes, Watch on the Rhine,* and *North Star.* She has now become the sum total of all her incredibly virtuous heroes and heroines in an incredibly villainous world. *Watch on the Rhine* was recently screened on television, and it was fascinating to listen to the Paul Lukas hero describing his profession as "anti-Fas-cist." Not "communist," mind you, or even "freedom fighter," but "anti-Fascist." One is reminded of Orwell's rueful words: "The sin of nearly all left-wingers from 1933 onward is that they have wanted to be anti-Fascist without being antitotalitarian." Of course, American right-wingers can be pilloried for wanting to be anti-Communist without being antitotalitarian, and they are so pilloried much of the time these days.

As a centrist, I see the left as a mirror image of the right in the realm of libertarianism. I hated Joe McCarthy. I hated the House Un-American Activites Committee. I hate all witch-hunts, and I hate all sectarian self-righteousness. I despised the movie moguls and the television tycoons for caving in to the mangiest "patriots" in residence. Sadly, the motion picture industry has a long history of Arbuckling under to any tinhorn moralist within mailing distance of the studios. Even today, the Motion Picture Association of America cowers before every two-bit district attorney in the boondocks. But when I look at *Watch on the Rhine* and *The North Star*, in which good leftists solemnly teach themselves the historical necessity of killing fascists and even obstacle-creating opportunists in cold blood, I conclude that the left has little to teach us about liberty or justice.

—February 1978

The Candidate

Cinema, like politics, makes strange bedfellows. Take *The Candidate*, for example. (I couldn't.) It so happens that I find myself more in critical harmony with Bella Abzug's recent blast in the kvetch section of the Sunday *Times* than with the raves for the film written by Vince Canby and most of his colleagues. I was away communing with the cosmic vibrations of the ocean when *The Candidate* opened to almost unanimous acclaim. Indeed, I have been told that there was spontaneous applause at a critic's screening. And yet most of the word of mouth I've heard from nonprofessional moviegoers has been bad. It may be that the critics have sold themselves a bill of goods only to find that the public isn't buying. But why would so many critics fall for a piece of cheese like *The Candidate*? Robert Redford cultism? Partly, I suppose. Redford seems to have convinced a great many people that he has more integrity than any other 30 actors put together. He comes down from his kingly mountain-top in Colorado only rarely and only reluctantly to mingle in the madding crowd for the sake of his muse. He never hangs around at Sardi's with all the other phonies trying to make the scene. No, he's too pure for that. Of course, he does take options on film properties, and currently he is campaigning for his slice of the profits in *The Candidate* with all the meditative monasticism of a Fuller Brush Salesman. But we never hear about this side of his soulful nature in all the interviews he manages to squeeze into his spiritual days. All we hear is how hard the corrupt world is trying to rape pure Robert, and how manfully Robert is resisting the rape; and, this, in short, is the main thesis of *The Candidate*.

Robert Redford plays a good-looking poverty lawyer named Bill McKay, who is minding his own business in sunny California with his black and chicano and eco-freak clients and a youthfully adoring staff when who should appear but Mephistopheles himself as Lucas (Peter Boyle), the bearded manipulator of bourgeois politicians. We never find out too much about Bill McKay beyond the fact that he is the son of a former governor (Melvyn Douglas) and hence tainted by heredity with the curse of electoral politics. Young McKay doesn't really want to run for senator. It's too much like selling out, but Lucas mysteriously persuades him to run with the promise of certain defeat. I say mysteriously because Jeremy Larner's script is very short on motivational rhetoric so that the why is generally fuzzy even when the what is reasonably lucid. Indeed, the best things in the movie are nasty insights into the systematic bruising of egos along the campaign trail: the losing liberal contender and his gallant family at the very beginning of the movie suggesting nothing so much as the faintly comical notion that family members that pose together too much for television begin to look too much like each other for real life; the semipolitical academic at a McKay rally trying to make it with a real-life Natalie Wood and being very sweetly shunted back into the academic woodpile; the staff subordinates standing up on their hind legs every so often for the sake of their self-respect, and then rocking back on their heels when their point has been made and ignored. It would seem that Larner's experiences with Gene McCarthy's children's crusade have permanently soured him on the political system.

Well and good, but *The Candidate* still doesn't qualify in my eyes and ears as "one of the few good, truly funny American political comedies ever made." Off the top of my head the following American movies strike me as better and/or funnier and/or more likeable than *The Candidate: Convention City, Mr. Smith Goes to Washington, Flamingo Road, The Great McGinty , Advise and Consent, The Best Man, State of the Union, The Manchurian Candidate, The Man Who Shot Liberty Valance, A Face in the Crowd, The Last Hurrah, The Phenix City Story, The Sun Shines Bright, A Lion Is in the Streets, Wilson, The Glass Key, Citizen Kane, The Great Man Votes, Judge Priest, The County Chairman, Meet John Doe, All the King's Men, Hail the Conquering Hero,* and even *The Man.* Which should indicate how low on the list I place *The Candidate*, but also how much more often Hollywood has dealt with politics than most reviewers realize. Some years ago Dwight Macdonald complained in his monthly *Esquire* column that there were very few American films about politics, and Stuart Byron promptly wrote in a long list, and Macdonald blithely printed the list with no suggestion of embarrassment. At the time Macdonald and I were engaged in a bitter feud, and I chose not to comment on this particular contretemps. As an animal probably more political than cinematic, Macdonald obviously fancied politics as a fascinating subject for movies, and despite Byron's solid research, the fact remains that a relatively small percentage of the American cinema has concerned itself explicitly with the political process, and for good reason. Most films on politics have not done nearly as well at the box office as they deserved to do. In this respect, films about politics are as jinxed as films about sports, and for much the same reason.

What is interesting about an election or an athletic event is not so much what *should* happen as what actually *does* happen. In the good old unconceited terms of movie morality, chess virtuoso Bobby Fischer should be the biggest heavy since Richard Widmark pushed the old lady down the stairs in *Kiss of Death*, but if he beats Spassky he will be king just the same and not knight-errant. Jack Nicklaus may not be as colorful as Arnold Palmer or Lee Trevino, but he is still probably the greatest golfer of all time. Similarly, uncharismatic Rod Laver is probably the greatest tennis player of all time; and cool, stolid, often petulant Kareem Jabbar has simply added a new dimension to basketball. I wouldn't pay a quarter to see any of these titans do their life story on the screen or regale me with their philosophical observations, but I'll walk a mile to watch them perform in the here and now. By the same token, I am presently sitting still for George McGovern's profile shots against Mount Rushmore (and does Frank Mankiewicz really keep a straight face through all this?) because I think McGovern is endowed with the will to win, and this year I'd go along with Bugs Bunny against Nixon, and so it's Go-George-Go with no moral compensations for second place.

And that is why I despise Robert Redford's mealy-mouthed reluctant virgin of a politician in *The Candidate*. I think Nixon can be beaten in 1972, but not by reluctant virgins and pure ideologues. At the very end of the movie, Redford's McKay has pulled an upset win over the reactionary incumbent, and all McKay can do is ask, "What do we do now?" Well, for one thing, Senator-elect McKay can go to the Senate and vote against the confirmations of Renquist, Powell, Burger, and Blackmun, and whatever new hanging judges Nixon has up his sleeve for his second term when he may be able to shape the Court for the rest of this century. McGovern himself just a week or two ago cast the deciding vote on the minimum-wage law, and less than half a dozen votes in the Senate separate the doves from the hawks on Vietnam.

Bill McKay's opponent Crocker Jarmon (Don Porter) is presented in the movie as somewhat to the right of Spiro Agnew, whereas McKay, compromises and all, is somewhat to the left of George Mc-Govern. Anytime a McKay can beat a Jarmon in California by fair means or foul, it would seem to be a cause for rejoicing. But not here. McKay has paid too high a price. He has been soiled by the public, insulted in the men's room, lusted after by all sorts of females. As Molly Haskell has suggested, male stars nowadays are taking over all the traditional women's siren and suffering roles. Instead of aging actresses like Gloria Swanson and Geraldine Page mourning the past at their dressing tables, we have aging rodeo stars like Cliff Robertson, James Coburn, and Steve McQueen. Redford's Bill McKay is thus ultimately Katharine Hepburn's Morning Glory in drag, gaining stardom at the cost of happiness and integrity and morality. The women in *The Candidate* exist merely to set off McKay as a media stud who wants to be appreciated for his mind. The wife, especially, is denied the slightest trace of anti-bullshit independence common not only among the wives in American movies about politics, but in real-life politicians' wives like Abigail McCarthy, Eleanor McGovern, and even Pat Nixon, and, of course, especially Martha Mitchell.

Bella Abzug has raised the very interesting point of McKay's finances for his media blitz against Jarmon. It would take millions in a state as large as California. Who raised the money and how and from whom? When Jesse Unruh ran against Reagan for Governor, he was so strapped for cash that he had to stage impromptu press conferences on Reagan's lawn to get free media attention, and no one has ever accused Unruh of being excessively finicky in the realm of fundraising. But McKay never has to worry about money. That would make him ordinary and human, hardly the qualities of egocentric stardom with a piece of the action. What I find most presumptuous about *The Candidate*, however, is its notion that politicians are any more ridiculous than movie-makers, or movie-reviewers for that matter. Redford fancies himself so superior to the electoral process that he ends up with a completely fatuous characterization of a politician.

In line with his liking of *The Candidate*, Canby recently fabricated a cardboard cultist in order to make a distinction between the presumed merits of Michael Ritchie's direction in *The Candidate* and the irrelevance of that direction in the Ritchie-directed gangster movie *Prime Cut* which opened the previous day. Curiously, Ritchie's directorial vision has remained remarkably consistent with three different script writers (James Salter for *Downhill Racer*, Robert Dillon for *Prime Cut*, and Larner for *The Candidate*). The editing is nervous, the sense of rapport hopelessly fragmented. Scenes will end with some of the participants brusquely excluded from the final shot, a mannerism particularly evident in the two Redford movies. *Prime Cut* has an idiotic plot in the new vein of gangster sentimentality popularized if not universalized by *The Godfather*. Good gangsters don't do much of anything but flaunt their machismo in a regal manner whereas bad gangsters deal in narcotics, prostitution, and just plain deviltry. Lee Marvin's gangster in *Prime Cut* actually comes out of a Dickens novel as the savior of Little Nells victimized by Gene Hackman's Upton Sinclair-type gangster who compounds all his assorted villainies by expressing a loathing for the inner city from his vantage point in Middle America. *Prime Cut* is so cut and dried as a commercial staple that Ritchie was free to concentrate on scenic compositions as derisive counterpoint to the bang-bang stuff. By contrast, Ritchie and Redford together are remarkably compatible in their winning-is-losing puerilities in *Downhill Racer* and *The Candidate*.

It is something in the air. It can be found on stage in *The Championship Season* and on screen in *Marjoe*. It is a chic attitude that is completely false and condescending and misleading. It is a hatred for unfashionable people, an all-or-nothing Faustian fanaticism based on guilt, despair, and hypocrisy. It would be simply ridiculous if it were not potentially harmful in this year of very crucial decision.

—August 1972

The Man

MOST REVIEWERS seemed to be as hard on *The Man* as they were easy on *The Candidate*, perhaps as a function of what Francois Truffaut once described as the alternation system of movie reviewing, one good, one bad, one good, bad, etc. Certainly, *The Man* depends more on an initial contrivance, the deaths of the President and the Speaker of the House, the disability of the Vice-President, and the accession to the Presidency of James Earl Jones's President Pro Tempore of the Senate. Haw, haw, haw. A black as President of the United States. I haven't heard so much critical chortling since Otto Preminger proposed casting the late Martin Luther King as a senator from Mississippi in *Advise and Consent*. A cheap publicity stunt, everyone yelled, and King was pressured not to accept the role because it would not be in accord with his dignity. Only whites are allowed to have generous portions of ham and fantasy in their make-up. Blacks must be realistic at all costs. Whites can live vicariously with James Bond, but blacks must repudiate Shaft. He is poisonously unreal. Of course, most blacks don't see it that way. They don't want to plunk down their money for the opportunity to suffer through the poetry of cockroaches.

Still and all, I found James Earl Jones infinitely more believable and sympathetic as a man in over his head than I found Robert Redford as a man holding his nose. To be sure, *The Man* is an embarrassment. And no one is more embarrassed than James Earl Jones's very discreet token black politician. He has spent his life trying not to give offense, and suddenly he is giving massive offense not by his guarded existence but by his ineradicable essence. He can no longer hide behind a spurious universality. He must look at himself and into himself with great intensity, and he must learn to love himself. *The Man* is basically a very small movie, crudely compressed in its original television format. Rod Serling's lines are often too melodramatically pointed for comfort, but Joseph Sargent's direction tries rather valiantly to modulate the improbabilities of the plot with a kind of expressive understatement. The People in *The Man* are thus not the surly boobs they are in *The Candidate* but a mysterious force situated on the other side of the television lens. Most of all, *The Man* is a marvelous vehicle for the measured, too often monolithic, magniloquence of James Earl Jones. A detractor once described him as the black Raymond Massey, but there are parts so embarrassingly massive that only self-constructed actors like Massey and Jones can play them. Hence, *The Man* is for Jones what *East of Eden* was for Massey.

Anyway, it is very instructive to watch a black become President of the United States in these days when succession is so much on all our minds. The realists may argue that the present President Pro Tempore of the Senate is Senator James Eastland of Mississippi, third in line to the Presidency after Agnew and Albert, but is there any reason to doubt that someone like Senator Brooke of Massachusetts could not become President Pro Tempore of the Senate in 20 or 30 years? I kept thinking of Brooke as I looked at Jones, and who can say what is "realistic" and what is "fantastic" in these incredible times?

The Eagleton affair has left a bad taste in my mouth as it has for a great many people, and I wonder now if McGovern has not wound up with the worst of all the possible worlds. First of all, nothing that has been revealed about Eagleton seems to be as damning as what we know about Ted Kennedy, and yet the Vice-Presidential nomination was always Kennedy's for the asking. Is there one law for the Eagletons of this world, and another for the Kennedys? Mind you, I never understood why Eagleton was picked in the first place; but, once picked, he should have been kept. What interests me is the bloodthirsty reaction of the supposed idealists around McGovern. Matthew Troy, who was whining that the party would have to turn to Teddy Kennedy if McGovern lost the California challenge, demanded Eagleton's head on a silver platter as the price of his continuing precious support of McGovern. Jesse Jackson, who didn't even vote in his own party's primary, dictated the execution terms to Eagleton. And still Eagleton held on for dear life, and now that he is off the ticket McGovern has to worry about the millions of people who have had to undergo mental treatment and don't like the idea of being stigmatized for life.

Think of it. Eagleton went to a psychiatrist and received electric shock treatments. And now he is unfit to be considered in the same category with Agnew, Albert, and Eastland, heartbeats from the Presidency and the Nuclear Panic Button. What if Jack Anderson had discovered from his usually reliable sources that Eagleton had once been busted for smoking marijuana or that he had been booked in a raid on a gay bar or that he had been a draft evader or that Mrs. Eagleton had once had an abortion? So what is all this nonsense about amnesty and forgiveness and the New Morality? When it comes to winning an election, what we seem to need are upright Lord Fauntleroys like Nixon and Agnew. If the New Politics crumpled up so completely over the specter of mental illness, I hate to think how firm it will be on far more controversial issues. Many writers on *The Voice* talk bravely about what is "in" and what is "out," but when election time rolls around suddenly there seem to be millions and millions of people who wouldn't vote for a candidate with liquor on his breath. Under the circumstances, Eagleton should consider himself lucky that he wasn't burned at the stake. Even so, I can't help feeling that the people around McGovern panicked once more, this time perhaps fatally. This is a time also when old-fashioned people may have been far ahead of the new-fangled politicians. Certainly, if it is in Ted Kennedy's scenario to ride to the rescue in 1976, he had better forget it. I'm beginning to wonder if the brain trust around McGovern really want to beat Nixon at all. It may be that all they wanted all along was merely to stop Humphrey. The Eagleton affair is hardly on a par with the Parnell scandal, but I can't help feeling that the media have helped to turn us back to the dark ages. At the moment, I don't know who McGovern's new running mate will be, and I don't really care. At times like this, movies make more sense than politics.

—August 1972

The Godfather

IT SEEMS THAT the first question everyone asks about *The Godfather* is concerned with Marlon Brando's interpretation of the title role. That is the way the movie has been programmed and promoted. Brando, Brando, Brando, and more Brando. The word from advance hush-hush screenings was wow, all caps and an explanation point. More exclamation, in fact, than explanation. More than one whisperer intimated that Brando's make-up (by Dick Smith, the auteur also of Dustin Hoffman's Shangri-La face furrows in *Little Big Man*) was so masterly that the Brando we all know and love had disappeared completely beneath it. I must admit that some of the advance hype had gotten to me by the time I sat braced in my seat for the screening of *The Godfather*. I was determined to discern Brando beneath any disguise mere humans could devise.

The picture opened with a face outlined against a splotched blue background with no spatial frame of reference, a background not so much abstract as optically mod with a slow zoom to take us into the milieu by degrees. But that face! I was stunned. How had Brando managed it? The eyes, the ears, the nose, the chin. It didn't look anything at all like Brando. And the voice was equally shattering in its unfamiliar pitch. I began groping for adjectives like "eerie" and "unearthly." Gradually the face began to recede into the background, and I heard a familiarly high-pitched voice somewhere in the foreground. I suddenly recalled the plot of the novel and thus I realized that the face looming in front of me did not resemble Brando's simply because it wasn't Brando's. (I learned later that the face and voice in question for the role of Bonasera belong to a 20th-billed actor named Salvatore Corsitto who gets no points for looking like himself.)

When Brando himself finally materialized on the screen as Don Vito Corleone, I could see it was Brando all the way. There was no mistaking the voice even with the slow-motion throaty whine Brando used to disguise it. Brando's range has always been more limited by his voice than his Faustian admirers cared to admit. That is why his best roles have always played against the voice by negating it as a mechanism of direct communication. Brando's greatest moments are thus always out of vocal sync with other performers. Even the famous taxicab scene with Rod Steiger in *On the Waterfront* operates vocally (though not physically or emotionally) as a syncopated Brando soliloquy, a riff on the upper registers of sensitivity and vulnerability resonating all the more in counterpoint to Steiger's more evenly cadenced street glibness and shrillness. Curiously, Brando has come to embody, often brilliantly, a culturally fashionable mistrust of language as an end in itself. The very mystique of Method Acting presumes the existence of an emotional substratum swirling with fear and suspicion under every line of dialogue. Hence, it is surprising that Brando has not played gangsters more often. The Machiavellian bias of the Method is ideally suited to the ritualized conversations of organized criminals.

So to answer belatedly the first question everyone asks about *The Godfather*: Brando gives an excellent performance as Don Vito Corleone, a role Lee J. Cobb could have played in his sleep without any special make-up. Brando's triumph and fascination is less that of an actor of parts than of a star galaxy of myths. Which is to say that he does not so much lose himself in his part as lift his part to his own exalted level as a star personality. The fact remains, however, that though Brando's star presence dominates every scene in which he appears, the part itself is relatively small, and there are other people who are equally good with considerably less strain, among them the extraordinarily versatile James Caan as the hot-headed, ill-fated Sonny Corleone, Richard Castellano as the jovially gruesome Clemenza, and Robert Duvall as Don Vito Corleone's non-Italian consigliere, Tom Hagen. Al Pacino as Michael Corleone has much the biggest and most challenging role in the film, and gives the most problematical performance. It is with Pacino's role that fact and fantasy come most discordantly into conflict. And it is with the characterization of Michael Corleone that both director-scenarist Francis Ford Coppola and novelist-scenarist Mario Puzo seem to drift away from the rigor of the crime genre into the lassitude of an intellectual's daydream about revenge without remorse and power without accountability.

There were many ways to adapt Puzo's novel to the screen. (There is no question here of fidelity to a text that was merely the first draft of a screen treatment.) Puzo quotes Balzac, no less, in a foreword conveying a Brechtian implication: "Behind every great fortune there is a crime." Brando claims to have been representing a typically corporate personality from the ruthlessly American capitalistic system. But *The Godfather* as a whole does not sustain this particular interpretation as effectively as did Kurosawa's *The Bad Sleep Well* some years ago. That is to say that Kurosawa and his scenarists came much closer to conjuring up the quasicriminal ruthlessness of a conglomerate like ITT than do Coppola, Puzo, and Brando. Coppola's approach tends to be humanistic, ethnic, and almost grotesquely nostalgic. There is more feeling in the film than we had any right to expect, but also more fuzziness in the development of the narrative. *The Godfather* happens to be one of those movies that can't stay put on the screen. There are strange ghosts everywhere, like Richard Conte's authentically Italian gangster kingpin Barzini evoking memories of *House of Strangers* and *The Brothers Rico*, and Al Martino as Johnny Fontane (alias Frank Sinatra) reportedly walking off the stage of a New York supper club just before *The Godfather* opened and apparently disappearing into that thick mist of forbidden fictions.

The Godfather is providing additional ammunition, if indeed any were still needed, for the kill-kill-bang-bang forces in the film industry. No, Virginia, this will not be still another article on violence in the movies. The lines forming for *The Godfather* can speak for themselves. What interests me at the moment is less the apparently insatiable hunger of the masses for homicide than the curiously disdainful attitude affected by the popgunnery purveyors toward their material. Gordon Parks, for example, refers derisively to *Shaft* (and, I suppose, the upcoming son of Shaft) as the kind of popular entertainment he must concoct in order to obtain the opportunity to do more serious work. Since Mr. Parks displays no discernible talent in private-eye melodrama, it is to be hoped that he obtains more "serious" assignments as quickly as possible. Similarly, Francis Ford Coppola has made it abundantly clear that *The Godfather* was undertaken quite consciously as a "compromise" with the commercial realities of the film industry. And now even Mario Puzo is making noises to the effect that *The Godfather* was written merely to provide the freedom and leisure necessary to turn out something comparable to *The Brothers Karamazov*. *Tant pis* and all that when we recall that there have been at least a score of gangster movies that have been artistically superior to any of the film versions of *Karamazov*.

Not that there is anything new about the Puzo-Coppola brand of voluptuous Faustianism, which might be subtitled: I sold my soul to the devil for filthy lucre and the roar of the crowd, but I still have my eye on the higher things. John Ford was eulogized through the thirties for turning out three commercial flicks like *Wee Willie Winkie* for the moguls in order to pay for any one serious film like *The Informer* for the mandarins. In retrospect, *Wee Willie Winkie* was never all that bad, and *The Informer* was never all that good. But Faustianism has continued to flourish even to this depressed day when Hollywood swimming pools are hard to come by for even the most corruptible radicals. No one seems to have learned the hard lesson of movie history that the throwaway pictures often become the enduring classics whereas the noble projects often survive only as sure-fire cures for insomnia. Not always, of course, but often enough to discourage the once fashionable game of kitsh-as-catch-can.

That *The Godfather* is almost fatally tainted with condescension follows almost logically from the revelation that the Coppola-Puzo second choice for the title role (after Brando) was none other than Sir Laurence Olivier. There's nothing like a classy performer to get the public's mind off the questionable cultural credentials of a popular subject. Still, publicity is publicity, and I have no desire to single out Coppola or Puzo for derision. Any artist is vulnerable enough in the journalistic jungle to claim the privilege of saying that he is saving his best for some later project still safely beyond the claws of the snarling critics. Coppola, particularly, has done good work in the past. His first film, *Dementia 13*, is unknown to all but the most dedicated archaeologists of American-International Corman horrifics. Coppola's official first film, *You're a Big Boy Now,* was completely eclipsed by Mike Nichols' *The Graduate.* What I said at the time (in *The American Cinema*) is still pertinent: "Francis Ford Coppola is probably the first reasonably talented and sensibly adaptable directorial talent to emerge from a university curriculum in filmmaking. *You're A Big Boy Now* seemed remarkably eclectic even under the circumstances. If the direction of Nichols on *The Graduate* has an edge on Coppola's for *Big Boy*, it is that Nichols borrows only from good movies whereas Coppola occasionally borrows from bad ones. Curiously, Coppola seems infinitely more merciful to his grotesques than does anything-for-an-effect Nichols. Coppola may be heard from more decisively in the future."

Since 1967 Coppola has been heard from with varying degrees of decisiveness in two commercial disasters—*Finian's Rainbow* and *The Rain People*. Coppola had set up his own studio in the San Francisco area to revolutionize what was left of Hollywood. He sponsored George Lucas's *THX-1138* and was informally associated with John Korty in what might be called the San Francisco School of lyrical realism and dissonant humanism. *Finian's Rainbow* was a hopelessly anachronistic project to begin with, a moldy bone to the blacks tossed by self-satisfied liberals of the forties in the mistaken belief that bigotry was confined to that picturesque terrain South of Shubert Alley. Coppola did his best with Petula Clark and the badly miscast Fred Astaire, but the show simply sank into the realistic landscape. Another compromise perhaps? Certainly, Coppola's heart was more completely committed to *The Rain People*, an itinerant production of uncommon emotional intensity.

I met Coppola at Bucknell when he was making *The Rain People* aboard a land yacht, traveling, as it were, across the real face of America in search of sociological truth with an improvised scenario. I remember being as impressed by Coppola's intelligence as I was suspicious of his professed intentions. People who go out looking for America always seem to know in advance what they are going to find. Alienation and Anomie, Loneliness and Lethargy, Late Night Whining and Daily Paranoia. Coppola never succeeded in establishing the characterization of Shirley Knight's wandering wife, and thus his narrative drifted without a psychological rudder. Still, the wife's encounters with James Caan's punchy jock and Robert Duvall's sympathetically lecherous state trooper lifted the film to the behavioral heights (and fights) of *Petulia* and *Point Blank*, two of the more brilliant explosions of the San Francisco area, if not of the San Francisco school, the formal sublimity of Alfred Hitchcock's *Vertigo* representing, of course, a different tradition altogether.

The failure of *The Rain People* and *THX-1138* and the Korty films can be attributed partly to the inability of the traditional distribution and exhibition patterns to funnel a new kind of audience that is presumably panting for it. Or is there really that much of a new audience for movies? Whatever the explanation, Coppola had the satisfaction of having established his artistic identity as a director at the cost of his commercial solvency as a producer. He therefore approached *The Godfather* less as a creative opportunity than as a crutch for his stumbling career.

I am convinced that *The Godfather* could have been a more profound film if Coppola had shown more interest (and perhaps more courage) in those sections of the book which treated crime as an extension of capitalism and as the *sine qua non* of showbiz. Much of the time spent boringly in Sicily might have been devoted to the skimming operations in Las Vegas, and to the corporate skullduggery in Hollywood. A very little bit of the corrosively Odetsian wit of the fifties in *The Big Knife* and *Sweet Smell of Success* could have gone a long way here in relating the Mafia to our daily life. Instead, Coppola has taken great pains to make *The Godfather* seem like a period piece. Antique cars, ill-fitting clothes (especially for loose-framed Diane Keaton's WASP wardrobe), floppy hats, vintage tabloid front pages featuring dead gangsters of a bygone era all contribute to Coppola's deliberate distancing tactics. Worst of all is the sentimental distinction between the good-bad guys and the bad-bad guys on the pseudoprophetic issue of narcotics distribution.

The production stories connected with *The Godfather* seem to take pride in the concessions granted to organized crime so that the film could be shot on New York locations without being shot up and shut down. Hence, there is no reference to the "Mafia" as such or to the "Cosa Nostra" as such, but merely to "The Family." It is as if producer Albert S. Ruddy were trying to enhance the diabolical reputation of his subject so that audiences would feel the chill of gossipy relevance. Since *The Godfather* is about as unkind to the Mafia as *Mein Kampf* is to Adolf Hitler, it is hard to understand why the local Little Caesars didn't pay Ruddy a commission for all the free publicity. However, even if Ruddy had not made all his noble sacrifices to the Mob for the sake of his muse, it is fairly certain that a realistic director like Coppola would have insisted on shooting his scenario on authentic locations. After all, wasn't that the whole point of Coppola's original safari from Hollywood to San Francisco: to escape from Hollywood's synthetic sound stages and infinitely illusionist set designers?

And so we see Al Pacino and Diane Keaton walking out of the Radio City Music Hall ostensibly during the Christmas Season of 1945. How do we know it is 1945? The marquee has been made up to advertise Bing Crosby and Ingrid Bergman in *The Bells of St. Mary's*. And here we have one of the paradoxes of plastic realism. It just so happens that I saw *The Bells of St. Mary's* at the Music Hall in 1945, and the scene Pacino so painstakingly recreates before my eyes is false and strained in every way except the most literal. As the production notes tell us, "crowds gathered to stare at the old-time automobiles and ancient taxis with the legend '15 cents for first 1/2 mile' fare rates painted on the doors. Meanwhile, ushers ran up and down the street informing the public that the film playing was Elaine May and Walter Matthau in *A New Leaf* and the stage show was the 1971 Easter Show."

Nonetheless, the plastic realism of the marquee and the old cabs cannot compensate for the sociological distortion of the empty sidewalks and the absent hustle and bustle. Around Christmas of 1945 at the Music Hall was a pretelevision festive crowd tableau such as we shall never see again in our lifetime. An old-time Hollywood illusionist like Vincente Minnelli would have captured the populist lilt of that moment whereas Coppola has captured only the plastic lint. Minnelli's vision would have been that of the warm animal kingdom whereas Coppola's is merely that of the cold mineral.

Similarly, few of the "more than 120 locations around Manhattan, the Bronx, Brooklyn, and Richmond" justified the trouble they took with any special aura of authenticity. Indeed, too often the studied and constricted framing of the "real" location only emphasized the artifices of the scenario. So little of Mott Street is utilized for gunning down Brando that the entire effect could easily have been reconstructed on a back lot. Location shooting has always been more of a Pandora's Box than realistic pundits have ever wanted to admit. If I see one more set of play-actors cruising around the canals of Venice with all the natives looking for the camera (or for Erich Segal on one of the gondolas), I shall sing "O Solo Mio" a cappella. To escape from the alleged tyranny of the set it is necessary to conceive a much looser scenario than any now envisaged for most movies.

As it is, Coppola spends much too much time savoring each location as if he were afraid audiences might not sufficiently appreciate its authenticity. There is remarkably little elision of movement for a modern (or even a classical) movie. People walk through rooms, clump, clump, clump, as if they were measuring the floor for a rug. At times I would have welcomed even a wipe to jolly things along with page-turning dispatch.

Coppola's treadmill technique is merely a symptom of his sense of priorities. The trouble began with the scenario's lack of concern for the characters it could not wait to slaughter. The first murder is a genuine shocker, not simply because of its bizarre choreography (even more gruesome than in the book), but also because even after the unexplained first murder in *The French Connection,* we are still not accustomed to having people we barely know bumped off on the screen. Puzo always provided a background dossier on his victims in his novel, and some objective mechanism for doing these dossiers a la *The Battle of Algiers* might have been devised for the movie. Coppola prefers to skim the surface of the novel for violent highlights, and thus discard all the documentation. However, it has been my impression that the rumored involvement of Frank Sinatra and Dean Martin in the narrative was the big talking point of the novel. Who cares that much about Joe Profaci and his brood except on the mythic level of glorified gangsterdom? By contrast, Sinatra and his colleagues and conquests have always provided the stuff of forbidden fantasies for precisely the type of urban wage-slave that stands on line to see *The Godfather.* After Vegas and Hollywood, how can you keep 'em down on Long Beach?

Coppola does his best to narrow the focus of *The Godfather* to manageably monstrous proportions. His film is neither tragedy nor sociology, but a saga of monsters with occasionally human expressions. Even the irony of invoking the "family" as the basic social unit is not pursued beyond a desultory conversation between Michael (Al Pacino) and Kay Adams (Diane Keaton). The irony is not that the Corleone family is a microcosm of America, but rather that it is merely a typical American family beset by the destructively acquisitive individualism that is tearing American society apart. It is an idea that Chaplin developed so much more profoundly in *Monsieur Verdoux*: that if war, in Clausewitz's phrase, is the logical extension of diplomacy, then murder is the logical extension of business. This notion is mentioned here and there in *The Godfather,* but never satisfactorily developed. There is simply no time. Another shot, another murder. And the crowds are keeping a box-score on every corpse. Let's not disappoint them with a meditation on machismo and materialism. We can do that on the next picture, the "serious" one, the one the crowds will stay away from in droves.

—March 1972

Dog Day Afternoon

THE ARTEMISIUM at Ephesus was one of the great wonders of the ancient world. A virtual forest of wooden pillars, this religious temple dated back to the prehellenic conception of Artemis as a universal earth mother rather than the virginal huntress she later became in the Homeric Age. Hence, her many-breasted figure at Ephesus confirmed her authentic antiquity as a maternal goddess. One night in 356 B.C., an otherwise obscure Ephesian named Herostratus set fire to the Artemisium in order to secure immortality for this awesome act of sacrilege. The rulers of the city subsequently decreed that Herostratus would be punished secretly, and that all records of his existence would be destroyed. That the name of Herostratus has come down to us at all is due to the strange coincidence of the Artemisium's having been burned the very night on which Alexander the Great was born. Even so, Herostratus never succeeded in becoming a household name.

The story of Herostratus has always intrigued me because it is one of the few pro-Establishment stories I know. Here, then, is the formula for dealing with assassins, terrorists, hijackers, and vandals. Of course, it can be argued that this formula has long been followed by police states. Right and Left. You can bet your bottom ruble that the Russian equivalent of Lynette ("Squeaky") Fromme would never have gotten her picture splashed on the front page of *Pravda* as Squeaky did on the cover of *Time*. And it can be argued also that the vandals who recently desecrated revered art works by Michelangelo, Picasso, and Rembrandt did not gain an undue amount of personal publicity, much less fame and immortality, for their dastardly deeds. Still, one often gets the feeling that our relatively permissive and media-mesmerized society seems to breed assassins, terrorists, and vandals of every variety. Why can't an Oswald, a Ruby, a Ray, a Bremer, or a Manson be driven back into the pit of obscurity from which he has clambered with bloodied hands? What particularly irritates me is that every time someone commits an outrage, the blame eventually filters down from the System and the Society to every poor slob who's sitting in front of a television set. Under the aegis of Freud and Marx, the perpetrator is transformed into a Problem *we* all should have solved a long time ago.

Dog Day Afternoon brings Herostratus to mind because it very cleverly takes society to task for the deep unhappiness of its criminals. In effect, Ephesus is somehow to blame for the crime of Herostratus. It all depends on the point of view. If Hitler's story, for example, is told entirely from Hitler's point of view then the Jews can be blamed for causing Hitler to have sleepless nights. And if Hitler were to be played soulfully by Al Pacino then history would truly be turned on its head by histrionics. Something of the same sort happens in *Dog Day Afternoon*, where the crazies have a field day against the squares.

The day in question was Tuesday, August 22, 1972. The temperature was 97 degrees. I was driving out to Long Island on the expressway, and, as was my custom, I was listening lethargically to the endlessly repetitive news bulletins on WINS. I have been a news freak all my life, and news freaks don't need real news to feed their habit. Then suddenly there was real news of the most ridiculous kind. A bank was being held up in Brooklyn. The police had arrived. Hostages were being held. A state of siege was in force. Demands were being made. It was a familiar scenario, but with bizarre variations. One of the bankrobbers demanded that his wife be brought to him, and, when the police complied, it turned out that the "wife" was a transvestite. I began to suspect that Andy Warhol and Paul Morrissey had staged the whole operation as a tasteless parody of the terrorism around us. But what really amused me was the way the bystanders picked up on all their media cues. I was particularly struck by an employee of a brokerage house across the street from the bank. With his Arnold Stang accent, and his Woody Allen sangfroid, he very expertly described the course of events to a *WINS* newsman. Good God, I thought, Everyman has become Anchorman. I didn't follow the story through that evening since I had gotten to where I was going and there seemed to be better things to do. But from my point of view, *Dog Day Afternoon* would have been a Woody Allen vehicle to express the media-mania in all of us. The bank robbers would have been seen at a great distance as media marionettes dangling helplessly in the public eye.

In the months and years that have followed, the focus has shifted decisively. First there was a graphic article by P. F. Kluge and Thomas Moore in the *Life* of September 1972. From this article Frank Pierson developed the screenplay for Sidney Lumet to direct as *Dog Day Afternoon*, and Patrick Mann wrote a novel with material from both the *Life* article and Pierson's screenplay. Arthur Bell has written in *The Voice* on this episode as a gay *cause celebre* with Mafia-bar-conspiracy overtones. And now finally we have the movie.

Any impulse I may ever have had to laugh is dashed by the first shot of Al Pacino ("Sonny") and John Cazale ("Sal") as grimly dedicated hold-up men. Pacino acts more assiduously with the whites of his eyes than any movie actor since Valentino. Here in *Dog Day Afternoon* he has become the Evil-Eye Fleagle of film. To laugh at him is to risk being struck blind. In terms of what he does, he is a streetwise, gutter-bred punk. In terms of what he feels, he is a Freudian tragic hero, walking a wobbly tightrope between Eros and Thanatos. It is myth-making time at the movies once more.

John Cazale enlists our sympathy more subtly by the dread stillness of his demeanor. Whereas pain comes pouring out of Pacino's eyes, the dull ache in Cazale's psyche is rendered as a deadpan death wish. Between them, Pacino and Cazale drag in so much emotional debris (from *Godfather I* and *II* and other ethnic expressionism) that the scenario sags under the burden. Robbing a bank and holding hostages become minor footnotes to their clinical case histories. To end the suffering and frustration of the Pacino and Cazale characters, the audience is conditioned to accept their terrorism as a form of treatment, perhaps even as a kind of release from the constraints of lawful behavior. But Lumet, Pierson, Pacino, and company are not content to let the bank robbers out-emote everyone in sight for sympathy. A new character is added, a kind of cop-out from the robbery. The character "Bobby" (engagingly played by Gary Springer) introduces a note of juvenile hysteria to the proceedings. At this point *Dog Day Afternoon* should be on the verge of becoming *Big Deal on Madonna Street*, but Lumet's solemn style and Pacino's doleful basset-hound expressions kill any laughs before they can leap out of one's throat. Nonetheless, Gary Springer acts as the audience's surrogate much as Roy Scheider does in *Jaws*. By showing fear both Springer and Scheider give the audience someone with whom to identify in their cowardly and perhaps even malicious voyeurism.

Also, Springer and Scheider make Pacino-Cazale and Richard Drey-fuss-Robert Shaw seem romantically unflappable by comparison.

Once the bank robbery gets started, Pacino and Cazale begin more and more to resemble lovable nonconformists held at bay by a hostile, unfeeling society. The casting is the first tip-off. The bank employees are a drab and dismal lot. The facts are tampered with to make the bank manager less resourceful and more pathetic than he actually was. In fact it was the bank manager who ingeniously tipped off an associate at another bank that a robbery was taking place, but the movie would have it that the robbery was botched up by a gro-tesque accident. Two different movies are involved here. In the for-ties or the fifties, the story would have been told in such a way as to make the audience root for the bank manager, his employees, the police, and the FBI. The bank robbers would have been complete psychos—Richard Widmark, say, and Richard Conte. A bank manager with brains would have fitted in with this ethos, there would have been a few good-looking girls at the teller's windows to uphold the sexism of Old Hollywood, and James Stewart would have come along as the fearless FBI agent to give the bank robbers what-for. No more. The high point of *Dog Day Afternoon* is Chris Sarandon's soul-sear-ing telephone conversation with Pacino, a conversation full of para-noia, hypochondria, and hysteria not simply between two ex-lovers, but between two wounded creatures capable of an extraordinary emotional audacity. (Sarandon transforms the very ticklish role of Sonny's "wife" into a memorably dignified portrayal.) The feelings exchanged so fatalistically in this encounter make it one of the great telephone scenes in Hollywood history, but it throws the whole pic-ture out of kilter. There is no moral balance between complex pathol-ogy and simple virtue. Lumet has crossed the line between compas-sion and complicity. The crooks are cuddly, and the honest citizens are boobs and bores and bullies. As for the FBI, they stalk the screen in the zombie-like performances of James Broderick and Lance Hen-riksen like subfreezing sentinels from another planet. (Broderick's uncanny resemblance to Norman Mailer makes his characterization of the cold-fish FBI agent seem all that much more programmatically Brechtian.) The FBI has lost much of its lustre in recent years even with the booboisie, but a bank robbery is hardly the occasion to demonstrate the bureau's ruthlessly tyrannical nature. Yet it's all part of the pattern. Poor Al Pacino as sweet Sonny. All he wants to do is

rob a quiet bank in Brooklyn in order to finance a sex-change operation for his beloved. Then all hell breaks loose, everyone is on television—even his fat pig of a first wife. It's more than he can bear. Oh,
he has his moments of street theatre, and he knows how to keep the
police in place: just hold guns on people in a bank. Who are these
people, and what are their inner lives? Forget it. That's another movie
from long ago.

Even on its own level, however, *Dog Day Afternoon* possesses at
least one fatal flaw. Does Sonny consent by his silence to the FBI's
killing of his buddy, Sal? It is the one moment of genuine ambiguity
in the picture, and it is never resolved. I have the feeling that Lumet,
Pierson, Pacino, alone or together, may have sensed that Sonny
would have been fatally compromised as a street hero if it were
clearly shown that he had sold Sal to save his own neck. On the
whole, *Dog Day Afternoon* is not a bad job of moviemaking. It
should be seen, but not swallowed whole. In these days, particularly,
I can't see making heroes out of felons with a theatrical flair. It is too
short a step from there to utter chaos.

—September 1975

The Conversation

IT CAME OVER the car radio while I was driving out to wintry, stormy Long Island for the Memorial Day weekend. *The Conversation* had won the Grand Prize at Cannes, *The Sugarland Express* had been singled out for its screenplay, and Jack Nicholson had been named best actor for his tangy tour-de-force in *The Last Detail*. A few crumbs were tossed to the French Film Industry in the form of a nostalgia award to Charles Boyer for his stately presence in *Stavisky*, and a female acting award to some French actress or other (Marie-José Nat, I think) for her performance in a reportedly happy story of French Jews during the Nazi Occupation. The irrepressible Italians were palmed off with a "visual" consolation award for Pier Paolo Pasolini's *Thousand and One Nights*, and Carlos Saura was felicitated vaguely for continuing to persevere in Spain while an aging Franco was still breathing (or is it now wheezing) down his back. But the message was clear: American films are now considered the cream of the crop not only commercially as heretofore, but artistically besides. Is this really true? Or does it merely mean that the pendulum of snobbery has swung from a middlebrow American overestimation of European films to a middlebrow European overestimation of American films? It's hard to tell. The American films at Cannes this year tended to fall into the category of blown-up B pictures, very accomplished stylistically, but not very ambitious thematically, fairly deep in some instances, but never very complex. Unfortunately, the European films in competition at Cannes were not very good on any level, be it the profound, the pleasurable, or the pornographic, and thus the American entries shone by comparison.

Also, the Hollywood moguls of the supposedly good old days used to sneer at Cannes and all other film festivals with the smug assurance that their expensive product had no business competing with some half-assed home movie turned out by a commie existentialist in his garret on a roll of toilet paper. By and large, the American movies at Cannes this year were commercially in-between items with a pressing need for artistic prestige and critical commendation. There was no *Sting* or *Exorcist* among them in the way of guaranteed grosses, and, indeed, *Mean Streets* had already premiered in the New York Film Festival, and *The Sugarland Express* had opened the New Directors' series at the Museum of Modern Art. On the Croisette a critic for *Positif* talked about Robert Mulligan and Robert Altman the way an earlier generation of critics from *Cahiers du Cinema* would talk about Nicholas Ray and Don Weis. But this kind of esoteric auteurism is not and never has been the mainstream of Cannes thinking, which I would describe as a process of compromising impossible ideals, among which are such droll notions as the internationality and universality of filmmaking ability, the convenient conjunction of art and entertainment, personal expression and social edification, and the existence of a consensus of good taste among the right-thinking and high-spending.

Why then and how then did *The Conversation* win the grand prize? For one thing, it's not a bad movie, and placed, as it was, near the end of a dreary festival, it was bound to seem like manna from heaven. More important, it seemed to be very pertinent to Watergate, though Francis Ford Coppola has denied up and down that he had anything like Watergate in mind when he first conceived of the project back in 1966. I believe him. *The Conversation* seems to have very little to do with Richard Nixon's Watergate, and very much to do with Michelangelo Antonioni's *Blow-Up*. Not that *Blow-Up* necessarily gave birth to *The Conversation*, but that the Antonioni at least made the Coppola seem more feasible as the colorful projection of an artistic confessional, sound in Coppola's case as spectacle was in Antonioni's.

I don't wish to stress the connection between *The Conversation* and *Blow-Up* merely as a means of demeaning the originality of Coppola's creative achievement. In many respects the two films are very dissimilar, as dissimilar indeed as San Francisco and London, as dissimilar as hung-over seventies and stoned sixties, as dissimilar as Cindy Williams as a femme fatale on the one hand (Coppola's) and Vanessa Redgrave on the other (Antonioni's). Also, whether as non-heroes or antiheroes, the conscience-stricken wiretapper in *The Conversation* and the culturally ambitious and morally ambiguous fashion photographer in *Blow-Up* are not precisely brothers under the skin. The purpose of the connection then is quite simply to explain why, in my view, *Blow-Up* succeeds as dramatic spectacle and *The Conversation* fails.

Blow-Up was adapted by Antonioni and Tonino Guerra from a then little-known short story by Julio Cortazar, a fact the daily reviewers were never allowed to live down by the literati of the little magazines with infinitely longer deadlines. The differences in the two versions were very striking. In the short story, the writer-raisonneur-photograper-protagonist is aimlessly taking pictures along the Seine when he records an intimate scene, almost but not quite an embrace, between a young, innocent-looking male student and a slightly older woman of a chic sophistication which seems incongruous in this context. The woman demands the picture: the author refuses. The young boy runs off. A sinister man emerges from a car nearby. The author suddenly realizes that the woman was actually procuring the boy for this older man, and that the author's intervention with his camera has thwarted the intended seduction of an innocent. A few days later the author blows up his photograph, and it comes to "life" in his studio as a motion picture with depth and movement and the dimension of inexorable time. The dramatic spectacle of innocence preserved is reenacted for the writer-photographer-hallucinator, and his tears of joy end up through a kind of subjective transformation of the objective as cleansing rain on his photo-turned-movie.

Cortazar writes in the self-consciously Borgesian mode of the mirrored sensibility struggling through the labyrinth of its own conceits. Hence, Cortazar's multipurpose character is more histrionic than the subjects of his spectacle. The "ending," such as it is, is "happy," "moral," and "creative" all at the same time, but the emotion expended on what is essentially a homosexual fantasy—the loving mother-figure leading the son with her caresses toward his sordid destiny—seems artistically disproportionate to the stylistic apparatus of the story. Unfortunately, I have not read Cortazar's other works, and I did not read even his *Blow-Up* until long after I had seen Antonioni's adaptation.

The movie, of course, changes the homosexual intrigue of a foiled seduction into a heterosexual triangle culminating in a murder. Antonioni's protagonist (David Hemmings) becomes directly and physically involved with the woman in his picture, but his intervention with his camera does not prevent the murder, but rather pro-

vides unexpected evidence that the murder is about to occur immediately after the picture has been taken. Antonioni's blow-ups excite
us because they are suspended in time, and because they keep reminding us that a man's life hangs precariously in the balance in the
interval between the taking of one picture and the non-taking of
another an instant later. The agonizing helplessness of the Hemmings
character is thus transformed from the moral-psychological (Should
he call the police? Should he tell someone? Should he feel remorse
for being so emotionally detached from the fate of a human being
who happens to be on the other side of his lens?) to the aesthetic-
metaphysical (How does one reclaim lost time when a movement
forward would have led to truth whereas a movement backward led
only to mystery and uncertainty? Is the artist part of reality when he is
in the process of recording it or does he occupy a privileged portion
of the universe beyond scrutiny and judgment? Does the artist in
photography or in cinematography transcend his machines or do his
machines transcend him?).

The major difference between Antonioni's *Blow-Up* and, say,
Hitchcock's *Rear Window* is that Antonioni's camera seems to function as a substitute for character, ego, libido, and subconscious,
whereas Hitchcock's camera functions as an extension of impulses
shared by both the characters and the audience. Thus, whereas
Hitchcock is closer to Gothic romance, Antonioni is closer to the
more alienating forms of science fiction. Not the least of Antonioni's
achievements in *Blow-Up* is to make the characters in a photograph
more vivid than the characters in the surrounding cinematograph.
Antonioni's blow-ups are friezes unfrozen, and an essential element
in our appreciation of these melted stills is the relative passivity and
indistinctness of Antonioni's on-screen voyeur-protagonist.

By contrast, where Coppola has gone wrong in *The Conversation*
is in overloading his wiretapping virtuoso with so many complexes
that we begin to worry about which side of the keyhole to take up as
our point-of-view position. Significantly, the best shot in *The Conversation* is the stunning opening shot with its slow descent into the
sights and sounds of a locale which we await eagerly to explore for
the deadly secret it contains. Gradually, we separate the hunters from
the hunted, the snoopers from the transgressors. It is an opening aria
from which Coppola will develop many variations. He will even manage to trick us to a certain extent by switching the inflection on a

crucial sentence, or so it seemed to my relatively untutored ear with the life-and-death words "kill" and "us." But his blown-up sounds (on the good-old Watergate-vintage Uher 5000) and his cyclical images never pack the emotional wallop they should because Coppola has too little faith in the profundity of his mystery to allow it to mesmerize his snooper-protagonist out of his own excessive self-absorption.

II

In what amounts to a program note in the credit sheets for *The Conversation*, writer-director Francis Ford Coppola makes the following declaration:

> I don't remember how I first became interested in the subject matter, but right from the beginning, I wanted to make a film about *privacy*, using the motif of eavesdropping and wiretapping, and centering on the personal and psychological life of the eavesdropper rather than his victims. It was to be a modern horror film, with a construction based on repetition rather than exposition, like a piece of music. And it would expose a tacky-subterranean world of wiretappers; their vanities and ethics; the conventions that they attend; the magazines that they read; and the women they value. Ultimately, I wanted the film to come to a moral and humanistic conclusion.
>
> I had no idea of what was to come in 1973. White House plumbers, Watergate, Ellsberg files, of course, were unfamiliar phrases to me, and even now I'm not completely sure of how these names and events relate to this film, despite so many coincidences and prophecies (the "Uher 5000" tape recorder).
>
> As I think about it now that it's done, I realize that I wasn't making a film about *privacy*, as I had set out to do, but rather, once again, a film about *responsibility*, as was *The Rain People*.

I have quoted the filmmaker at length in order to stress that he cannot be blamed if reviewers insist on drawing a providential parallel between his film and the current headlines. Aside from a brief, forced reference to Nixon in a newscast, Coppola has not pressed the parallel unduly. So for the moment my quarrel is more with certain reflex reactions to the film than with the film itself, at least on the level of what the film seems to be saying explicitly.

And what is *The Conversation* saying explicitly? Let us examine the plot for some clues to its thematic intentions. When we first encounter Gene Hackman's Harry Caul, he projects a seedy, nondescript presence right out of one of those gloomy Graham Greene thrillers about guilt-ridden, world-weary detectives and spies. His shoulders sag and slouch as if he were huddling into his all-seasons plastic raincoat in search of an inner warmth that he can never locate in his grubby soul. Even before we know what Harry Caul is up to in the narrative, Hackman and Coppola are very busy building up a crumby character out of bits and pieces of ironic incongruity. First of all we literally look down on the character in the little-man-big-world mode of the descending camera on a crowded outdoor scene in a public park dominated by the counterculture sound and spectacle of bongo drums and street theatre. (There is even a brash mimic of sorts left over from *Blow-Up*.)

In this lazy atmosphere of letting everything hang out, Gene Hackman's Harry Caul epitomizes every contained creep who keeps everything bottled up until it finally explodes one day like a malignantly middle-American Molotov cocktail. On the iconographical level, Gene Hackman seems to be refining his overstuffed persona in *Scarecrow*, but only at first glance. His movements, gestures, and expressions are too purposive to accommodate the kind of allegorical wanderer for whom the whole world is an open road and an open book. Harry Caul starts out, at least, as the kind of character who is defined more by what he does than by what he is. Harry Caul is a wiretapper and eavesdropper. And he works for whatever the traffic will bear.

As the opening unfolds, a young couple emerge from the crowd as the target of Harry Caul's surveillance, and it is their conversation which is to become the crux of the film's mystery. Coppola induces us to imagine that the rights of this couple are being violated both by what he shows and by what he allows us to infer. Indeed, the director encourages us to draw on some of our oldest and some of our newest moviegoing prejudices. In the ancient category is the audience's assumption that good-looking people are morally superior to bad-looking or even just so-so looking people. Frederic Forrest and Cindy Williams as the stalked couple are not exactly Mr. and Miss America, but they virtually shine with well-scrubbed virtue next to the funkiness of the street-theatre types, and to the frumpiness of Caul and his covert crew of snoopers and eavesdroppers. Caul has four or five people working for him, and Caul himself has been hired by an organization with vast resources, and thus the young couple can seize immediately on the audience's instinctive sympathy for inferior size and number (a criterion which seems to operate everywhere except in the Middle East). Also, Mark and Ann (the token names of the Forrest and Williams characters) look much younger than Caul and his crew, and youth still retains cinematically its association with relative innocence next to the visually damning furrows and wrinkles of age.

Of the newer audience prejudices, the most decisive is the liberal knee-jerk rejection of any kind of electronic surveillance whatsoever. The loftier libertarians do not see the world in Manichean movie-genre terms of gangsters and criminals at war with the decent elements of society, but rather as a series of medieval murals in which presumptively innocent citizens are menaced by a cruel and capricious sovereign. Of course, a great deal depends on who is the hare and who is the hound, which is to say that in a quarter of a century we have witnessed the metamorphosis of a hound (red-hunting Representative Nixon) into a hare (Watergate-wallowing President Nixon). But at what point on the political spectrum does an unconscionable invasion of privacy become a courageous exposure of secrecy? Or is it simply a question of Our Privacy versus Their Secrecy, a question the answer to which helps separate the lofty libertarian from the pragmatic partisan.

Both ethics and ecology enter into the equation. It is bad enough to spy on your neighbor; it is presumably even worse to use modern machinery in the process. When Justice Holmes castigated wiretapping as "dirty business," he may have been thinking as much of the apocalyptic advance of technology as of the Constitutional rights of the individual against the State.

There has been a pastoral bias in American libertarian thinking since Jefferson's time with the result that the logical left in America has often been split between the liberals and the populists, as between mind and body and as between aims and needs. In this respect, *The Conversation* follows the relatively liberal San Francisco school (Coppola, Lucas, Korty, et al.) as opposed to the relatively populist Hollywood tradition. Indeed, when Coppola declares: "Ultimately, I wanted the film to come to a moral and humanistic conclusion," he sounds more like Bellocchio or Bertolucci than like Capra or Borzage. Not that the latter were any less moral or less humanistic than the former, but what to Capra and Borzage was a natural sentiment becomes for more self-conscious artists like Coppola, Bellocchio, and Bertolucci a stylistic flourish. With Capra and Borzage, the major characters are as one with the human condition; with Coppola and his contemporaries the major characters tend to be alienated from their own humanity by their debased function in the social structure.

Hence, Coppola's young couple become increasingly sinister and conspiratorial as we probe deeper into their mysterious conversation. Mark looks bland and plastic and yet manipulative behind his glasses; he has that look of the young executive on the make. Again, as with Hackman, the director has intentionally deadened an attractively sensitive actor with the numbing Novocain of the System. The Ann of Cindy Williams tends to become less and less convincing in her postgraduate course in well-tailored bitchery here after her emotional initiation in *American Graffiti*. The visual duet of Mark and Ann begins to strike sour notes of conformist calculation, and our attention and sympathy are diverted forcibly to the increasingly harried Harry Caul.

III

Gene Hackman's Harry Caul functions in *The Conversation* as a kind of push-pull-in-and-out-of-focus character with no clear line of development. We never learn exactly why he is what he is or even why he does what he does. Francis Ford Coppola's attitude toward his apparent protagonist switches from scene to scene between the derisive-objective (Caul as snoopy caricature) and the delirious-subjective (Caul as sniveling conscience). Caul's problems and hang-ups, however, seem only marginally related to his particular line of work. In the contemporary cinema no line of work is especially creditable except as a comical cover for a caper (vide the wall painters in *The Sting*, the ice-cream vendors in *Thunderbolt and Lightfoot*, the road crew in *Gravy Train*, et al.). In *The Conversation*, moreover, Caul and his eavesdropping elves seem less sinister than their supposedly legitimate employers. These facelessly corporate types are both slicker and slimier than the buffoonish spies they recruit for the wretched tasks of industrial espionage. If in *The Godfather* Coppola tended to treat business as a crime, and not just any business, but all business, except possibly show business, even here Coppola may be implicating himself somewhat in Caul's confessional booth. Coppola is not as brutally explicit about the innate ruthlessness of big business as

Kurosawa was in *The Bad Sleep Well*, but there is, if anything, even more disdain in Coppola's attitude toward the trappings of capitalism than there is to be found in Kurosawa's angriest attacks on the system.

And since the system itself is rotten beyond redemption, Caul's very virtuosity in serving its most vicious needs is his spiritual undoing. Indeed, the whole plot hinges on Caul's extraordinary ability to rescue a crucial conversation from tapes teeming with noises. People with some experience of their own in sound recording assure me that some of Caul's technical feats are beyond belief. Even so, there is no joy in Caul's effort, no joy and no pride of accomplishment. Whereas the sleuthing photographer in *Blow-Up* engages the audience in his quest, there is something so unsettling about the way Caul clutches the tapes of the conversation as to make the whole operation seem as ill-advised as the opening of Pandora's Box. Since we are living in an age when anything done well ends badly, the safest thing is to do nothing, to sit alone in a room belting out old jazz standards on a self-centering saxophone. It is at this point of modishly alienated narcissism that Caul comes into focus most clearly as Coppola's mouthpiece, literally and figuratively. We do get the director's musical signature, but the artistic flourish is more affected than affecting. It is as if Coppola were concerned more with the cultural credentials of his enterprise than with the creation and illumination of a character.

Caul's relationships with women are clearly cases of don't-Caul-me-I'll-Caul-you. As it happens, Caul limits his activities to dames rather than girls since his profession presumably incapacitates him for any genuinely deep involvement with the Other. Nonetheless, after the two sexual encounters we are privileged to witness, the first dame deserts him, and the second betrays him much as Vanessa Redgrave betrayed David Hemmings in *Blow-Up*. With the supposedly sweet young thing of Cindy Williams on the tapes turning out to be a murderess rather than a victim, the sexual (or rather heterosexual) pattern of *The Conversation* degenerates into paranoia and sexophobia unlimited. But it is here that Coppola comes closest to outright banality. After all, there is nothing particularly unusual or idiosyncratic about Caul's cautiousness and suspiciousness in dealing with women. A man does not have to be a wiretapper in order to yearn for a one-way relationship with a woman with no strings attached. Bogie even made Bacall walk around him in *To Have and Have Not* to establish the absence of strings. And what man has not at some time or other in his sordidly carnal strivings echoed Ambrose Bierce's bitter lament: "Woman would be more charming if one could fall into her arms without falling into her hands." Caul's misogynous misadventures are therefore simply the latest variation on the old something-for-nothing shell game between the sexes.

In other respects, however, Caul is very much the product of Coppola's realistic concern with the rootlessness and instability of modern life. Coppola is compassionate enough to show pain in his character, and yet is also sophisticated enough to prevent the pain from becoming a form of dramatic paralysis. Life and death go on in a Coppola movie, pain or no pain. Nonetheless, *The Conversation* strikes me as the least successful of Coppola's trinity of very personal projects. In retrospect, *You're a Big Boy Now* was a more fully rounded and more keenly articulated projection of adolescence and young manhood than was the wildly overrated *The Graduate*. It just happened to be Coppola's misfortune that Peter Kastner did not give *You're a Big Boy Now* the mythic boost that Dustin Hoffman gave *The Graduate*. Not that everything worked as it should have in *You're a Big Boy Now*. The humor, especially, seemed to wobble uncertainly between giddiness and heavy-heartedness. It was as if Coppola's visions were too cloudy and too complex for the chiaroscuro contrasts of a knockabout farce on roller skates. With *The Rain People*, Coppola seemed to have come of age artistically in that he had found reasonably complicated characters to function in a relatively mobile milieu. He had escaped Hollywood in every sense. His directing and screenwriting were anticliché to the point of being anticlassical as he took to the road like a Charles Kuralt with ants in his angst, and he was free to improvise to his heart's content. His casting—Shirley Knight, James Caan, Robert Duvall—was as nonjudgmental and as nonstellar as his conception, itself a model of morbid compassion for people truly and profoundly cast out from themselves. Again, the paying customers didn't show up in large enough numbers, and Coppola might have been permanently written off by Hollywood's new demimoguls if his fairy *Godfather* had not intervened at an opportune moment.

The most disconcerting flaw of *The Conversation* is the tendency of its plot to cover up its own improbabilities with facile flourishes of absurdism. It is hard enough to accept the premise that the whole conversation was merely staged to deceive Caul and his employer (and the audience as well). It is even harder to understand why Caul and all his electronic gear were hauled into a simple murder plot in the first place. Why is it so necessary for the corporate conspirators to lure Robert Duvall's cameo tycoon into a hotel room laboriously designated on the tape of *the* conversation? Coppola never lets us in on any of the tactical details. Obviously, he opts for surprise over suspense, but even his surprises are muffled by his solemn gaze. In the end we are asked to believe that Caul's erstwhile employers have penetrated his own jealously guarded pad with an electronic bug and even a hidden television camera. (A spectacularly unmotivated camera movement simulates the hidden video viewer with a kind of spectral imitation of HAL's lip-reading eye-movement in *2001*.) Again, why should ruthless industrialists content themselves with merely spying on a most dangerous witness to murder when it is so much easier and cheaper to kill him? It is, of course, ironic that Harry Caul should be obsessed with his own privacy after a hard day invading everyone else's. Ironic and even plausible. But never very funny.

Coppola is hitting too close to home in that Caul's isolation is a mirror image of Coppola's introversion. And are not Caul's doubts and fears simply fantasized extensions of the doubts and fears of a contemporary filmmaker in search of new truths to replace the old formulas? Is there not a bit of a snooper and the eavesdropper in every filmmaker, and, indeed, in every narrative or dramatic artist worth anything at all? Eric Rohmer, for example, is said to have written many of his scripts after listening to taped improvisations of his actors in the roles they were going to play. Indeed, as I watched the first shot of *The Conversation*, I wondered whether Coppola had stage-managed the whole scene with self-conscious extras or had instead snooped on a real-life setting with a few "ringers" (Hackman, Forrest, Williams, et al.) from his cast.

As a modern filmmaker, Coppola must face up to the representation or simulation of the most sacredly intimate moments of existence. Orson Welles once declared in an interview that he could never believe in the emotional truth of sex or prayer on the screen because in his mind's eye he could see the production crews hovering about a supposedly private experience. Such an attitude may sound quaintly mid-Victorian today, not only because of changing mores but also because of changing technologies. As Marshall McLuhan once suggested, did we ever really believe that we could string up so much electric wire without connecting some of it to our innermost souls?

I believe that Coppola is very aware of these gray areas in the intellectual-industrial complex of which he is now such a prominent part. But he has not broken through the barriers of his own self-consciousness in *The Conversation*. Hence, Harry Caul, who enters the movie as a mere extra, eventually emerges as a massive enigma, settling down neither as the audience's Everyman, nor as the artist's ego. As he tears apart his apartment in search of that elusive electronic bug, I thought of the furniture-smashing frenzy in *Citizen Kane*, of the red-wall-into-firewood demolition derby in *The Red Desert*, of the systematic stripping down of living-room surroundings in *Life Upside Down*. Indeed, I thought of the entire age of absurdism with all the gloom and doom and Weltschmerz.

Still, it struck me that art has never been absolved of its obligation to be more illuminating than life. Even as an ignoble, ignominious descendant of Sam Spade and Philip Marlowe, the guilt-ridden Harry Caul remains a private eye from whom the audience expects a full accounting. Unfortunately, Coppola has not thought through the plot twists of *The Conversation* on their own terms. He has instead retreated into the inner space of the supposedly suffering artist as if there were nothing more to be done with the outer space of this wicked world. Nonetheless, he has posed a mystery for the audience, and all mysteries have the property of awakening an atavistic yearning for a rational order in the universe. Movies themselves are so inquisitive and indiscreet that the moviegoer becomes irrevocably implicated in the prying and probing of the medium. Once the projector starts turning it is too late to turn back with the prim attitude that certain secrets are best left unseen and unheard. The truth must be known, and it had better make sense. *The Conversation* could have used a great deal more vulgar curiosity about its own plot and its own characters. Coppola's good taste has been misplaced on this occasion, but he remains one of our most promising new filmmakers nonetheless.

—June 1974

The Front

LET US NOW dispraise infamous men. *The Front* takes dead aim at the television blacklisters of the 1950s and shoots loads of buckshot at these baddies. Director Martin Ritt and scenarist Walter Bernstein know whereof they speak when they reenact the era of Joe McCarthy and his minions. Ritt and Bernstein were themselves blacklisted at the time, along with cast members Zero Mostel, Herschel Bernardi, Joshua Shelley, and Lloyd Gough. Woody Allen, who clearly sympathizes with the sufferings of this period, plays the "front" who peddles scripts by blacklisted writers to the unsuspecting networks. So far, well and good.

The House Un-American Activities Committee has been attacked on-screen only once before, in Charles Chaplin's *A King in New York*, a film made, alas, in exile. Chaplin's curious mixture of pratfalls and polemics in the midst of McCarthyism struck even his politically sympathetic critics as artistically inappropriate for the period. Chaplin implied in the film that he had never been a Communist and that it had been absurd to accuse a man as rich as he of being one. The trauma of past Communist association is transferred in the film to a little boy Marxist (played by Chaplin's own son Michael) who starts out spouting class-struggle maxims and ends up naming his own parents as members of the Communist party. The clumsy sentimentality of this plot gambit does not bear very close scrutiny. Shirley Temple was accused in the thirties by HUAC (when Martin Dies was chairman) of being a dupe of the Communist party. Miss Temple was nine at the time, and the ensuing laughter did not represent a net gain for the cause of anticommunism. Still, Chaplin's attitude toward America in *A King in New York* seemed remarkably gentle, wistful, and affectionate, in view of the treatment he had received

By contrast, *The Front* starts out on a sour and supercilious note with a mock montage of America in the fifties (Truman, Eisenhower, McCarthy, DiMaggio, the Rosenbergs, American bombs over Korea, etc.) to the syrupy strains of Sinatra's rendition of "Young at Heart."

The filmmakers thus seek to impose upon the viewer an orthodoxy fully as odious as that preached by the rabid Red-hunters of the period. It is as if we were laboring under the delusion that the fifties were all *Grease* and *Happy Days*, and we need Ritt and Bernstein to enlighten us.

Once Woody Allen makes his entrance, however, the focus shifts from McCarthyism to Making It, particularly with a girl idealist played too earnestly by Andrea Marcovicci. Allen's character is named Howard Prince and is supposed to be a lowly wretch who tends the cash register in a bar, makes book on the side, and is virtually illiterate, but who persists in making incriminatingly witty-Woody remarks like: "The only sin in my family was buying retail." The long-range strategy of the film is to milk Allen's familiar brand of ratty opportunism for all it's worth before arranging his political redemption at the final fade-out. Hence, Allen shamelessly cavorts as a bogus celebrity after he has agreed to front for three blacklisted television writers (Michael Murphy, Lloyd Gough, David Margulies), taking 10 percent of their earnings and 100 percent of their professional reputation. Allen serves also as the uninvolved Everyman who will eventually be awakened by the murderous obscenity of the blacklist.

Ritt and Bernstein do not make the three writers wronged innocents on the rack of the inquisition, but rather committed Communists who never retreat from their convictions. *The Front* therefore diverges from the purely libertarian point of view of the recent teleplay, *Fear on Trial*, based on the real-life clearing of radio entertainer John Henry Faulk of all the charges brought against him by the blacklisters. Through the recalcitrant writers in the movie, Ritt and Bernstein seek to make opposition to America's role in the Cold War in the late forties and early fifties ideologically consistent with later opposition to the war in Vietnam, thus bridging the gap between the Old Left and the New Left. It is a hard-nosed approach to the subject and one that raises more questions than it resolves.

I would hazard a guess that Ritt and Bernstein would never agree to the liberal proposition that the inquisitorial rituals of the McCarthy era provided a mirror image of the Moscow trials. They are entitled to their opinion, of course, but they leave themselves open to the charge of oversimplification. It is one thing to say that a Communist should not be deprived of his or her livelihood in the arts. It is quite another to suggest that anyone who did not vote for Henry Wallace in 1948 was guilty of red-baiting.

Ritt and Bernstein hedge their bets somewhat with the more pathetically victimized character of Hecky Brown (Zero Mostel), based partly on Mostel's own experience and partly on the tragic fate of Philip Loeb. Of all the victims of the blacklist, the performers were the most vulnerable and the most helpless. No one could front for them, and in their relative prominence in the public eye they made particularly tempting targets.

It is never made clear in the script or in the editing whether Hecky Brown has succumbed to the suggestion of the blacklisters that he spy on Howard Prince. One suspects that Mostel would never play the part of an informer after what his own defiance has cost him. He at least has earned the right to be vindictive. But Woody Allen seems on much weaker ground in the final fantasy of defiance as he tells the House Un-American Activities of a quarter of a century ago to go fuck itself.

It is so easy to imagine that that was another time and another place, as if each age did not breed its own scapegoats. There are perhaps fewer victims at the moment, but I have not detected a great rush to the side of Daniel Schorr and Harry Reems in their recent encounters with the enemies of the Bill of Rights. Ritt and Bernstein and Allen have restaged an Old War with a falsely optimistic ending. It's a shame, because the Woody Allen character had the comic potential of a truly Brechtian character. Like Dr. Johnson's dog on its hind legs, however, *The Front* deserves a great deal of credit for having been done at all.

—October 1976

Lenny

THE LINES have been forming for Dustin Hoffman in *Lenny* at Cinema I in the Bloomingdale Belt of funky chic, and I have a feeling that many of the same people were standing on line for Dustin Hoffman in *The Graduate* back in 1967 and 1968. Two blocks east of Cinema I at the even funkier First Avenue Screening Room, the cinematic ghost of the real, live Lenny Bruce haunts the screen every Thursday at midnight in a documentation entitled *Lenny Bruce Performance Film.* In 1966, the year before Dustin Hoffman became a great star almost overnight, Lenny Bruce was found dead in his own bathroom, naked before his enemies and detractors, the tell-tale paraphernalia of the dope addict strewn about him. In the years since his death two visions of his life have been swirling about in the public consciousness, one of Lenny Bruce the Saint in accordance with the gospels of Murray Kempton, Nat Hentoff, Dorothy Kilgallen, and other scribes who witnessed the Murtaugh-Kuh crucifixion of a saloon Socrates, if I may mix my martyrdoms, and the other of Lenny Bruce the Sinner as chronicled with Suetonian severity in *Ladies and Gentlemen, Lenny Bruce!!* by Albert Goldman and Lawrence Schiller. Then there are the play and screenplay by Julian Barry, who seems to have hedged his bets by mixing the apostle and the addict, the persecution and the paranoia. In Tom O'Horgan's stage version (with Cliff Gorman as Lenny), the tribal tom-toms of Amerika are blamed for Bruce's downfall, and as usual, there are in the staging many pathological overtones which tell us more about O'Horgan than about Bruce. From O'Horgan's Lenny Bruce Superstar we move to the pseudo-objectivity of Bob Fosse's ostentatiously low-key exercise in black and white.

Under the circumstances, Dustin Hoffman does about as well as could have been expected with a legendary performer everyone claims to have known intimately. In recent years it has been considered chic in some circles to poke fun at Hoffman for allegedly having lucked himself into a legendary reputation. I can't fault him here as a performer. He's got Bruce's voice and cadence down right enough, and his "hey man" reverberates with all the self-pitying hysteria of the fifties and sixties. But the big trouble is with the fatal evasiveness of the total conception as the movie hints at this and hints at that, but never comes down solidly on anything. Thus, there is not enough social overview on the Saint, nor enough insight into the Sinner. Fosse's portentously shadowy style demands more psychological analysis of his characters than he seems able to provide. Perhaps, Fosse and Barry were fatally inhibited by the need to cooperate with Bruce's ex-wife, Honey, and his mother, Sally Marr. Perhaps also, the demands of the Dustin Hoffman myth happened to clash with the actual dimensions of the Lenny Bruce legend in both its nobility and its notoriety. Indeed, there is more than a passing resemblance between the audience appeal of Hoffman's Lenny and that of Hoffman's Benjamin. In both films, Hoffman gets off on the right foot by putting down his elders and showing himself indifferent to material temptations. He then falls in love madly and sincerely, and then society makes him suffer for his madness and sincerity. But whereas Benjamin prevails in *The Graduate,* Bruce perishes in *Lenny* without leaving much of a clue to his ultimate intentions.

I have no desire to play God with the life and death of a man I never met, and, in fact, never even saw perform in the flesh. For weeks and weeks now I have been running into hipster freeloaders badmouthing *Lenny* for allegedly not telling it like it was. There seem to have been about a dozen huge screenings for free, and it is hard to believe that there is in this town anybody who's supposed to be anybody who hasn't seen *Lenny* for free. Now it seems to be the turn of the relative nobodies to plunk down their money at the box office and make their own feelings felt by word of mouth. I would suspect that most of the unreconstructed Lenny Bruce fans are among the somebodies, and that most of the unregenerate Dustin Hoffman fans are among the nobodies. And, for commercial purposes alone, one must never underestimate the subliminal Playboy Playmate potential of "artistically" unveiled Valerie Perrine as Honey the Stripper. It is here, especially, where the thin line between exposure and exploitation is crossed irrevocably as Bruce goes beyond Saint and Sinner to Satyr and Spectator. As the material becomes increasingly sensational, Fosse seems to strain for a self-consciously Godardian style of solemn contemplation out of the early shock contrasts of *Citizen Kane.* We have come a long way, but not all that long, from *Time on the March!*

to *Ladies and Gentlemen, Lenny Bruce!!*, the recurringly Pirandellian refrain in *Lenny*.

Nonetheless, a film is a film is a film, and it should be considered as a self-enclosed entity. Anything to avoid the addled literalism of the dreary realists who confuse mimesis with mimicry. In this context, however, it seems to be a bad idea for one celebrity to attempt to impersonate another. It is almost a matter of soul-stealing in that any degree of inexactitude in the reproduction is considered a betrayal of the original. Also, there is a tendency in practice for showbiz personages to be "done" once and once only whereas historical personages—Lincoln, Napoleon, Hitler, etc.—are done many times as if they pre-existed in literary forms like *Hamlet* and *Madame Bovary*. Hence, James Cagney's George M. Cohan in *Yankee Doodle Dandy* is likely to be the only lead-role impersonation of Cohan on the screen. Larry Parks's Jolson and Keefe Brasselle's Cantor and Kathryn Grayson's Grace Moore are likely to stand side by side with the original portraits of Jolson, Cantor, and Moore as the only examples of fakes. As if to underscore the problem, albeit unconsciously, there is a curious joke in *Lenny* involving Honey's linking of Bruce's addiction to the alcoholism in *I'll Cry Tomorrow*. "You mean Lillian Roth?" her interrogator inquires. "No, Susan Hayward," Honey replies to a ripple of laughter from the audience, which is invited to feel culturally superior to Honey because (a) she looks at movies instead of reading books, and (b) she confuses the actress playing a biographical character with the character herself. In other words, the audience for *Lenny* has been inveigled to laugh at itself.

Given the problems inherent in the project itself, what is one to say of the movie called *Lenny*? First, there is very little material to indicate exactly how funny Bruce could be at his best. The London Palladium recording, one of the greatest comedy albums of all time, was missing from both the play and the film. The Warner Brothers Prison Movie routine with the demand for a gay bar in the west wing was in the play, but is not in the movie. And where, oh where, are those fantastically prophetic Lenny Bruce routines on Eisenhower and Nixon which later found their way on to the Watergate White House tapes! If most of us have suffered from a feeling of *déjà entendu* in the past two years, it is because Lenny Bruce prepared us for the incredibly ratty sound of men in high places with his uncanny ear for a universal viciousness and hypocrisy through a buzz of saloon chatter. To demonstrate how funny Bruce could be might have been considered a form of pandering to audiences which prefer to be punished for their sins, real or imaginary. Perhaps, the sadly self-destructive trajectory of Bruce's existence might have become evident in the transition from comedian to crusader. A feeling of loss might have been supplanted by a feeling of waste. In any event, Dustin Hoffman's Lenny is not nearly as funny as the original, but then the new rock generation has never demonstrated much interest in the style of stand-up comics.

We are left then with the notion of Lenny Bruce as prophet, as the taboo-breaker ahead of his time. But was he? Is he? How many stand-up comics have you heard lately making jokes about the mastectomies of Betty Ford and Happy Rockefeller? In his own time, Bruce spoke approvingly in public of Eleanor Roosevelt's tits, and noted that Jackie Kennedy was hauling her ass out of the car at the time of the assassination, and that he wouldn't want his own girl to come home one day and be ashamed because she ran from danger instead of staying put. People don't stay, man, he said, more or less, they run. This section is in both Lenny Bruce films on view at this time, and it makes one pause with its profound feeling. I think it does a disservice to Bruce's uniqueness as an entertainer and as a human being to suggest that his audacity and soul-searching bad taste have been matched by anyone else to this day. I am not sure that I would have ever been prepared to accept every feverish improvisation that gurgled out of his unconscious. His art, such as it was, was generally too raw and abrasive and unreflective for my taste. I can do the libertarian bit as well as any one else. I voted for Morgenthau, or—more precisely—against Kuh, to demonstrate my disapproval of Bruce's ancient inquisitor, but I think we are a little too quick to congratulate ourselves on our cultural progress. The young, particularly, delude themselves if they fail to realize that they are replacing one set of taboos with another, and that somewhere on the horizon there lurks someone who is prepared in all bad taste to tell them precisely what they do not want to hear, just as Lenny Bruce himself is currently tricked up to tell them what they do want to hear.

Finally, I think that both the play and the film and, perhaps, even Bruce himself may have missed a bet in not devoting more time to an examination of the very devious art of comedy as it was practiced by other comedians. When other comics used to say that Bruce was "dangerous," I suspect that what they meant was that he neglected to follow the unwritten rules of the guild by involving the audiences too deeply in his own fear and desire. As poltergeist and Portnoy, Bruce was as disturbing as he was disturbed. Still, he would not serve so conveniently as a legend if his sense of humor had not largely deserted him in the end. Perhaps, being "merely" funny is more subversive than anything else. The most ludicrous aspect of Fosse's implicational cutting between the "reality" of Lenny's life and its "repetition" (in the Kierkegaardian sense) in his art is that it takes us back to those old musical biographies in which poor Franz can't finish his symphony because his lady love has walked out on him. In Lenny's case, we go directly from a soft-core episode in Honey's lesbian life to a Bruce routine on dykes. Life and Art may be close, but *that* close is indecent. And somewhat inane. As for Jan Miner's Mama Bruce, every mother in America should applaud. But in the background of the applause, I hear very faintly from the real Lenny Bruce: "Hey, man, that was *my* life!"

—November 1974

The Assassination of Trotsky

JOSEPH LOSEY'S *The Assassination of Trotsky* is the most underrated movie of the year largely because audiences seem to have anticipated one kind of experience, and Joseph Losey and his scenarist Nicholas Mosley have provided another. I must admit that I too was suspicious of Losey's intentions before I saw the film, not so much because Losey was a self-proclaimed non-Trotskyite, and was therefore not emotionally committed to his subject, but rather because history is in itself more constraining than fiction. People had complained of being bored by the film, and I believed them to the point of finally having to drag myself to the Baronet Theatre where my early departure would not be too noticeable. Also, I preferred not to endure the hostile vibes of the New York Festival audience.

But as I watched the film, I experienced the double epiphany of appreciating it for its own sake and also perceiving why it was disliked by other people. It is the old story. People are always demanding intellectual entertainment, but deep down they want to be emotionally raped. Oh, why aren't there more movies made about intellectuals and about intellectual subjects, but beware if you don't invest the screen intellectual with the endearingly crochety mannerisms of Paul Muni in his bearded period or with the voluptuous vacuity of Peter O'Toole's somnambule.

Richard Burton's Trotsky is all the more admirable for being so dryly and (until the pick-ax of Alain Delon's Jacson comes crashing into his skull) so bloodlessly intellectual. That is the whole point of Losey's meditation on the vulnerability of the political animal at bay. A man, like Trotsky, who believed in the power of the Word to change the world could never have sniffed out his assassin in advance. A bureaucratic beast like Stalin, by contrast, placed his faith in the world as it was and employed the word merely as psychological camouflage. Stalin, with his seminarian's scent for the preternatural, would have recognized Alain Delon's Jacson as the Angel of Death. But Trotsky saw in Jacson merely a potential convert to the Fourth

International, a shy journalist manqué who needed only some of Trotsky's editing and encouragement to become an effective polemicist in the cause.

Losey's style is very rigorous in this regard. He never lets us warm up to the emotional space between the victim and the assassin, and thus he never exploits the facile paternal-filial feelings which flowed through the film version of Jean-Paul Sartre's *Dirty Hands* some years ago with the victim-assassin histrionics of Pierre Brasseur and Daniel Gelin. It must have struck Losey from the beginning how fitting it was for Trotsky's assassin to aim for the brain as Robespierre's assailant had once assaulted the eloquent mouth. Why else would Losey have staged such an inglorious guignol when he might have cut away to the emotional ripple and reverberations attending the death of a Great Man?

Indeed, it seems almost perverse of Losey to take so long to take us to Trotsky and then so long to take leave of him. But I don't believe that Losey has thus diminished Trotsky any more than Straub diminished Bach by not placing him in the jazzier movie Ken Russell has in mind for the compulsive composer. What Losey, Mosley, and Burton among them have devised is a rare portrait of an intellectual, dying as he has lived, with full faith in the rational processes of history. Losey could have inserted more of Trotsky's words, but he might have had to sacrifice thereby some of the music of Valentina Cortese's emotional radar as Natalaya, Trotsky's wife, and the counterpoint and balance to Trotsky's noble obtuseness.

—November 1972

Sacco and Vanzetti

Sacco and Vanzetti is a skimpy, confused, incoherent, unconvincing movie on a subject so vast and intricate that we are almost justified in the belief that Italian fools rushed in where American angels feared to tread. Almost but not quite. American companies have had 50 years to do a movie about Sacco and Vanzetti, and they passed up the opportunity while turning out no fewer than three versions of the Dreyfus Case. Indeed, the Sacco-Vanzetti affair is our own Dreyfus Case with a more downbeat ending. Nicola Sacco and Bartolomeo Vanzetti were arrested on May 5, 1920, in Brockton, Massachusetts (later memorialized as Rocky Marciano's home town), subsequently tried and convicted for a South Braintree payroll robbery that had resulted in two felonious murders, and finally executed more than seven years later (August 23, 1927) after entire continents were convulsed by the most controversial judicial proceeding in American history.

And ironically, what is most memorable about this chapter in American history—that is, the victims themselves—is also what is most moving about the otherwise inadequate movie that commemorates them. Riccardo Cucciolla and Gian-Maria Volonte not only resemble in their make-up the contemporary photos of Sacco and Vanzetti when they were still walking on this planet, but their visual eloquence also corresponds to the verbal eloquence of their models. It is possible to look at Volonte's face and think of him as the man who declared: "If it had not been for these things, I might have lived out my life talking at streetcorners to scorning men. I might have died unknown, unmarked, a failure. This is our career and our triumph. Never in our full life can we hope to do such work for tolerance, for justice, for man's understanding of man as now we do by an accident." Unfortunately, Volonte muffs the speech itself, a symptom of the verbal catastrophe in the film as a whole. After all, spaghetti English can get by on the mythic vistas of a Sergio Leone western, but not

59

in an epic of language like the Sacco-Vanzetti case with its trial transcript alone taking up more than three million words.

It might be noted also that John Dos Passos has written passionately on the case in *U.S.A.*, and that Maxwell Anderson's *Winterset* is based loosely, romantically, and ultrapoetically on the search for truth by the son of a Sacco-Vanzetti-like victim. There is also a longer version of Vanzetti's speech as an issue of academic freedom in *The Male Animal* by James Thurber and Elliott Nugent. Finally, I recall taking a sociology course at Columbia in the late forties at which time Professor Casey would open the course with a lengthy discussion of the Sacco-Vanzetti case, particularly of the detailed identification of Sacco, an identification that sounded laughable as Professor Casey read it. It was not until much, much later that I realized that a distinction must be made between proving someone not guilty and believing someone to be innocent. In all that I have read of the case, I am convinced that there was enough doubt to exonerate Sacco and Vanzetti of the crime, but that there was never enough evidence to establish their innocence beyond the shadow of a doubt.

Giuliano Montaldo's approach to the inherent ambiguities of his material is to ride roughshod over them. Hence, he is not content merely to caricature unfriendly witnesses; he must undercut their testimony with objective reenactments of events which occurred at a time and place from which Giuliano Montaldo has been forever barred by history and geography. Thus by pretending to know the unknowable, the director merely creates his own credibility gap. The movie's tendency to canonize Sacco and Vanzetti while caricaturing their prosecutor, Katzman (Cyril Cusack), and their persecutor, Judge Thayer (Geoffrey Keen), would indeed seem intolerably unfair if it were not for the innate dignity and depth conveyed even in caricatures by Mr. Cusack and Mr. Keen. The best that can be said for *Sacco and Vanzetti* is that it ends up being not too offensive in the shrillness of its special pleading. And if that isn't damning with faint dispraise, I don't know what is.

—November 1971

The Case of the Naves Brothers

The Case of the Naves Brothers is worth more than passing interest in this era of lawlessness and disorder. This account of a spectacular miscarriage of justice in Brazil some decades ago provides some of the most harrowing scenes of official torture I have ever witnessed on the screen, and I am not speaking now of grand guignol effects, but of a feeling of hopelessness and helplessness inspired by the very senselessness of the situation. The two Naves brothers are accused by the authorities of having disposed of their partner so as to steal his share of the business. The alleged victim has mysteriously disappeared, and the Naves brothers insist that it is *he* who has absconded with *their* money. The alleged victim's family suspects the Naves brothers; there is gossip around town; and then a newly installed police chief decides to take matters into his own hands. He begins torturing the suspects and terrorizing their immediate families. After a period of resistance, they confess to anything he suggests, and they are convicted of murder on the basis of their confessions. A civil liberties freak in the area takes their case, but he is unable to secure a judicial reversal. Years and years later, the alleged victim is apprehended in a faraway city in Brazil, and the Naves brothers are released from prison. The newspaper headlines announce the correction of a "judicial error."

One of the problems of the picture is that the audience never becomes sufficiently involved with the Naves brothers to identify with them. Hence, they remain sensationalized human interest characters in a tabloid drama, to be pitied without being understood. That an antiauthoritarian scenario of this stripe should have gotten past the censors of Brazil's military dictatorship would seem a bit odd if it were not for the extraordinary audacity of the Cinema Nuevo in recent years under the most oppressive social conditions imaginable. Of course, there are allegorical overtones for today in this "real-life" story from yesterday's newspapers, but the film is far from satisfying allegorically. There are none of the usual salivary signposts of race

61

and class conflict. The torture victims are white middle-class entre-
preneurs, and several of their tormentors are black policemen. There
seems to be no particular political issue involved beyond the most
abstract notions embodied in our Bill of Rights and common law,
notions that do not seem to travel well to warmer climates, as many
young American hashish fanciers languishing in Old World jails for
extended periods without benefit of counsel have discovered to their
sorrow after escaping the confines of repressive America.

Often, the histrionics are more harrowing than the supposed
tortures, and the film drones on and on in the most tedious legalese.
But the very pointlessness of the proceedings only adds to the numbing horror. I saw the film a few years ago and regarded it as one of the
more naive tracts on innocent Man enslaved by his evil society. I
didn't like it at all, and couldn't fit it either into ethics (too one-
sidedly one-dimensional) or aesthetics (too hysterical and uncon-
trolled). But I've never forgotten it. There is an embarrassingly authentic banality about its brutality, and at the very least, it reminds us
all too forcefully of the vast number of potential victims on this
planet.

—September 1972

State of Siege

I

IF *State of Siege* had happened to arrive in America under ordinary circumstances as a commercial enterprise seeking a payoff and a playoff in a capitalistic country, a political analysis of the material would have seemed supplementary if not indeed superfluous. A movie is a movie and all that. Unfortunately, *State of Siege* has been rather conveniently converted into a *cause célèbre* under the auspices of the allegedly American Film Institute. The issues have become George Stevens, Jr., and Freedom of Expression rather than the images, sounds, and alleged "facts" of *State of Siege*. Ever since George Stevens, Jr., disinvited *State of Siege* from the opening series of screenings at the AFI Theatre at the Kennedy Center, we have had alarums and excursions and pronouncements and perorations. Indeed, people were busy signing petitions and striking moral poses in support of freedom of expression even before they had seen the movie. As Nichols and May once reminded us in their classic skit on the quiz-show scandals, moral issues are ever so much more fun than real issues. And especially when the culprit is such an easy, harmless, safe target as the infinitely vulnerable American Film Institute. For the record, however, my own position on the moral issue of freedom of expression has never varied by a hair's-breadth over the years. I am flatly opposed to all censorship, be it applied to *State of Siege* or *Deep Throat* or *Birth of a Nation* or *Triumph of the Will* or every last racist flicker of the old cowboy-injun flicks. My commitment to cinema and all other forms of artistic expression is unconditional.

As it happened, I had submitted my resignation from the Board of Directors of the American Film Institute a few days before the controversy over the Costa-Gavras movie erupted. As only one out of 37 members of the board, I hardly intended to overdramatize my departure. I have too often criticized others for grandstand plays not to feel uncomfortable over one of my own. Also, I have always been very careful to make a distinction between reasons and excuses. My

63

basic reason for resigning? I had too many other obligations. That's all, folks. I did not resign because George Stevens, Jr., had the temerity to ignore my political predilections by inviting Richard the Third to the John Ford dinner. I did not resign because *State of Siege* was disinvited, and I did not resign because George Stevens, Jr., had refused to resign or even relent.

My role at the AFI was always too marginal for any administrative megalomania to take hold. I enjoyed my association with Roger Stevens, George Stevens, Jr., and all the other members of the board and the staff. I must confess also that sitting on the board with such star eminences as Gregory Peck and Charlton Heston always gave me a Through-the-Looking-Glass feeling of being a villainous character actor in a movie about Greg or Chuck as an idealistic executive looking right through my darkly circled night-school CPA eyes into my evil corporation-raiding soul, and thus foiling all my nefarious plans. I mean that I was suddenly on the wrong side of the movie screen, and my muse beckoned me back into the creative and critical sanctuary of that darkness in which I had always been destined to function in my proper role.

Nonetheless, I still stand behind the American Film Institute and its objectives, particularly in the crucial area of archival preservation. I believe also that the Institute should assume more responsibility in the encouragement of film scholarship, a domain that has been shrinking in the AFI budget ever since the ouster of Jim Kitses, Estelle Changas, and Paul Schrader from Greystone. After all, it is a community of film scholars we can thank for the continuing interest in John Ford's career through the sixties and the seventies, and not the assembled Hollywood and Washington stuffed shirts at the Ford dinner. Render therefore unto Caesar the things which are Caesar's; and unto the Cinema the things which are the Cinema's.

I have talked with both parties to the dispute: George Stevens, Jr., and Roger Stevens for the AFI, and Costa-Gavras for the film. I have now seen the movie, and checked the reviews of Vincent Canby, Judith Crist, Kathleen Carroll, and Archer Winsten. I have also benefited from some instant research on the subject. But it is very hard to know where to begin, and so I will just sort of spill all over from Rome and Paris to Montevideo, from New York to Washington, from *The Battle of Algiers* to *Z*, from fact to fiction all the way to dialectical distortion and the poisonous poetics of partisanship.

First, I can understand why George Stevens, Jr., was upset when he saw the movie and thought of it being screened a few yards from a bust of John F. Kennedy. As a Kennedyite and Washingtonian (and McGovernite too, let us remember), Stevens remembers too many flag-draped coffins, and too many widows' weeds and grieving children to accept the murder of an American on the screen as a parable of Marxist justice. Even an American like Daniel A. Mitrione, for whom few tears were shed around the world at the time of his death. An ethnic police chief from Richmond, Indiana, on a dubious mission for the A.I.D., first in the Dominican Republic, then Brazil, then finally and fatally in Uruguay, is hardly the stuff of which memorable martyrs are made.

Costa-Gavras and Franco Solinas have concentrated on Mitrione as the focal point of all American foreign policy, and indeed of all social evil in the world. However, the film is fictionalized to the extent of using assumed names. Hence, Mitrione is called Philip Michael Santore, but the American flag and the Alliance for Progress, and every aspect of American involvement with Latin America is tied up with Mitrione in a Montevideo cellar. Of course, *State of Siege* was shot not in Montevideo or in any part of Uruguay, but in nearby less chilly Chile. One senses the steep topography of Chile in the early shots of police roadblocks snarling traffic. For the Marxist sensibility, all of South America and indeed all the world is governed by the same laws of oppression, exploitation, and expropriation. The well-publicized statement of Franco Solinas, screenwriter of *State of Siege*, is clear enough:

We haven't sought to make a suspense film. We wanted to ask the public a question—not in the classic sense, will he die? But is he or is he not responsible? Guilt not in the traditional sense—he has killed, he has robbed—but much greater. A responsibility of a political nature. Our point of view is not romantic. We are not giving a discourse on morality. We do not seek to establish whether Santore is good or bad. Santore interests us because he represents a system which is bad for the majority of men.

In his telegram to the members of the Board of Directors of the American Film Institute, George Stevens, Jr., declared:

Sometime ago we announced plans to premiere *State of Siege* in the AFI Theatre at the Kennedy Center. Though I had not, a' that time, seen the film, I made the decision based on my respect for the filmmaking abilities of its creators. I have now seen the film and discovered it deals with a theme which makes it an inappropriate choice for the showing that has been planned for it as part of our opening at the Kennedy Center.

State of Siege deals, according to published statements by the authors, with an event which actually happened in 1970, the political assassination of an American A.I.D. official, Daniel Mitrione, at the hands of guerrillas in Uruguay. Our decision to provide this film with its U.S. premiere in the opening days of the new motion picture theater in the Kennedy Center was a serious mistake, particularly in the wake of recent events which saw the assassination of the American Ambassador and the chargé d'affaires in the Sudan by Arab terrorists.

Moreover, it appears to me that this film rationalizes an act of political assassination; and I think it undesirable to initiate programing at the John F. Kennedy Center with such a film. I hope any disappointment Costa-Gavras might feel over this will be balanced by the knowledge that his film and the statement he makes within it will be available to the American public in theaters throughout the country of which the film is highly critical.

Stevens later told me he had first been alerted to a possible problem with *State of Siege* when he was having dinner with Max Palevsky, the film's financial backer. Palevsky reportedly remarked that he was surprised to see *State of Siege* go into Kennedy Center. Stevens then made his request to see the film. I first learned of the cancellation when a reporter from the *Washington Post* called to ask my reaction, first to the cancellation, and then to the fact that Stevens had substituted for *State of Siege* one of my alleged "faves," Jacques Rivette's *L'Amour Fou* as if I had engineered the whole thing to pay off Jacques Rivette. For just an instant, I felt a twinge of Nixonian nastiness toward the *Post*, but it passed, and I pleaded ignorance of the whole dispute.

When I attended the press conference given by Don Rugoff to explain his own position and that of the film's director and screenwriter, there were several interesting plays on words, first as to whether Stevens really meant "rationalization" or "justification." Costa-Gavras and Solinas insisted on making a distinction between the former, which they considered a valid approach to the subject, and the latter, invalid. Don Rugoff then made the distinction between assassination and "reluctant" execution, and I popped up to ask what the difference was as far as Mitrione was concerned, and I felt waves of hostility surging over me from all over the auditorium. Mitrione was a nonperson that morning, even though an unreasonable replica is now serving as mayor of nearby Philadelphia, and another may be in City Hall come 1974.

My curiosity over the film now thoroughly whetted, I went to see *State of Siege* at the Beekman at its first public performance in New York. At first, I felt the kind of documentary diffuseness I associated more with *The Battle of Algiers* than with *Z*. I was thoroughly familiar with both Costa-Gavras and Solinas, having seen all their work with other writers and directors, and thus spotted the tensions between them. Costa-Gavras flashy, intuitive, fatalistic, almost tragic; Solinas solid, theoretical, dialectical, almost lucid. With Costa-Gavras there was the swirling public occasion with the sardonic Greek Marxist chorus, on this occasion O. E. Hasse as the raisonneur. With Solinas there was the documentary authentication of fictional detail, the torture gadgets shipped in diplomatic pouches from a Disneyland training ground in Texas. Step by step, Solinas will instruct us in all the picturesque details of an American conspiracy to enslave the world. It is the same story everywhere, one of the guerrilla interrogators declares: Algeria, Cuba, Vietnam.

Of the reviewers thus far, only Vincent Canby has expressed any reservations about the factual background of the narrative. One would never know from this picture that Uruguay was in a state of civil disorder largely because of the malaise induced by a rampaging inflation, the same kind of inflation which brought Hitler to power in Germany. However, Costa-Gavras and Solinas cannot be faulted for neglecting the bread-and-butter issues of economics. Nothing would be more effective in keeping audiences away from the theater. American complicity in South American torture is a much more effective ploy for the box office, and there is undeniably American complicity in our support and recognition of regimes which torture their citizens, but I really wonder if Algeria, Cuba, and North Vietnam are exempt from the distressingly long list of countries whose dictatorial regimes practice some form of repressive torture. Where does the guilt begin and where does it end, and do Costa-Gavras and Solinas really mean to imply that repressive torture is exclusively the mechanism of capitalistic countries? Why is Mitrione any more the logical product of capitalism than Stalin is the logical product of Marxism?

When I spoke with Costa-Gavras and Solinas, they countered my objection that there was a tendency nowadays to attack the evils of one country's regime against another country's landscape. Thus, I argued, the film versions of the Solzhenitsyn novels were shot in Norway (*One Day in the Life of Ivan Denisovich*) and Denmark (*The First Circle*), *Z* was shot in Algeria, *The Confession* in France, and now *State of Siege* in Chile. But, they responded, the purpose of ideological cinema is not necessarily to convert the enemy, but to enrich the consciousnesses of one's supporters. Why shouldn't the left have its own entertainments?

I can't find much to quarrel with in this unusually modest statement of intention. I could even agree with Costa-Gavras and Solinas that all cinema is ideological either by commitment or default. In this sense, *The Godfather* may well be Nixonian by default as *Sound of Music* is Eisenhowerian by evangelical zeal. Why then should I quibble over the discrepancies and distortions in *State of Siege* when there is so much in the film that does attest accurately to the state of the world in our time? I suppose it is because I don't like it when a film tries to outsmart me by juggling its categories between fact and fiction. And also, I feel that Costa-Gavras and Solinas have chosen to exploit libertarian ideas in which they do not really believe. Hence, there is in *State of Siege* a recurring reference to the supposedly sacred Constitution, to the principles of democracy and judicial restraint and parliamentary pluralism, and to the rights of nations to govern their own affairs without outside interference. However, the Tupamaros were a small group of middle-class intellectuals who rejected democratic methods of persuasion. They hardly qualified as victims of capitalistic exploitation, being closer to our own Weathermen than to Fanon's *Wretched of the Earth*. But from the moment they first appear on the screen, they are romanticized in a way that can only be called Hollywoodian. They seem to travel perpetually in pairs, virile young man with pretty but idealistic young girl. No overt macho here. The Theodorakis percussive rhythms accompanying the capers of the Tupamaros are sympathetically pulse-stirring. There are flashes of comedy relief and humor. It's all such a lark to "expropriate" cars by luring dumb drivers with pretty decoys, and then brandishing guns all over the place. It *is* funny to wrap a middle-aged American in a rug so that his bald pate is sticking out. I could hear the audience giggling. It wasn't quite as exciting as blowing up French men, women, and children in *The Battle of Algiers*. That was really an orgasmic thrill. Perhaps Costa-Gavras and Solinas are not quite ready to rationalize the "reluctant" execution of the Jewish athletes in Munich, but Mitrione, alias Santore, alias Yves Montand as dialectical antagonist for the hooded inquisitors of the left, will do for the moment.

Yves Montand's casting is the movie's biggest coup. Montand gives Santore more gravity, dignity, lucidity, and moral stature than any mere police chief from Richmond, Indiana, would ever dream of demanding from central casting. And it is this inspired casting which gives the movie the tiniest semblance of the objectivity and ambiguity granted to it by those reviewers who have chosen to swallow it whole. Otherwise, every frame of the film is loaded with one-sided propaganda. Indeed, the frames themselves are often gilded with obtrusively oversized officer's hats left over from *Catch-22*. Renato Salvatori, who is especially adept at playing the fascist buffoon for Costa-Gavras, acts more with his ridiculous hat than with his sympathetically primitive face. The fascists are often distorted through the mercilessly derisive lenses of grotesque caricature; the Tupamoros are almost invariably seen in modestly heroic middle shots.

What then of the double layer of the film? It serves merely to imply a causal relationship between every manifestation of the American system and Mitrione. But is it Mitrione as an American, or is it Mitrione as a policeman in any society in the world that is at issue here? Let us say that we comfortable Manhattanites prefer not to know what our Mitriones are doing in the back rooms of station houses throughout the city, the country, and even the world. The order which we seek and which perhaps we now even crave cannot be purchased cheaply. But how much terror would it take in our own immediate neighborhood for us to call Mitrione back from his grave to save us?

Costa-Gavras and Solinas can mince all the words they want. If they do not rationalize or justify assassination by the Tupamaros, they certainly romanticize and sentimentalize it. For example, we see the atrocities of the repressive regime in all its graphic (almost pornographic) detail, but Costa-Gavras never shows us the Tupamaros actually killing Yves Montand. Why not? We saw Montand clobbered again and again in *Z* when he was the good guy being assassinated by the bad guys. Why not now when he is the sympathetically bad guy being "reluctantly" executed by the good guys? Were Costa-Gavras and Solinas afraid that their "rationalization" of leftist terror would leave a bad taste in the viewer's mouth if the viewer were treated to the spectacle of a breathing human flame being snuffed out in the name of a principle?

In *Z*, if you remember, a postscript told us of subsequent developments in Greek politics, all depressingly bad and reactionary. Strangely, there was no postscript to the activities of the Tupamaros. The American fascists go on as before under the watchful Eye of the People, but of the Tupamaros what? Normally, a movie ends when it chooses to end, and the critic has no business pushing it forward in time. Unfortunately, no one thus far seemed interested in checking out what ever happened to the other two officals kidnapped along with Mitrione, namely, American agronomist Dr. Claude L. Fly and Brazilian consul Gomides. On the bus in which the various guerrillas meet in turn to vote on the execution of Santore, the leader is asked about the fate of the other two captives, and the leader answers that they are innocent and will be released in a few days unharmed. The audience is left with the impression that this is precisely what happened. Both men *were* released, but only after a million-dollar ransom was paid for the Brazilian, and only after Claude L. Fly suffered a heart attack during his eight-month captivity. Eight months, not three days. Meanwhile, this same group of Tupamaros had kidnapped the British ambassdor to Uruguay, and later another group kidnapped a French woman journalist. A million-dollar ransom was asked for Fly also, but his family couldn't raise the money, and they severely criticized both the Nixon administration and the Uruguayan government for not negotiating with the Tupamaros. The Tupamaros later kidnapped the attorney general from Montevideo, released him after two weeks, and then kidnapped for the second time in three years one U. Pereira Reverbel, President Pacheco's confidant and director of the state-owned telephone company, while he was sitting in a dentist's chair. He pulled a gun but was beaten unconscious and taken out of the building bundled in a blanket.

The British ambassador, describing his ordeal upon arriving in England, said that the kidnappers looked like Ku Klux Klansmen in their masks and theat they were about university age. He termed conditions of his imprisonment "abominable," but added that the kidnappers gave him books to read. In that respect, Claude L. Fly wrote a 600-page diary which the Tupamaros delivered with him when he was released. I have not been able to determine whether or not Fly's death a short time later was a result of his ordeal, but it was a chance comment of Roger Stevens's that led me along this line of inquiry. There is at once a comic opera aspect and a note of prophetic horror in the full story of the Tupamaros. *State of Siege* does not begin to tell this story in all its historical, sociological, and psychological complexity. But if Costa-Gavras and Solinas had not come along with their provocative movie, I would never have bestirred myself to brush away all the cobwebs from the Mitrione affair. They have thus made me rethink much of my politics and poetics.

What upsets me most in *State of Siege* is not the anti-Americanism, and certainly not the anticapitalism, but rather the dramatized deliberation of a group of idealists as they prepare to kill an ideological enemy in cold blood. If I believe in the total abolition of capital punishment everywhere in the world, and especially in the United States, I don't believe premeditated political murder can ever be sanctified by a poll of the murderers, and, consequently, I cannot participate vicariously in the murder of Mitrione when we have seen already that even Eichmann's execution failed so dismally as psychological retribution that there seems to be an unconscious fear in Israel of another Nazi war criminal doddering into the dock with traumatic irrelevance to the horror of history.

I am willing to believe Stevens rejected *State of Siege* more for its imagery than for its ideology. Still, Stevens was ethically wrong in first inviting and then disinviting a film, the makers of which never sought the honor of an AFI screening in the first place. The feelings of an honored filmmaker should be considered of more import than the feelings of official Washington. Even on the most tactical level, Stevens would have lost nothing by having allowed official Washington to be outraged a bit. So far New York doesn't seem to be outraged at all. Our national self-hatred seems so insatiable that the ideological disapproval of America shared by Costa-Gavras and Solinas seems mild by comparison. There is at least a part of me wondering why Costa-Gavras and Solinas don't go home to take pot-shots at Pompidou and the Pope. It is that same part of me that warms to Jane Fonda, but gets turned off by Vanessa Redgrave. Social criticism should begin at home, and if America has had a bad habit of exporting its presumed virtue abroad, Europeans have an equally bad habit of thinking they can diagnose all America's ills with a quick course in Berlitz and a very short interview with Allen Ginsberg. The strange thing is that *State of Siege* is a great deal more fun as a movie-movie than I seem willing to give it credit for, and both Costa-Gavras and Solinas are a great deal more sympathetic than I seem willing to concede. Perhaps it is the critical and audience reaction that has turned me off from this very skillfully wrought spectacle. So go see it without fail while I prepare to plunge more deeply into its curious paradoxes in Part II, now that I have discussed some of its surface aspects.

II

All Greeks are exiles at heart. When they are not in flight from their impoverished geography, they are in retreat from their glorious history. They are officially the most beloved of all minorities, and emotionally the most beleagured. After all, the rocky, arid, unproductive soil of Greece is hardly the ideal terrain for a national pedestal. Being of Greek descent myself, I believe I have as much right as any non-Greek to have a theory about Greeks.

All my life I have heard condescendingly kind words about Greeks and Greece from non-Greeks. These kind words seemed always to have been designed to make me feel like an unfortunate orphan who had lost his illustrious ancestors a very long time ago. It was therefore in character for the so-called civilized world to repay its debt to Greece by looting the country of almost all its art treasures. There is consequently more of the glory of Ancient Hellas in New York, London, Paris, Berlin, and other museum metropolises than there is in the barren wastes of Greece itself. In this respect, we might say that Lord Elgin loved Greece with the dreadful efficiency of Genghis Khan.

But then who could expect Hellenophiles around the world to entrust modern Greeks with the heritage of Ancient Greeks? Even Byron was supposed to have become disillusioned with the brawling Balkan tribe he found foraging on the sites of his romantic visions. He journeyed in quest of nineteenth-century Pericleans, and all he found was a procession of pushcart vendors, who can be found nowadays on any streetcorner in New York beginning the very tedious task of amassing great fortunes.

However, I do not profess to be a professional Greek even in this supposed year of the ethnics. I have very rarely socialized with my ancestral compatriots unless their cultural interests happened to coincide with mine at any given moment. And although I have visited London and Paris fairly regularly since 1961, I never managed to make it to Greece until 1968, and even then and in the following year I never bothered to venture beyond Athens, with its open-air cinemas at the walls of which young Costa-Gavras used to leap up and down to get a free view of the screen. The respective birthplaces of my father and mother are not too far from where Costa-Gavras was born, but I have little desire to visit these ancestral locales. Somehow I don't want to repeat Byron's mistake by forcing a pathetic patina of rot and ruin and poverty to fulfill the heroic fantasies my father left behind as his only legacy. Besides, my roots and memories are in Brooklyn and Queens and Manhattan, and not in the Pelopennesian ports from which Greek kings once sailed to reclaim Helen from the Trojans. Still, there were moments in 1968 and 1969 when I sat in the syntagma in Athens with the ghostly feeling that I had been sitting there always in spiritual harmony with my true people, and that some part of me would never leave again.

Perhaps it is true that you can't go home again, but it may also be true that you can never entirely escape the ghosts from the grave. Modern Greece has been politically and often bloodily divided ever since King Otto assumed the throne in 1830. The Monarchists and the Republicans have struggled for power ever since. Nowadays they call each other Fascists and Communists. Even the language has reflected this division with the Cretan dialect of Venizelos and Kazantzakis contending with the Constantinian Katharevousa, in which I was instructed by a succession of very genteel Greek-American teachers.

From anything I have read of the early life of Costa-Gavras in Greece, I know instinctively that his mother and my mother would never get along. I have had many affectionate arguments over Papadopoulos with my mother, but in the crunch I don't think I could turn her over to revolutionary or even reformist authorites for political rectification. Nor would I be particularly overjoyed to see my bourgeois relatives in Athens butchered or even badgered in an "objectively" justified revolution. I don't argue their case or their cause, but there is enough of them in me, and of me in them, to keep me effectively apathetic about the political situation. If the alternative to Papadopoulos and the coarse colonels were some ideal democratic Eden which combined economic justice with political and intellectual freedom, and which excluded the influence and domination of Big Powers, East or West, I would have no problem making the sentimental choice Costa-Gavras has suggested in his last three movies. But I find it naive to think that any small country (except possbily

Switzerland) can find happiness and prosperity in the Big State-Multinational Corporation maelstrom of today's power politics. Hence, Greece, Czechoslovakia, Uruguay—each in its own way is a pathetic anachronism, a clucking victim of those Big Power Predators: the Eagle and the Bear.

But what of the tortures and arbitrary imprisonments Costa-Gavras complains about in his movies? Of course, I'm opposed to torture and arbitrary imprisonment. Who isn't? But is it more important to condemn a wicked system in which torture and arbitrary imprisonment are possible, or to single out wicked men at random in a melodramatic fashion? If indeed the late Daniel Mitrione practiced torture in Central and South America, and I notice now that that fact is in some dispute, would not a concern with *habeas corpus* and due process be relevant to the situation? But such a concern applies only if we are talking about politics rather than poetics. When we shift to poetics, the problem is of a different order. Then we must ask if the melodrama surrounding Mitrione is a valid pretext for indoctrinating the audience with a Marxist view of American economic imperialism in South America and the Third World. Most reviewers seem to think it is. Look at the ITT scandals and the Watergate follies, they say. Look at Daniel Ellsberg and Ray Dirks in the dock and on the carpet for exposing chicanery in high places while the worst culprits get off scot-free. Certainly, the most morbid Marxist would be hard put to think up a plot as sordid as Watergate or the Equity Funding Corporation with a computer actually programmed for fraud.

We are ready to believe the worst about anyone and anything. Thus, Costa-Gavras and Solinas do not have to prove their case against Mitrione alias Santore. They merely have to shout: *"J'accuse!"* and the mob will do the rest. For some reviewers, the daily headlines fill in the blank spaces of *State of Siege*. Judith Crist, for example, considers the machinations of ITT in Chile as full confirmation of what Costa-Gavras and Solinas impute to Mitrione in Uruguay, Brazil, and the Dominican Republic. Now, no one can accuse Judith Crist, Archer Winsten, and Kathleen Carroll of being systematic Marxists or anti-Americans. None of these critics has ever been unduly enchanted with Jean-Luc Godard's brand of Marxist-Leninist cinema in recent years. It isn't really a movie, they complain of just everything Godard has done in the past five years, and even before. Godard seems boring and self-indulgent whereas Costa-Gavras seems exciting and entertaining. But if anything, Godard's politics are more radical than Costa-Gavras's. Having recently interviewed Godard and Jean-Pierre Gorin at the Algonquin, I retain an image of two field-jacketed fugitives from Mao's Ninth Field Army walking across the media-hardened indifference of the dining room. By contrast, Costa-Gavras and Solinas at the relatively palatial Pierre evoke the elegant middle-class leftism of the brightest salons in Paris and Rome. And yet in the esoteric reaches of world structuralism, Godard is still regarded as a stylistic force, and Costa-Gavras merely as a manipulative entertainer with a weakness for sacrificing form to effect. It is this perverseness in the structuralist scene in Paris against which Mary McCarthy was reacting when she declared in a recent symposium in the *Partisan Review* that she did indeed enjoy *Z*, as if the topmost towers of *Tel Quel, Cinethique*, and the newly structured *Cahiers du Cinema* would topple in shock from such vulgar impudence. My own reading of Costa-Gavras from his films has always been that he was nothing if not passionately pragmatic.

But when I finally did meet him, I found that my previous insights were only partially confirmed. In a sense, we both belong to a multinational firm of film sensibilities and we are both limited in our power, our choices and options, he as a filmmaker and I as a film critic. On the gut isssues, he is probably closer to radical anarchism, and I to liberal skepticism, and this is perhaps the widest chasm possible between two sensibilities in the modern world. I state my bias openly so that my instinctive resistance to his movies may be taken by the reader as a personal idiosyncrasy. I have read elsewhere that Costa-Gavras's father fought on the EAM or losing side of the Greek Civil War, which in its way was as traumatic a struggle between left and right as the Spanish Civil War. One could not expect a direct victim of the Truman Doctrine to grow up with a warm feeling for American Manifest Destiny anywhere in the world. But have the movie-movies of Costa-Gavras radicalized the world any more than has the anticinema of Godard? Or do they serve, as Luis Buñuel suggested to Carlos Fuentes of all subversive movies, merely as a means of expressing a margin of dissent from established authority?

It is significant that violence and/or torture figure very centrally in all three Costa-Gavras political films. Costa-Gavras told me that he had imported a tragic vision of life into the French cinema from both his Greek background and from the American movies he always admired. Orson Welles once remarked that tragedy in the English-speaking world had become inseparable from violence. By contrast, French tragedy since Racine is locked in the mind. Thus, as Shaw once noted, whereas English-speaking intellectuals tend to disguise their feelings as ideas, French intellectuals tend to disguise their ideas as feelings, the difference precisely between Shakespeare and Racine.

Curiously, the most feeling I ever sensed in a Costa-Gavras came through in his very first movie, a nonpolitical exercise entitled *The Sleeping Car Murders*, particularly in the relationship between the wisely world-weary detective played by Yves Montand and his surrogate son played by Jacques Perrin. There was an odd sweetness and intensity to this relationship, which, in retrospect, takes on an autobiographical coloration. I am beginning to understand Costa-Gavras's feeling for tragedy as I have always understood his image of himself as an exile. It is a feeling that is evidenced in the looks people give one another in flashbacks as if they already know that things are going to end very badly. With a natively somber artist like Costa-Gavras, life does not really begin until someone has died. But tragic feelings and tragic looks do not constitute a tragic vision. There is more of a tragic vision in Mizoguchi and in Ophuls and even in Sergio Leone than there is in Costa-Gavras. And least of all is there a tragic vision in *State of Siege*. Why not? Simply because Costa-Gavras and Solinas do not display the slightest interest in Daniel Mitrione as a human being. Time and again, the recurring images of memory and celebration threaten to break through into personal reverie, but they always stop safely on the other side of congealed politics. What was it really like for a police chief from Richmond, Indiana, to await death in a Montevideo cellar? For that matter, what was it really like to be a police chief in Richmond, Indiana? Costa-Gavras doesn't really care. He has convinced himself somehow that life is a collective experience within certain prescribed ideological limits, and the Enemy is invariably vulgar, corrupt, perverted, and, when Yves Montand plays the lead, pathetically deceived. But tragic feelings divorced from individual, idiosyncratic personal destiny result only in sentimental politics.

Hence, *State of Siege* reminds me of nothing so much as those old Warners historical allegories like *The Life of Emile Zola* and *Juarez* with a touch of *Watch on the Rhine*. The assassinated pacifist leader in *Z* was a combination Zola, Dreyfus, and Juarez, and the "reluctant" execution of Maximillian in *Juarez* bears more than a passing resemblance to the "reluctant" execution of Mitrione in *State of Siege*. It remained for Lillian Hellman's *Watch on the Rhine* to dramatize how some murders were less evil than others, and how the end sometimes justified the means, especially when Mother Russia was being menaced by fascist Finland. But then why shouldn't the left have its own John Wayne-type genre entertainment? I prefer to see left and right as arbitrary points on a circle of human illusions rotating endlessly around lonely, alienated exiles from Eden in search of a meaning to life before the darkness of death. My poetics are therefore even less in tune with *State of Siege* than are my politics. However, it is possible that Costa-Gavras may have decided that to let his tragic feelings come through all the way in his political films would make him tactically guilty of the Sin of Despair. Art and Revolution. Choose One. I choose Art.

—April 1973

The Mattei Affair

FRANCESCO ROSI'S *The Mattei Affair* lingers in my mind as the most fascinating political film of the year thus far. It was relatively well received by the local reviewers and was granted a reasonable run at the Little Carnegie, but the audiences simply didn't turn out for it. I caught it during the end of its run in a virtually empty theater. I didn't brood about this circumstance particularly; I have enjoyed some of the greatest films of all time in virtually empty theaters. Quality and popularity have a very erratic relationship in any art. Very recently, however, a political journalist of my acquaintance pointed out to me the ironic coincidence of the film's being at one and the same time dialectically opposed to the American oil companies, and yet officially distributed by the movie company arm of Gulf and Western. (Actually, Gulf and Western has no connection with oil.) The journalist in question is clearly not to be classified as paranoid in terms of the overwhelmingly conspiratorial times in which we live. Still, he wondered why the studio had not backed up *The Mattei Affair* with a bigger publicity campaign. Could this lack of support be interpreted as a devious maneuver by Gulf and Western to keep audiences away from the biography of a man whose mission in life was to pour oil on troubled waters and who may have been assassinated by a conspiracy of multinational interests?

I'm not that sure that a bigger publicity campaign would have gotten that many more people into the theater. It's been my experience over the years that political people talk a good game of political cinema, but when it comes time to go out at night they line up for *Last Tango in Paris* or *The Last Picture Show*, and not for the latest exclusive *cinéma-vérité* interview with Eldridge Cleaver. "Where are our movies on Vietnam?" we were asked rhetorically for years and years. And yet when a local theater owner showed antiwar documentaries for free, hardly anyone showed up. Of course, the Movement as a mass phenomenon has turned out to be one of the biggest pipe dreams of the sixties and seventies.

But I am not arguing now about the futility of preaching to the converted. I am suggesting instead that even the converted stay away in droves from the cinematic ceremonies of political revivalism. This is especially true of intellectually complex reconstructions of the ambiguities of history and biography such as Rosi's *The Mattei Affair*, and, before that, *Salvatore Giuliano*. Rosi's cinema does not cajole his audience with sentimental certitude in the patented Costa-Gavras manner. Nor does it cater to the voluptuous helplessness and pseudo-innocence of the audience in the face of obvious evil. Rather, Rosi chooses to pose political mysteries for our contemplation, and he is aided in *The Mattei Affair* by the dynamically unsentimental performance of Gian-Maria Volonte as Mattei, that curious eruption of recent world history, that odd blend of bluff, bluster, idealism, insecurity, and intransigence, that volatile mixture of grown-up self-discipline and childlike wanderlust. Above all, Mattei is a creature of global economics, a would-be magician trying to fly around the earth on a cheap mixture of Italian methane and hot air, floating from Lenin's tomb to the Arabian sands in search of oil and power for his own people. But there are no easy answers for Mattei or for Rosi or for us, and power of any kind and in any cause can be perilous.

The Mattei Affair is a masterly political biography, and I very much doubt that Gulf and Western would pass up a dividend to discourage American audiences from seeing it. It is more likely that even the most cultivated moviegoers prefer to use the screen for escape rather than for elevation. And what could be more irritating for a supposedly knowledgeable New Yorker than a cinematic reminder that he is a mere babe in the woods when it comes to international economics. Whereas *The Mattei Affair* indicates that a course in high (and lowdown) finance might be in order, *State of Siege* contents itself with a rousing chorus of "The Internationale." And as a New Yorker cartoon of ancient vintage suggested, if you don't know the words, you can just hum.

—October 1973

The Sorrow and the Pity

MARCEL OPHULS'S *The Sorrow and the Pity* runs about four and a half hours without an intermission (about five hours with); but, in terms of moral, intellectual, and emotional absorption, it is one of the shortest movies of the year. I mention this temporal paradox at the outset simply to warn any prospective American distributors and exhibitors that there is no fat to cut from *The Sorrow and the Pity*. No fat and no fatuousness. Only the irreducible wholeness of a delicately balanced meditation on the mysteries of courage, cowardice, and commitment. Thus, far from wearying most members of the audience at the recently concluded New York Film Festival, the film's relative thoroughness managed to whet their appetites for more revelations and illuminations on a dramatic but hitherto idealized chapter of French history: the German occupation from 1940 through 1944. To be exhaustive without being exhausting requires more than mere tricks of showbiz pacing and spacing. It requires a coherent and consistent vision of the world, nothing less than a veritable laser beam of concentration capable of piercing a bewildering array of surface idiosyncrasies to find the universal core underneath.

As it happens, *Le Chagrin et la Pitie* opened unobtrusively in a small art house on the Paris left bank until the turnaway crowds persuaded the fat-cat exhibitors to move it over to the Elysian Fields, and without any elisions in the film. But that was France, some people may say. What does the film have to say to us here in the good old guilt-ridden USA? My initial soundings indicate that the film is rich enough to sustain a great many interpretations both as history and as allegory. Local ideologues who feel they have been howling in the wilderness while life around them went on as usual may feel vindicated by some of the testimony in the film. Just as some Frenchmen, even more than the worst Germans, were the worst enemies of other Frenchmen, so do some Americans consider other Americans *their* worst enemies. We have been tossing around the notion of self-hatred too easily here in America. Perhaps it isn't ourselves we hate so much as our immediate neighbors. After all, even the late Joe McCarthy hated Owen Lattimore far more than he hated Chairman Mao or Uncle Joe. Most murders are transacted between people who know each other fairly intimately. Even those classical monsters, the Nazi death-camp killers, are now treated in some circles as relative humanitarians next to LBJ and Dick Nixon, and to argue the contrary is treated in these same circles as evidence of excessively Zionist zeal.

Hence, I noted a smattering of applause when a former officer in the Wehrmacht defended his wearing of military medals granted by the Nazi regime. "They still give out medals for the same sort of thing," he argued. True enough. Perhaps our whole apparatus of collective guilt was built on nothing more substantial than the power of winners to lecture losers. But if I felt that *The Sorrow and the Pity* were merely a pretext to rehash the same old left-right, red-black, pink-brown debating points, I would consign it to the ever mounting pile of idiotically ideological cinema. Fortunately, Marcel Ophuls and his colleagues do not so much exploit their subject as ennoble it. How? Certainly not by any fancy cinematics, but merely by allowing the witnesses to shape the course of the trial.

Oh, almost everyone these days pays lip service to the doctrine of letting the material of documentary establish the message. No preconceptions, no preconceptions, say the Wisemans, the Leacocks, the Maysles, and their disciples. And all the while these professional scavengers, these preening snobs, take their cameras up the nostrils of their victims so that elitist audiences may recognize once and for all the inescapable mediocrity of mucous. Wiseman, in particular, seems to enjoy ridiculing his social and cultural inferiors under the guise of institutional criticism. And only people who were socially and culturally intimidated by Wiseman's phony credentials as a sociologist with a camera would sit still for his boringly malicious ego trips at their expense.

By contrast, Ophuls seeks to illuminate an era by tracking down its noblest and most articulate survivors: Pierre Mendès-France, former Premier of France, aide to de Gaulle in the Resistance period, captain of the "Lorraine" Group; Lord Avon, better known to Americans as Anthony Eden; Dr. Claude Levy, biologist and writer; Emmanuel d'Astier de la Vigerie, founder of the "Liberation" movement; Georges Bidault, president of the National Resistance Council; Emile Coulandon, called "Colonel Gaspard," head of the Auvergne maquis;

Marcel Fouche-Degliame, director of the "Combat" movement; Maurice J. Buckmaster, head of the English underground; Denis Rake, an English secret agent; General Spears, liaison between Churchill and de Gaulle; and, above all, Louis Grave, a heartbreakingly virtuous peasant resistance fighter with a capacity for forgiveness (from the edge of the yawning furnaces of Auschwitz) almost beyond belief.

If I have omitted Jacques Duclos, head of the clandestine French Communist Party, from the roster of the lucidly good guys, it is because his very rhetorical answers to questions seemed to smack less of a personal credo than of a party manifesto. Also, Ophuls and his colleagues never pursue the implications of resistance rivalries between the Communists and the anti-Communists, and indeed of the questionable behavior of the French Communist Party between the signing of the Nazi-Soviet Pact on August 24, 1939, and the Nazi invasion of the Soviet Union on June 22, 1941, an interval in which, as the late George Orwell observed, French Communist Party Chief Maurice Thorez remained safely in Moscow while Nazi legions streamed across the French Capitalistic Countryside. Ophuls and his colleagues cannot be reasonably criticized, however, for not covering every aspect of their vast subject. Indeed, they have conscientiously restricted most of their coverage to the town of Clermont-Ferrand near Vichy, and to the memories of those who passed through it. The only time I thought the irony was becoming heavy-handed was when René de Chambrun, lawyer, and son-in-law of Pierre Laval, made a desperate attempt to redeem the reputation of his notorious father-in-law. Laval is too much to stomach, even for Ophuls. But not Christian de la Mazière, a veteran of the French Waffen SS ("Charlemagne" division), and one of the artistic triumphs of *The Sorrow and the Pity*. In the very castle where Pétain and Laval sought refuge across the Rhine from the advancing Allied armies, de la Mazière walks with Marcel Ophuls, son of the imperishable Max, and talks about commitment, and suddenly the emotional focus of the film shifts unexpectedly from the question of right choices and wrong choices to the feeling that any choice, right or wrong, right or left, is preferable to no choice at all. We begin to wonder how many of the people who cheered Pétain turned around and cheered de Gaulle when the tide had turned the other way.

I asked Marcel Ophuls if he had wondered himself, and he merely smiled, and said that he had, but that he hadn't wanted to press the point too strongly. I asked him about Maurice Chevalier, and he asked me what I thought about his treatment in the film, and I said that I found Chevalier in this context grotesquely egocentric, and Ophuls thought I was being too hard on Chevalier whom he (Ophuls) admired as the ultimate entertainer, the kind of man who always adapted himself to whichever way the wind was blowing. I told Ophuls that I had seen more extensive footage of French actors and actresses (Darrieux, Delair, Préjean, etc.) traveling through Germany during the Occupation, and that said footage had been shown to me under the auspices of the East Berlin Cinematheque. Ophuls himself had no access to East German archives and relied instead on French, English, and West-German sources for the most part. And, of course, there was an enormous amount of material he couldn't use.

I suppose every viewer will find some moment or other to treasure in this testament. I don't suppose I will ever forget Mendès-France's description of the anti-Semitism that swept through Casablanca after the fall of France, and of the indignities his own wife suffered as a consequence. I suppose Rick's Place will always seem a little more rickety after listening to Mendès-France. (Ophuls told me that the only time Mendès-France broke down was when he began to speak of his wife's suffering in this period.) But what has remained on the screen is the ability of a great many extraordinary people to look at themselves from the outside as participants in a historical drama, and to tell us better than we could ever imagine what it was really like in those days. Of course, the French have had a great deal of practice with this mystical conception of the Germans as the embodiments of what was evil and reactionary in France. The same morality play was acted out in 1789 and 1870. In 1918 the happy ending of melodrama could not conceal the mountains of corpses, and in 1940 it was the hero of Verdun who preached "Peace at any price."

Anthony Eden was very wise when he noted that no country that had escaped enemy occupation could afford to feel superior to France under the Vichy regime. As I looked around me at Lincoln Center, I wondered how many of us would take to the Catskills to mount a resistance, and how many of us would stay on as usual in Manhattan, and make the best of a bad situation. It would depend somewhat on the ideology of the occupiers, but not entirely. Courage and cowardice are abstract qualities, and no one can predict them in one's self or in others. What mysterious link could there have been between a self-professed homosexual actor like Denis Rake and a self-professed socialist peasant like Louis Grave, and yet there they were and there they are, brothers in arms, possessors of a quality in common that lifts them far above most of us mere mortals.

It is to the credit of Marcel Ophuls and his colleagues that they accept the harsh judgment of history by presenting authentic heroes not so that we can identify with them, but so that we can admire them from afar. Above all, these heroes are allowed to speak in the context of an intellectual tradition of documentary which seems to come mostly out of France (vide Resnais's *Night and Fog* and Rossif's *To Die in Madrid*). Perhaps the Anglo-American documentary movement could be salvaged with an emergency transfusion of glorious language, but bad aesthetic habits seem to linger forever. So go see *The Sorrow and the Pity* for genuine eloquence in three languages.

—November 1971

The Nasty Nazis:
History or Mythology

THE MORALIZERS are out in full force to pontificate on two allegedly decadent divertissements entitled *The Night Porter* and *Lacombe, Lucien*. Who would have thought back in 1945 that the time would come (less than 30 years later) when Nazis could be treated as period costume figures in sado-masochistic spectacles? Hello? Central Casting? Send me a dozen guys who can swagger in an SS uniform, and about 50 skinny types of all ages and sexes for concentration camp background. By the way, do you know where we can locate Martin Kosleck?

Even so, irony was already corroding the moral armor of the subject matter in such late fifties and early sixties meditations as *Night and Fog, The Diary of Anne Frank, Judgment at Nuremberg, Hiroshima, Mon Amour, L'Enclos, Kapo,* and *The Pawnbroker*. The tone of these testaments was almost excruciatingly solemn, but the blinding sacredness of the subject was being dimmed. It was no longer permissible to avert one's eyes from the horror. Spare Us Not Lest We Forget. To boo took precedence over taboo. And soon there were other, fresher horrors to contemplate: Hiroshima, Algeria, Vietnam, Biafra, Bangladesh. One by one, nation by nation, we were all guilty, and the Nazis became the invidious standards by which we were judged. Consequently, these once universally condemned creatures with their Sieg Heils and goose steps began to lose their historical specificity. The booming business in Hitlerian artifacts gradually shifted its selling campaign from straight horror to kinky nostalgia. Indeed, the Nazi experience was even absorbed into a slightly subterranean branch of Jewish humor (vide the "Springtime for Hitler" number in Mel Brooks's *The Producers*). An Odetsian gossip columnist's wife in *The Sweet Smell of Success* (1957) calls her mildly repressive husband a Hitler in an atmosphere of New Yorkish chic. A Jewish playgoer gets a big laugh when he declares that he would have

85

surrendered to the Germans rather than stay in the attic with the actress playing Anne Frank on the stage. Meanwhile, anti-Semitism crept back into intellectual fashion under the guise of anti-Zionism. What *had* we learned from the Holocaust? Simply not to trust another little man with a mustache, which meant that the next Hitler was already programmed as a big man with a beard. Besides, if every successive American President could be casually castigated as another Hitler, how uniquely monstrous could Hitler himself have been? In a sense, every narrative, dramatic, and documentary "treatment" of the Holocaust only cheapened it and made it more titillatingly thinkable. If it had been transformed immediately into a religion, it might have found a transcendent symbolic form, and today we might all be practicing Holocaustians.

But such was not to be. History was not to be interrupted. Instead, the movie rip-offs on the subject became increasingly sensational. From the beginning there had been a sub-genre of political pornography devoted exclusively to the death camps. Indeed, it isn't very far in ghoulish commercialism from the official footage of the atrocities to the most mendacious of "Mondo Cane" extravaganzas derived from these archives. By the same token, otherwise undistinguished scenarios could use the subject of Nazis to gain the kind of easy pathos associated with the Let's-Take-the-Titanic-for-Our-Honeymoon-Dear school of screenwriting complete with A-Little-Town-in-Pennsylvania-called-Gettysburg dialogue. This process of amplified pomposity is known also as The-Ship-of-Fools syndrome.

For my own part, I consider *Night and Fog* the only film on the Nazi era to have truly transcended its subject without betraying it. Even *The Sorrow and the Pity* tended to have moments of mitigation without justification. For the rest, it was more exploitation than explanation. In the East, Hitler remained a safer target than Stalin or even Ivan the Terrible. In the West, Hitler descended from melodrama to vaudeville. Finally, *The Damned* and *Cabaret* demonstrated to the film industry how audiences could be made to wallow in decadence in the name of social consciousness. We had come from Der Tag to Der Drag in one generation.

Hence, I gritted my teeth when I first heard what *The Night Porter* and *Lacombe, Lucien* were supposed to be about. Call it prejudice or preconception, but films about Nazis are in my view almost invariably doomed to bad faith and mediocrity. As it happens, *La-*

combe, Lucien has been favorably received in New York whereas *Night Porter* has been dismissed as drivel. I get the impression that many of the reviewers are jumping on Joe Levine and his hard-sex sell more than on the film itself. I can understand not admiring nor enjoying *Night Porter*, but I can't understand not respecting it. To be sure, there are problems with some of the minor characters dubbed in derisory English, and, as usual, the ear is quicker and more decisive than the eye in the average American screening room. Nonetheless, Liliana Cavani's visual style is so seductive and so obsessive that one has to be willfully blind to ignore it. One can quarrel with the tendency of her lyricism to overwhelm her frail narrative. But I really can't see how anyone can think for one moment that *The Night Porter* is intended as a realistic reconstruction of the Nazi era. One of my colleagues complained, for example, that it was highly unlikely that Nazi war criminals would ever form encounter groups to achieve some primal absolution for their sins. I agree that such activities form a very shaky premise for the plot, but coupled with the continuing elimination of incriminating witnesses by these same Nazis, this grotesque parody of group therapy functions more as ironic exposition than as realistic revelation. *The Night Porter* is no more concerned with the inner workings of the Nazi mind than *Last Tango in Paris* was concerned with the economic possibilities of dance halls. As *Last Tango* was more mythology than sociology, thus is *Night Porter* more mythology than history. A large part of the mythological emphasis in both films can be attributed to the casting. Marlon Brando, after all, played a night porter of sorts. (*Last Tango* was inspired at least partly by an obscure novel entitled *The Night Clerk*.) Still, no one is expected to believe in the sociological probability of Marlon Brando's characterization. *Last Tango in Paris* is a far cry from *An American in Paris*, and a mythic actor named Marlon Brando does most of the crying. If Brando had played opposite Dominique Sanda as was originally intended, Bertolucci might have fashioned two myths instead of one. Instead, the relatively unfamiliar Maria Schneider functioned as the sociological sex object (awakened French female of good family) to Marlon Brando's mythological sex subject (surly Saint Marlon of all the orifices).

By contrast, *The Night Porter* is reciprocally mythological in its casting of Dirk Bogarde as Max the SS man turned night porter, and Charlotte Rampling as Lucia, the wife of a symphony conductor from

America (even more mythology there), but formerly a concentration camp inmate on perversely intimate terms with Max. Max and Lucia meet again in the Vienna of 1957, and the past flows gracefully and inexorably into the present until the film and its protagonists are flooded by erotically sado-masochistic reminiscence. Cavani's camera movements are not as wildly ostentatious as Bertolucci's, but they do their work well as the shared memories of Max and Lucia are transformed into the slow dances of sleepwalkers drifting away from everything in the modern world except their own fear, desire, and disgust. Theirs ultimately is a forbidden love dredged up from the murky depths of their unconscious, rendered in space by Cavani's lofty overhead shot of the night porter in his darkened office as he awaits the dangers of the dawn. We are back with Orpheus and Eurydice once more, but this time they are both enjoined (by a commune of ex-Nazis representing Pluto) from looking back into Hades. They are both doomed by their desire to recreate the past in all its chained ecstasies. The last part of the film is all lyrical expression at the expense of narrative development, and this may be considered an artistic miscalculation on Cavani's part. I suppose it all depends upon whether you are as enthralled as I am by the very morbid spectacle of Dirk Bogarde's archangel of sexual anxiety grappling with Charlotte Rampling's archangel of sexual anguish. Since Bogarde and Rampling have consolidated their iconographical identities within the past decade, they tend to evoke the absurdist disorder of the sixties and seventies rather than the existential disorder of the forties and fifties, and this tends to make *The Night Porter* even more remote from historical reality than it would have been otherwise. Still, Cavani's *Cannibals*, with its artfully anachronistic treatment of the Antigone legend (dead bodies on city streets), did not set up long lines at the box office. Her art may need the alibi of the "big subject" in order to pass muster with the masses. If so, it would not be the first time in film history— even on the supposedly exalted level of a Bergman (the alibi of erotic violence) and Kurosawa (the alibi of samurai misanthropy).

Louis Malle is much cannier than Cavani. Indeed, Malle is a past master at being just one small step ahead of his audience and critics. His career has unfolded since 1957 more as a procession of projects than as a stream of personal expression. His first film, *Frantic (Ascenseur pour l'echafaud)* with Maurice Ronet and Jeanne Moreau, was made when the director was 24. It is still one of his most interesting films, ending as it does with a chic pre-*nouvelle vague* image of developing photographs emerging from the liquid mix with incriminating evidence of Ronet's and Moreau's passion for each other, thus linking them to the murder of Moreau's husband. What brings *Frantic* to mind most vividly in the context of *Lacombe, Lucien* is an interesting subplot involving a young joyriding couple counterpointed with the upper-class, cartelized world represented by Ronet and Moreau. Malle's sophisticated sense of class alignments has always distinguished him somewhat from his *petit-bourgeois* contemporaries on the French film scene, and it is his ability to perceive the ultimate virulence of class envy that provides *Lacombe, Lucien* with its most perceptive moments.

After *Frantic* came the *nouvelle libertinage* of *The Lovers*, again with Jeanne Moreau, but this time as the incarnation of every French housewife's fantasy of all-consuming adultery. For one reason or another, American audiences found the picture silly. In retrospect, Malle displayed much the same brittle upper-class effrontery in *The Lovers* that he later displayed in the much overrated *Murmur of the Heart*. His next film, *Zazie,* seems in retrospect somewhat of a prophecy of Richard Lester's strenuous strategies with a kind of zany surrealism in the mid and late sixties. *A Very Private Life* was Malle's failed *La Dolce Vita*, despite the box-office insurance of Brigitte Bardot and Marcello Mastroianni. Barely past 30, Malle was at a low ebb in the French film industry. *The Fire Within* recouped some of his critical prestige, especially in America. It was based very loosely on (and titled in France as) *Le Feu Follet*, a work of the late Drieu La Rochelle, a precious symbolist of the twenties and thirties, who was executed as a collaborationist in 1945. The film was influenced as well by Antonioni-Pavese speculations on suicide, then so cinematically fashionable. *The Fire Within* was a strange mixture of decadence and detachment, of self-pity and ennui. There seemed to be something irremediably dilettantish in Malle's artistic temperament. He seemed to be following the public pulse more closely than his own inner voice. His style always seemed tentative, provisional, dispensable. *Viva Maria* and *Le Voleur* were nothing if not exercises in style, trendy as all get out, but not quite audacious enough. Then the "comebacks" of *Murmur of the Heart* and *Lacombe, Lucien*, and the soporific *succès d'estime* of *Phantom India*. It can be argued (though not by me) that Malle has been unfairly maligned by auteurist critics because he is more in the tradition of the *objet d'art* directors such as Clair, Mamoulian, and Wyler than the river of personality directors such as Renoir, Lubitsch, and Ford. I prefer to think that Malle's career is notable more for its intelligence than its inspiration. Certainly, *Lacombe, Lucien* is nothing if not an intelligent film. Malle himself seems sensitive to the charge that his film is a bit of a rip-off from *The Sorrow and the Pity*, or even that the unexpected success of Marcel Ophuls's revisionist documentary may have made Malle's project more feasible. I tend to accept Malle's disclaimers at face value. From the very beginning of his career, Malle seems to have gone against the grain of bourgeois complacency not so much formally as thematically. Murder, adultery, suicide, revolution, burglary, incest, treason, and genocide have been flung into his audience's face with a kind of derisive finesse as if to declare that we are all more culpable than we care to admit.

His rather middle-brow point in *Lacombe, Lucien* is that any historical event, even the most sacred, is seen from literally millions of different points of view. Also, the past is never entirely inexplicable in terms of the present. Thus, that sullen young man who delivered your groceries last night may turn out to be your executioner tomorrow morning. Or even your gauleiter. *Lacombe, Lucien*, the bureaucratically inverted name of Malle's eponymous nonhero, represents every neatly dressed wretch who ever hit the streets in search of a job, only to answer an endless stream of ads with Sisyphian futility, and always last name first for purposes of degradation and dehumanization. Then one day the Gestapo offers a position of power and authority. What follows is a slow, low-key saga of the banality and bureaucracy of evil in Occupied France. What keeps the film going is the endless variety of put-downs possible in a position of such brutal authority. In this respect, Lucien Lacombe serves a useful purpose in reminding us of the fundamentally populist appeal of such dreadful demagogues as the late Joe McCarthy and the lingering George Wallace. One of the most interesting scenes in the film involves an act of vandalism on Lucien's part in destroying an exquisitely crafted ship model, the handiwork of an upper-class youth of the Resistance. The audience's sympathies are thus shrewdly divided between lower-class rebelliousness in the service of fascism and upper-class smugness in the name of humanism. Indeed, the scene is almost too shrewdly Marxist for its own good.

The most disconcerting image in the film is that of a black Gestapo agent. I asked Malle if this bit of off-beat casting were based on
historical fact, and he assured me that he wouldn't have dared cast
the part as he had if he hadn't had the research to back him up. There
were apparently several African agents working for the Gestapo in
Bordeaux. Indeed, there were more than a few Jewish agents in the
Gestapo all through the War.

Lacombe, Lucien, unlike *The Night Porter,* provides a *tabula rasa*
for the audience's fantasies in the casting of unfamiliar and inexperi-
enced players in the two lead roles: Pierre Blaise as Lucien, and Au-
rore Clement as France, Lucien's young Jewish mistress. Without the
iconographical distractions of a Bogarde or a Rampling (or a Brando
for that matter), it is easier for the audience to accept the factual
"authenticity" of the narrative. At times, the inexpertness of the two
lead performers slows the action down unconscionably, but what is
lost in tempo is often gained in unpredictability, and thus Malle
comes out ahead on balance. Despite unfortunate lapses into sentimentality and overly calculating humanization, *Lacombe, Lucien*
stays in the mind as a minor classic of universal underdogdom turning on its masters with a vengeance.

—October 1974

Slaughterhouse-Five

A minimum of unconsciousness is necessary if one wants to stay inside history. To act is one thing; to know one is acting is another. When lucidity invests the action, insinuates itself into it, action is undone and, with it, prejudice, whose function consists, precisely, in subordinating, in enslaving consciousness to action. The man who unmasks his fictions renounces his own resources and, in a sense, himself. Consequently, he will accept other fictions which will deny him, since they will not have cropped up from his own depths. No man concerned with his equilibrium may exceed a certain degree of lucidity and analysis. How much more this applies to a civilization, which vacillates as soon as it exposes the errors which permitted its growth and its luster, as soon as it calls into question *its own* truths.

—E. M. Cioran, *On a Winded Civilization*

I HAVE BEEN meaning to deal with the movie version of *Slaughterhouse-Five* for a perilously long period in terms of the journalistic time clock of movie reviewing. Indeed, it probably is too late for any credible shooting-from-the-hip review, nor for any supposedly impulsive blast from the barricades. *Slaughterhouse-Five* has not only been running for weeks and weeks at the Sutton; it has also been moderately hailed at the recently concluded Cannes Film Festival, about which we are to be deluged with Doomsday declarations from our professional pessimists on the scene. Doomsday declarations in film date back at least to Louis Lumière, who proclaimed that the cinema had no future, and this at a moment in history when the medium in question had had no opportunity to build up a past. Nowadays, of course, it is the world itself, and not merely its newest medium, that is coming to an end; and somehow film is supposed to reflect this apoplectically apocalyptic feeling or be judged hopelessly irrelevant. What nonsense! If the world is indeed coming to an end, then the state of the cinema is the least of our problems, and if it isn't, then it behooves us to shift our focus from doom to zoom.

As it happens, I did knock off a peremptory first-reaction review of *Slaughterhouse-Five* back when it opened, but I held it up for publication because it seemed both too caustic and too cryptic. I reprint it now simply to confront the anger that I felt at the time: "*Slaughterhouse-Five* leaves me unmoved and unimpressed. It is much, much better than *Happy Birthday, Wanda June,* but is that enough? I doubt it. Kurt Vonnegut bothers me. Perhaps his books are too cinematic for my taste, and by the time they get to the screen they seem curiously insubstantial. Vonnegut seems to want it every which way, inside his character for tears, and outside for laughs, grotesque situations for satire, gruesome situations for social protest, and gravitational situations for adolescent fantasies. And how the kids love it, I'm told. He ridicules machismo on the surface while nourishing it underneath with the creation of only two kinds of women: blobs (mothers, wives) and bunnies (breast-feeding play-mates). The movie is very pretty to look at, and George Roy Hill must be conceded a flair for fantasy; but the digestive after-effect is decid-edly low-protein Resnais."

Actually, I stand by my first impression. I have no intention of reneging or revising, but perhaps a certain amount of amplification is in order. By some standards, *Slaughterhouse-Five* is a success. Audi-ences like it. Its point is clear and trendy: war is not merely hell, it is childish. And especially World War II, that biggest of all jokes on the historians. Vonnegut's vision, such as it is, has been well served by George Roy Hill's direction, Stephen Geller's screenplay, Miroslav Ondricek's photography, and Dede Allen's editing. Except for the efforts of a minicult at Doc Films around the University of Chicago, not much attention has been paid to the directorial career of George Roy Hill. He seems eclectic as all get-out, but after *The World of Henry Orient, Butch Cassidy and the Sundance Kid,* and now *Slaugh-terhouse-Five,* a certain stylistic pattern begins to emerge, but a pat-tern very badly marred by emotional and plastic facility. The ease with which Hill slides back and forth between reality and fantasy, between objectivity and subjectivity, goes beyond conventional slickness into idiosyncratically odious oiliness.

Stephen Geller wrote the novel on which *Pretty Poison* was based. Now that neo-auteurists have eliminated director Noel Black and scenarist Lorenzo Semple from serious consideration, it may be of slight interest to note the thematic affinity between Geller and Vonnegut, and how at home both writers are with the derisive and the grotesque. Similarly, the casting of Michael Sacks as Billy Pilgrim comes as close to an anti-macho, anti-Wayne, anti-Sinatra casting of a reluctant warrior of World War II as it is possible to come without becoming clinically perverse or resurrecting the miscast-in-real-life Audie Murphy. But as I sat in the theatre feeling the audience around me wallowing with voluptuous helplessness in the sandbox of history, I became hopelessly alienated from the spectacle on the screen. It was the *Catch-22* cashing-in swindle in operation once again. Because Errol Flynn once lied to us, we can never believe anything again, and what fun it is not to believe in anything (except one's own sincerity) and still feel superior to people who do. Some of the film's admirers talk about its compassion. I didn't feel any. Perhaps I didn't get the joke. So it goes.

The whole thing started with Kurt Vonnegut's alleged desire to write a novel about the bombing of Dresden, a desire he exorcised by writing an antinovel on the subject. The title page sums up his motives, methods, and even alibis: "Slaughterhouse-Five or The Children's Crusade: A Duty-Dance with Death by Kurt Vonnegut, Jr., a Fourth-Generation German-American Now Living in Easy Circumstances on Cape Cod (And Smoking Too Much), Who, As An American Infantry Scout Hors De Combat As a Prisoner of War, Witnessed the Fire-Bombing of Dresden, Germany, 'The Florence of the Elbe,' a Long Time Ago, And Survived to Tell the Tale. This Is a Novel Somewhat in the Telegraphic Schizophrenic Manner of Tales of the Planet Tralfamadore, Where the Flying Saucers Come From. Peace."

Within this one paragraph one can discern the skillful blend of Bradbury (Tralfamadore) and Brautigan (Shaggy Dog Confessions) with just a sliver and slobber of Salinger. The stuff about a Fourth-Generation German-American is particularly canny in this context. It disarms any vulgar criticism of Vonnegut's moral priorities. Both in the book and in the movie, an officious academic brings up the question of the slaughter of the Jews, and the implied weariness in both media seems to convey the same message. Don't bother me with second-hand history, when I am peddling an eye-witness account. I vas dere, Charlie and Franklin and Eleanor. At Dresden, that is, not at Auschwitz or Buchenwald. Hence, there is more gut than von in Vonnegut's reaction to the desecration of Dresden. Believe only what you see and experience directly. Don't believe what you read in the papers. Perhaps that's too strong. You can believe it, but don't take it too seriously. As it happens, I believe Vonnegut about Dresden, as I believe the survivors of Auschwitz and Buchenwald. But I believe also that my mind can still encompass a fabric of history in which these two orders of atrocity are interwoven as complementary strands. But whatever happened back then and there, I don't believe it happened so that we could smile at it superciliously, as if we had been liberated from history by an interplanetary potion of irony.

—June 1972

Promised Lands

SUSAN SONTAG'S *Promised Lands* (at the First Avenue Screening Room) was filmed so soon after the October Yom Kippur War that the screen shows corpses still strewn across this ancient crossroads and battlefield between East and West, paganism and monotheism, Jew and Roman, Saracen and Crusader, Moslem and Jew, Moslem and Christian, Arab and Turk, Arab and European, Arab and Jew, and, perhaps most perplexingly of all, Palestinian and Israeli. By choosing this emotionally explosive subject, Miss Sontag makes it very difficult for the reviewer to judge her film apart from its larger contexts in history and politics. Indeed, there are so many ideological implications to each image in *Promised Lands* that it is possible for people to see and hear in the film whatever their prior prejudices want them to see and hear. Unfortunately, Miss Sontag never makes her own attitude entirely clear. There are many elusive hints of her ultimate sympathies, but little hard evidence.

Promised Lands never gives us even a glimpse of the Susan Sontag of the very explicit and very expressive essays, but supplies instead a skimpy documentarian who alternates half-heartedly between the contrasting approaches of Roberto Rossellini's *India* (visual irony) and Marcel Ophuls's *The Sorrow and the Pity* (verbal incandescence). That *India* and *The Sorrow and the Pity* are arguably the two most profound documentaries of the past two decades cannot be explained entirely in terms of the intelligence and inspiration of the artists involved. Entering into the equation also are the artist's rapport with the subject, and the subject's own appeal, expressivity, and cinematogeneity for its audience. Alain Resnais and Raymond Queneau once collaborated on an extraordinarily evocative documentary on glass-blowing (*Le Chant du Styrene*), , but one glorious movie on glass-blowing is enough for this viewer-reviewer. Yet I never tire of the most uninspired "documentaries" on basketball, tennis, and the vanishing Victorian art of the strip-tease. And any idiot knows that there is more commercial mileage for the documentarian in rock groups than in rock piles.

In this context, the Israeli-Arab imbroglio has turned out to be as unproductive a subject for Susan Sontag as the current Irish troubles turned out to be for Marcel Ophuls. Neither in Israel nor in Northern Ireland have the hopeless absolutes of ancient hatreds lost their capacity to kill indiscriminately. It is not the time in either region for drawing very fine distinctions between good and evil, justice and injustice, rights and wrongs. When blood is still running in the streets and valleys, the mind is ill-advised to fashion elaborate ambiguities and facile dialectics. I have no answer for either area, and I fear the worst for both. Still, no one seems to regard Ireland with the degree of apocalyptic anguish with which so many of us regard Israel. It is like reliving a nightmare in which we are forced to choose between one Holocaust (the genocide of the Israelis) or another (a nuclear confrontation between the Great Powers).

It was much easier the first time around—with Hitler and his Nazi cohorts. Back in the thirties even the Jews did not fully believe in the likelihood of their own extermination, and there were no Watergate-type reporters to reveal leaks from high-level Nazi meetings at which the Turkish decimation of the Armenians was cited as an historical precedent for a "final solution" with no lasting stigma for the German people. Strange as it may seem today, the Nazis were not entirely immune to the influence of world opinion on their place in history. A few stronger words from the world's leaders might have saved millions of lives, but the devotees of detente in the thirties were positively traumatized by the thought of another World War. The slaughter in the trenches was remembered with revulsion for years and years after the Great War of 1914-1918, the useless war to end all useless wars. And so many wild atrocity stories had been circulated about the bestial Huns and their brutalization of Belgian nurses that when Hitler and his gang came along it was too soon to cry wolf again with any hope of being believed. Whereas Kaiser Wilhelm had been maligned as if he were a Hitler, Hitler himself was given every benefit of the doubt as if he were a Kaiser Wilhelm.

Through the world's misadventures in Manchuria, Ethiopia, and Spain, the appeal of Peace at any Price as a policy never lost its power to stir the multitudes. Then when the horror of the concentration camps was revealed and filmed in 1944, every member of the casually anti-Semitic Grand Alliance spat on the evil German people not merely for consenting to this mind-boggling crime aginst humanity, but also for exposing the bad faith of European civilization. There was enough guilt to go around for all the victors, and the state of Israel was born in 1948 largely out of this guilt. That other people had been living in Palestine for four and a half thousand years did not seem to concern Israel's American and European sponsors at that time of breast-beating protestations. Of course, if the European conscience had been all *that* stricken by the Nazi Holocaust, the Jews might have been given Switzerland or Sweden or even South Dakota as moral compensation. Instead, they were given part of Palestine as if they were to be put out to pasture as the first remittance race in human history, out of sight, out of mind. Only it didn't work out that way, and now, four Wars and many crises later, the soul-searching on all sides seems to be just beginning, and history seems to be repeating itself in the most gruesome manner.

What to do, which is to say, what to do besides pontificate to no purpose? Susan Sontag does not provide any leads in *Promised Lands*. Her tone is one of discreet disenchantment as her camera ponders the paradoxes and contradictions of Israel, and her chosen spokesman seems to be one Yoram Kaniuk, identified in program notes, though not on the screen, as a left-wing liberal writer-novelist, and author of *Adam Resurrected*. Kaniuk is very articulate as the spokesman for antigovernment opinions in Israel. He is given more screen time and photographed from a less awkward camera angle than Yuval Ne'Emmann, "defender of government position, Rector at Tel Aviv University, nuclear physicist, Nobel Prize Candidate, and Colonel in the Israeli Army." But Ne'Emmann gets his licks in just the same, and I found myself agreeing with him more than I did with the otherwise convincing Kaniuk. Kaniuk is very eloquent about the plight of the Palestinians, and about the tragedy of the same lands having been promised to two different peoples, and tragedy is the operative artistic form for Kaniuk, not drama nor dogma, but tragedy. The Jews, he insists, not once, but twice, do not understand tragedy like the Greeks. When Kaniuk postulated Jewish nonunderstanding of tragedy the first time the thought tripped with pleasing profundity to the ear, but the second time the thought positively stumbled with the strain of Kaniuk's self-contemplation apart from his own people. One might say with equal justification that the Arabs do not understand tragedy either and that they prefer to live in an epic fantsy of their own invention.

For the record, I am neither Jew nor Arab, neither Israeli nor Palestinian. I feel obliged to define the dimensions of my nonethnicity because of the exclusionary rhetoric of the recent Walton-Willis debate in the pages of *The Voice*, with Richard Walton arguing that American Jews tend to be too quick on the trigger with the charges of anti-Semitism against anti-Zionist non-Jews, and Ellen Willis retorting that she preferred not to discuss the fate of Israel with "liberal" non-Jews. Only last week, the indefatigable Ethel Strainchamps proposed the replacement of the medieval epithet "Jew" by the more respectful-sounding "Judean." (Why not change "Jew" to "Joy" to rhyme with "Goy"?)

Actually, I don't think that the word "Jew" poses as much of a problem as the word "Zionist." I suppose that there is a precise history of Zionism apart from the forgeries purporting to be the Protocols of the Elders of Zion, which my late father believed rather religiously. Hitler was undoubtedly aware of the Zionist movement in Palestine when he made his famous speech that poked fun at FDR's pathetic plea for restraint in world affairs. The ironic intonation with which Hitler lingered over "Palestinen" in the roll-call of nations drew guffaws from his nationalistic audience. The idea of a Jewish state was a joke to the Nazis, and the word "Zionist" had a wildly visionary connotation, but even the Nazis acknowledged the presence of Jews in Palestine. It isn't as if they were smuggled into the country by the CIA to prevent a coup d'etat by Arab socialists.

After the Holocaust, the advocates of assimilation found themselves at a considerable debating disadvantage. Still, a surprising number of Jewish voices were raised even then against the involvement of Jews with Israel. There were the religious arguments against the betrayal of the eventual Messiah; Jewish Marxist-Leninists restated Rosa Luxembourg's eloquent rejection of any parochial restrictions on her universal conscience. Later there was to be an increasingly intense moral conflict over Israel between the Meaning-of-Life Jews and the Making-a-Living Jews. Jews, however, have every right to reject Israel and Zionism. I am not so sure that European-American-Christian non-Jews have the same option in this matter. After the Holocaust, anti-Zionism has become for the non-Jew merely a polite form of anti-Semitism. When the Arabs claim that they don't hate Jews, but only Zionists, they are merely expressing a preference for the Jew as victim to the Jew as victor. Still, the Arabs have of their own history a long and misty-eyed view which few Americans or Europeans, Jewish or non-Jewish, have even attempted to understand. That is why I remain very pessimistic about a permanent peace in the area. The Jews have had their Holocaust, and the Palestinian Arabs have had their Hegira, and there is no forgetting for either people.

For that matter, how long is the Left, Old and New, Jewish and non-Jewish, going to persist in its jolly anti-Teutonism? For how much longer are Germans to be considered criminally responsible for the Holocaust? Today, any German 30 or under was not even born when the camps were opened in 1944. Any German 60 or under was not old enough to have voted Hitler into power. Thus, for how much longer can anti-Teutonism persist before it begins to seem as irrational as anti-Semitism in burdening the children with the alleged sins of the fathers? Yet, many Left people who shed copious tears for the division of Vietnam manage to muster a smile over the equally cynical and equally unjust partition of Germany. Few non-Germans of any political persuasion believe that the reunification of Germany is worth another World War. Still, Hitler was aided in his rise to power by a combination of triple-digit inflation and the Treaty of Versailles. Another Hitler could well be waiting in the wings while we continue wagging our fingers at the wicked Germans. But the Prevailing Philosophy seems to be to settle for one day of peace at a time. Why then should Israel be bludgeoned to become, in Tacitus's phrase, a desert so that we can call it Peace?

Promised Lands is misleading in attributing the trauma of the Yom Kippur War simply to War itself. Even Hitler didn't like War itself, but only as a means to an end, and even then only as a last resort. I wonder how Americans would feel if they had been involved since 1948 in four wars with Canadian-Mexican forces armed to the teeth by the Soviet Union. The Canadians and Mexicans didn't hate us Yanks as people, they hated only our imperialistic leaders who had misappropriated the Promised Lands of Texas and Alaska despite a series of UN resolutions. I'm sure that there would be a great many American intellectuals who would argue that we Yanks didn't really need Texas and Alaska as much as we needed peaceful frontiers with our next-door neighbors. Unfortunately, there seems to be a law of aggressive momentum in the territorial imperatives of nations. The early Zionists had a vision of Israel, but they also perceived a power vacuum in the area. The Palestinian Arabs are probably correct in their prognosis: Israel must grow or die. Hence, time is on the side of the Arabs. A loss of confidence in the future of Israel would be almost as beneficial from the Arab point of view as the loss of Israel itself. Israel is still collecting moral IOUs from the West for the Holocaust, and most private citizens in the West still back Israel against the Arabs. But for how long? Despite the pro-Israeli polls, no European government has fallen because it played footsie with the Arabs. The exigencies of oil economics seem to be steadily eroding the practical support for the poor, beleaguered, besieged Israelis.

And from whom among the fragmented Arab leadership are the Israelis to receive dependable guarantees of a lasting peace? Susan Sontag and Nicole Stephan could not have taken their speculatively inquiring cameras into Damascus or Cairo or Bagdad. Peace is a matter of an Israeli-Palestinian dialogue, not of an Israeli monologue or of an inter-Israeli debate. Besides, the events of the Yom Kippur War suggest that Israel is unable to survive without the shelter of the American nuclear umbrella. Indeed, it is still debatable whether the Nixon-Kissinger alert actually saved Israel from extinction at the hands of 50,000 Russian paratroopers with a previous track record of speedy expertise in Czechoslovakia. Against this backdrop of global power politics, the ruminations of dissident Israeli intellectuals suggest to me only that a land in which dissent flourishes shows more promise for human happiness than a land in which obsessive self-righteousness tends to stifle dissent. I suppose that I sound too much like an old-fashioned liberal when I suggest that dissent is more praiseworthy than descent even in the Middle East. When I see the Arab equivalent of *Promised Lands*, I may begin to believe in Peace in the region as a two-way street and not simply as a temporary tactic.

—July 1974

Hearts and Minds

There's no doubt the people will go for fine things. But their immutable demands must be understood and met first; the thing must be put over on them, and that is the job, the true test of good faith and skill—that, not empty words. Look at the case of the Resettlement Administration's film about the Great Dustbowl, *The Plow That Broke the Plains.* It was a grand subject and the treatment had good ideas and scattered brilliance. But the film was definitely ticketed for the experimental-amateur audience, which is numerically lean pickings. Yet when the big distributors turned it down there were charges and yelling: the people were denied something which was good for them and for which, what is more, they were crying out. But were they? Was the picture really made as their oyster? Those who exhibit to the people saw at once that it had no exploitation angle to pull them in off the sidewalks; it had no real punch once you'd got them in by other means; and it was a three-reeler, i.e., of a length that is the showman's bane. Nevertheless Arthur Mayer (an independent exhibitor—which means he can show what he chooses but must choose what the chains don't want) sneaked the film into his New York Rialto Theatre program, to catch the audience reaction anyway—and rejected it when his audience went to sleep. Then some critic came out saying the film wasn't shown because no one dared. So Mr. Mayer, still short of product, and liking a bit of a fight on principle, got *The Plow* back and bolstered it up with the ready-made ballyhoo ("See the picture no one DARED show"). He got a small audience of the cautious, had a little fun losing a little money, and detected no sinister pressure, before, during, or after. Subsequently the film (which had been available right along) was booked by at least two small New York exhibitors who worked the "no-one-dared" angle (plus a certain snob appeal) for what could be got out of it.

The point is that whether or not there are ogres abroad in the land, this film could never be the test case of it, not having what it takes. And we might put a little time into studying why not and how to correct this—if in fuming about the popular good we are indeed sincere at all. If not, we can, I suppose, go right on proving irrefutably how the public still cries piteously for the bread of beauty and truth, and is tossed instead a million-dollar Hollywood bone.

—Otis Ferguson, *The New Republic,*
August 5, 1936, reprinted in
*The Film Criticism of Otis
Ferguson*

THERE ARE MOVIES one is ashamed to like, and then there are movies one is ashamed not to like. Peter Davis's *Hearts and Minds* is clearly a movie one is ashamed not to like. Unfortunately, the movies one is ashamed to like make considerably more money than the movies one is ashamed not to like. This is simply a fact of life. People talk a good game of high art and noble purpose, but when it comes down to putting their three and a half or four dollars on the line they sneak around the corner to *The Sting* or *The Godfather*, leaving the exhibitor to hold the bag with *Starvation in the Sahara*. The critic is then left in a curious position. He or she can scold the audience for its insensitivity to human suffering, and the readers will simply lower their heads in shame as they continue scurrying around the corner to *The Sting* or *The Godfather*. Or the critic can note, even if only in passing, that *Starvation in the Sahara* is not the best of all possible movies on starvation, in which case the readers will raise their heads a bit as they scurry around the corner to *The Sting* and *The Godfather*. See, they'd say, it isn't even a good movie about starvation. Not that they would plunk their money to watch all that suffering on the screen even if the film were the product of a collaboration between Bergman and Fellini, but the critic would have let them off the hook. Also, the critic would risk the wrath of the permanently politically activated who would write letters beginning, "I haven't seen the movie, but how can you ignore the problem of starvation in the Sahara. Have you no heart? Have you no soul?"

As it happens, I don't like *Hearts and Minds*, or, rather, I didn't like it when I saw it at the Cannes Film Festival back in May. I found it simplistic, tendentious, disorganized, and repetitious. Its onesidedness verged on vulgarity. It is the cinematic equivalent of the political campaigns of George McGovern and Ramsey Clark. Still, I voted for McGovern and I voted for Clark, and I didn't bad-mouth either one of them afterward for not being chic enough to win. I campaigned for Gene McCarthy, and I cheered in print when Nixon was forced to resign. Unlike Victor Navasky, I didn't use the defeat of Clark as an occasion to ridicule Jane Fonda in the *New York Times*, and I am still waiting for *The Voice* to provide a political analysis of why Norman Mailer publicly supported Javits after Jake the Snake red-baited Clark for that innocent's pilgrimage to Hanoi. If Vietnam should still be on everyone's mind, why is it no longer on the front pages of the *New York Times, The Village Voice*, the *New York Post*, and the *New York Review of Books*? Why is Lucian Truscott in Israel rather than in Vietnam? Why then should a film about Vietnam be considered so timely and urgent today? Is it not at least conceivable that director Peter Davis and producer Bert Schneider miscalculated on the Zeitgeist to the tune of about a million dollars? So here they are stuck with all this footage of American atrocities in Vietnam for a public bedeviled by fears of a new Depression presided over by a Model T Ford whose world view antedates the T-formation. And the name of the fear now is not so much War as it is Terror, not so much strategic bombing as satchel bombs.

There are a few interesting revelations in *Hearts and Minds*. George Bidault's assertion that John Foster Dulles once offered the French two atomic bombs in 1954 to hold firm against the Viet-Minh (not one; not three; two) amounts to a sensational scoop. Also, General Westmoreland's callous statements about the cheapness of life in the Orient are almost as startling as General Brown's recent anti-Semitic comments. By contrast, Walt Rostow never seems to get a chance to speak his piece. In its treatment of the American presence in Vietnam, *Hearts and Minds* seems to indulge in reverse racism, in that the Vietnamese are shown exclusively in terms of victimization and virtue, whereas the Americans are shown as innately violent and rapacious. We are never shown the civilian toll from North Vietnamese rocket attacks on Saigon, or what happens when a land mine or a hand grenade explodes at a G.I.'s feet. It is one thing to say that the United States has followed a misguided policy toward Vietnam since 1946; it is quite another to imply that war is a one-sided process in which the bad guys (The Americans) maim and mutilate the good guys (The Vietnamese). Ultimately, the images in *Hearts and Minds* vulgarize the enormous complexities of the subject. And to what end? To preach to the converted or to convert the unbelieving? A short run at the First Avenue Screening Room should take care of the converted in this city willing to plunk down their money for what should have been a television special on one of the networks for maximum social impact. Of course, Peter Davis can show his scars from network cowardice against the Nixon Administration over his *The Selling of the Pentagon*, an exposé of one-sided advertising masquerading as Public Affairs Information. Davis demonstrated on that occasion that he was an expert at spotting distortions in an argument. I find *Hearts and Minds* no less distorted. Indeed, for most of its two hours the film strikes me as an insult to my intelligence, and I do not flatter myself that I am any more intelligent than my readers or even those masses of people out there presumably waiting to be enlightened by agitprop exercises like *Hearts and Minds.* I call 'em as I see 'em, and I don't believe in a double standard or a different threshold of boredom for myself and my readers, "*mes semblables, mes freres.*" Not that my readers always agree with me. Far from it. I am bracing myself for a storm of angry letters. But I will not presume to read their hearts and minds. And if they should prove me wrong at the box office, I would be very happy to stand corrected.

On the consumer research level, Vietnam may be too far away in time for exploitational sensationalism, and too near for historical perspective. Stephanie Harrington has made the comparison in the *Times* (November 17, 1974) between *Hearts and Minds* and *The Sorrow and the Pity.* I don't see any connection. Marcel Ophuls mixes good and evil, courage and cowardice, in tantalizing proportions, and his touch is much subtler and more civilized. Besides, the dust has settled, and the blood has congealed. *Hearts and Minds* is still red-hot with fury and indignation. Vietnam remains an open wound, but we have come away from it with no false legends, and no feelings of nostalgia. There are no Dresdens and Hiroshimas in Vietnam, no war heroes turned war criminals. There is instead a legacy of shame and defeat. Johnson is dead. Nixon has been deposed, and the putative war hero Westmoreland wasn't even able to get elected as Governor of South Carolina. For their parts, Rusk and Rostow were blacklisted from most of academe. Lest I be misunderstood, let me state that Vietnam was the most thoroughly exposed and demystified war in human history. When I say that there are no Dresdens or Hiroshimas in Vietnam, I mean that there are no horrors lurking there in the guise of glorious triumphs against evil. Also, where are the newsreel pictures of the wars since Vietnam? Did India and Pakistan fight with snowballs? Did the Arabs and the Israelis fling rubber darts at each other? Are missile gunners any more intimately involved with their targets than bombardiers? Does it matter all that much whether you're killed by napalm or by a flame-throwing tank? The Nazis made their own atrocity movies about the pugnacious Poles. It is a game anyone can play, and a genre anyone can exploit. But only in America does it seem to be big business to play it against one's own government, and presumably against one's own people. Or is *Hearts and Minds* simply the final ploy of the counterculture against its discredited elders? I can't tell. The whole enterprise seems so obvious that I may be missing something. I was recently raked over the coals at a meeting of the friends of the New York Film Festival for possibly having had something to do with the nonacceptance of *Hearts and Minds* for the New York Film Festival. I never imagined in May that *Hearts and Minds* would be unreleased in December. If *Hearts and Minds* should be held up from release another year, I pledge here and now to vote for its inclusion in the 1975 New York Film Festival so that at least part of the public can make up its own mind.

—December 1974

Fascinating Fascism
Meets Leering Leftism

SUSAN SONTAG'S essay entitled "Fascinating Fascism" appeared for the first time in *The New York Review of Books* issue dated February 6, 1975. The two books ostensibly reviewed on this occasion were *The Last of the Nuba* by Leni Riefensthal, and *SS Regalia* by Jack Pia. Sontag's essay was later included in *Women in Film: A Critical Study*, edited by Karyn Kay and Gerald Peary.

Back in 1975 Sontag created a stir around New York by abandoning her customarily cool, deliberative, cerebral tone to deliver a ringing, prosecutorial denunciation of Riefenstahl's self-exculpatory account of her own involvement with the Nazi Regime. Much of Sontag's accusatory rhetoric is directed against the copy on the dustjacket of *The Last of the Nuba*, and many of her debating points tend to be unduly pedantic: "For starters, not only did Riefenstahl not make—or star in—a talkie called *The Mountain* (1929). No such film exists. More generally: Riefenstahl did not first simply participate in silent films, then, when sound came in, begin directing her own films, in which she took the starring role. From the first to the last of all nine films she ever acted in, Riefenstahl was the star; and seven of these she did not direct."

At times Sontag goes after Riefenstahl woman-to-woman with the ferocity and contempt Edna Ferber once lavished on Clare Boothe Luce in the heat of the 1944 Roosevelt-Dewey contest: "And here is a fascinating layout of twelve black-and-white photographs of Leni Riefenstahl on the back cover of the book, also ravishing, a chronological sequence of expressions (from sultry inwardness to the grin of a Texas matron on safari) vanquishing the intractable march of aging." (The touch of the "Texas matron" sounds more like Mary McCarthy than Susan Sontag.)

In a very contrived comparison of Riefenstahl with the Soviet experimental documentarian Dziga Vertov Sontag enters the fray as a filmmaker in her own right: "*Triumph of the Will* and *Olympiad* are undoubtedly superb films (they may be the two greatest documentaries ever made), but they are not really important in the history of cinema as an art form. Nobody making films today alludes to Riefenstahl, while many film makers (including myself) regard the early Soviet director Dziga Vertov as an inexhaustible provocation and source of ideas about film language."

That many film historians (including myself and Dwight Macdonald) find Dziga Vertov more exhausting than inexhaustible does not necessarily disqualify him as a source of Sontag's ideological inspiration. Nonetheless, I would argue very strongly that whereas *Triumph of the Will* and *Olympiad* are "superb films" because of Riefenstahl, *The Man with the Movie Camera* is interesting almost in spite of Vertov. Furthermore, Sontag's stress on "ideas" in filmmaking reminds me of Mallarme's rejoinder to Degas when the painter complained that he wanted to write, but had no ideas. One writes with words, not ideas, the poet replied. Sontag is therefore beside the point and anticlimactic besides with her curiously structured derogation of the lens-hound Leni: "nobody, not even her rehabilitators, has managed to make Riefenstahl seem even likable; and she is no thinker at all."

Riefenstahl's alleged rehabilitators make reasonably safe targets for the readers of *The New York Review of Books.* Only Jonas Mekas, formerly of the *Village Voice,* is mentioned by name as a supposedly naive worshipper of "beauty" in Riefenstahl's films. Otherwise, an anonymous hodgepodge of documentarians, film feminists, and pop theoreticians serves as Sontag's composite straw man to be blown down with the righteous rhetoric of one who professes to remember the Holocaust. She quotes from the few film historians who support her position, and ignores or insults the rest. The late Siegfried Kracauer's very questionable *From Caligari to Hitler* is trotted out as if it were holy writ, its mandate for 20-20 hindsight renewed. Still, the problem with either a prosecution or a defense of Riefenstahl is that so much of the evidence has disappeared in the rubble of the Third Reich that we can never be quite sure whether Leni was Little Eva (as she claims) or Lucretia Borgia (as Sontag suggests) or (more likely) an opportunistic artist who has been both immortalized and imprisoned by the horror of history.

What is particularly incongruous about Sontag's indignation is its suggestion of a widely held assumption of Riefenstahl's absolute innocence. Talk about smoking guns! *Triumph of the Will* is so unambiguous a deification of Der Fuehrer and of the German nationalism which he preached that there is a tendency to stipulate the politics as a given, and to concentrate one's critical energies on the aesthetics. But such an approach runs the risk of being labeled "immoral formalism" if the properly pious disclaimers are not appended. And this is precisely the label that has been affixed to much of Sontag's writing ever since she burst into prominence with her *Notes on Camp* in the mid-60s. At that time no less a moralist than John Simon took her to task for allegedly honoring a distinctively homosexual taste. Sontag retorted with some justification that she was merely describing that taste, but her subsequent essays on style, pornography, pop phenomena, radical initiatives in theatre et al., seemed to irritate many of the liberal arbiters of culture. Her own style was spare, severe, humorless, ideologically concentrated, with little of the expansive small talk of the Anglo-American belle-lettrist. Her specialized training in philosophy, and her shrewd instincts as a journalist enabled her to pull ideas from various periods into the foreground of an urgent present. She had absorbed Levi-Straus and Barthes before the full dimensions of the structuralist upheaval in Paris had been detected on the seismic recorders of the English-speaking countries. Her cogent essays on Godard, Bresson, and Bergman displayed an impressive flair for relating images to ideas in intellectually sensuous prose. The suspicion persisted, however, that she lacked a moral overview and humanist balance, and that she endorsed with too few reservations the anarchic outrages of the counterculture.

Against this background, Sontag's attack on Riefenstahl immediately endeared her to Hilton Kramer, not only for the attack itself, but also for the accompanying critique of many contemporary life-styles with Fascist overtones and regalia, and for the suggestion (from an unlikely source) that moral principles could enter into aesthetic discussions. Sontag, who had once stationed herself against much of the cultural establishment by her crusade "Against Interpretation," was now welcomed back with open arms for her obligatory rhetoric against Riefenstahl. This would be the most cynical motivation one could attribute to this essay, but there are other less cynical possibilities as well. By discrediting Riefenstahl as a human being, Sontag removes her from the center of any discussion of *Triumph of the Will* and *Olympiad,* and is free to discuss fascist art in a more generalized fashion. (Significantly, Riefenstahl is not mentioned in Sontag's own title for her essay, but is employed as a cover-teaser by *The New York Review of Books*). According to Sontag's argument, it is not Riefenstahl's art that appeals to us still, but, rather, something fundamental in fascism itself: "the ideal of life as art, the cult of beauty, the fetishism of courage, the dissolution of alienation in ecstatic feelings of community; the repudiation of the intellect; the family of man (under the parenthood of leaders)."

Sontag then proceeds to amplify Walter Benjamin's dialectical distinctions between communist art ("utopian morality") and fascist art ("utopian aesthetics"), but she is too honest an observer of totalitarian mendacity not to report that the similarities between communist and fascist art outnumber and possibly even outweigh the differences. Perhaps, leaving well enough alone, she does not further complicate her argument by such anomalies of the Nazi era as Stalin's personal congratulations to Riefenstahl for *Olympiad,* and Dr. Goebbels' professed admiration for *Potemkin* and *Mrs. Miniver.* Also in her otherwise thorough account of Riefenstahl's filmmaking career, Sontag neglects to mention Riefenstahl's collaboration on the script of *The Blue Light* (1932) with Bela Balasz, a left-wing screenwriter and film historian. Hitler admired *The Blue Light,* but so did the late Charles Chaplin, who arranged to have it play on a double bill with reissues of *The Immigrant.* Of course, Hitler's approval had more lasting consequences for Riefenstahl than Chaplin's. She obtained the opportunity to make *Triumph of the Will,* a careerist coup for a young woman filmmaker. Sontag finds it hard to believe that Riefenstahl could have had trouble with Goebbels when Hitler himself was so forthcoming. But it is hard to explain Riefenstahl's relative inactivity after *Olympiad* in any other way. It seems reasonable to assume that Hitler had other things on his mind besides advancing Riefenstahl's career past the bureaucratic roadblocks set up by Goebbels. More important, there is nothing in either *Triumph of the Will* or *Olympiad* that makes us see the Holocaust in all, or even any of its ultimate horror. Sontag herself concedes the absence of racism in Riefenstahl's conception of beauty. Unfortunately, there is a tendency to flatten out the historical perspective of the Nazi era so that the Holocaust is seen as a tapestry out of time, instead of as a gradually accelerating process of the Nazi death-machine through the stages of annexation, appeasement, conquest, war, and defeat. Even in the Nazi-controlled cinema, the most virulently anti-Semitic propaganda film—Dr. Fritz Hippler's *The Eternal Jew*—did not materialize until 1940. Until the Night of the Broken Glass of Nov. 9, 1938, it was still thought possible abroad that a *modus vivendi* could be devised for the Jewish population in Germany. To this day Lillian Hellman reflects thirties leftist attitudes on the Jewish Question when she quotes the martyred Julia on wanting to help not just the Jews, but all sorts of political prisoners. One would have thought that the perception of the outside world changed traumatically and irrevocably with the first exhibition of the death camp footage in 1944 and 1945. For a long time everything German was on trial, and Kracauerism ruled the roost in film studies to such an extent that Jewish and anti-Nazi filmmakers in the Weimar Republic were condemned for not having made movies that would have somehow prevented the rise of Hitler. Films of the Nazi era existed in limbo, and even Riefenstahl's contributions were omitted from the standard film histories in the West.

When *Triumph of the Will* (and even *The Eternal Jew*) finally resurfaced in the fifties the viewing experience was a completely morbid one despite the "educational" trappings of the screenings. *Triumph of the Will* was thus seen by most of us for the first time apart from its own time. Even today, most people tend to concentrate on a few privileged, charismatic moments in the spectacle at the expense of a considerable amount of political oratory turgid enough to qualify for a May Day Celebration. There are also very interesting visual tensions in the palpable insecurity of the brown-shirted S.A. who have just been eclipsed by the black-shirted S.S. in the very bloody Night of the Long Knives of June 29, 1934. But what are such picayune details in comparison to a sustained glimpse of this century's arch-fiend in the company of many of his most loathesome underlings? That Riefenstahl was under the illusion that she was photographing a god rather than a fiend only adds to the *frisson* of fascination. *Triumph of the Will* in itself, however, does not "explain" Belsen and Buchenwald any more than *Ten Days that Shook the World* "explains" the Gulag Archipelago.

My own judgement of Riefenstahl tends to be more charitable than Sontag's if only because I cannot find enough evidence of malignity and hatred in her art to make her seem as evil as her political masters. And, anyway, she never claimed to be working for British Intelligence while she was making *Triumph of the Will*. At the very least, I can understand her behavior in the early thirties when confronted with the realities of power. Among artists, the filmmaker is probably the most vulnerable to social and governmental pressures. What is amazing about the Nazi era is how many non-Nazi and even anti-Nazi filmmakers tried to continue making movies in Germany until the last bit of hope had been lost. It is never easy to play the hero or heroine by abandoning one's *métier*, one's culture, one's country, one's language. Not that Riefenstahl was ever tempted to play the heroine, but she was not the first filmmaker nor the last who would be willing to accept backing from the devil himself.

Incidentally, Riefenstahl never demonstrated any particular affinity for talking narrative films. Her direction of actors in *The Blue Light* left much to be desired, and in *Triumph of the Will* and *Olympiad* the visual imagery and the music overwhelmed the intermittent speech. The operatic grandeur of her conceptions made it unlikely that she could ever get down to earth for a psychological analysis of characters. Even as an actress she projected a demanding, uncompromising sensuality, muddled hopelessly by repression and longing. Her art thus expresses a flamboyant chastity that releases itself in orgasmic spectacle. Far from costing her a career, her encounters with Hitler and the Olympic athletes may have provided her with the only possible subjects of sufficient scale for her mountainous sensibility. The fact remains that something enduringly magical occurs in *Olympiad*, which explains why in a recent poll of international film scholars on works worthy of preservation the three entries from 1937 are Jean Renoir's *La Grande Illusion*, Walt Disney's *Snow White and the Seven Dwarfs*, and Leni Riefenstahl's *Olympiad*.

Have we then so distanced ourselves from the Holocaust that we can indeed "rehabilitate" Riefenstahl? I do not think that that would have ever become an issue if there had not been an alarming postwar resurgence of anti-Semitism, masquerading on the right as anti-Communism, and on the left as anti-Zionism. We were already distanced from the Holocaust when we began to reshape the camp footage into cinematic art objects. When radical journalists chose to describe the late Hubert Humphrey as a war criminal on a Hitlerian level, the Holocaust began to lose much of its sacred uniqueness. Certainly, many people will never forget nor forgive what happened in the death camps. But almost from the moment the ghoulish spectacles of extermination were projected on the screen, a self-conscious satanism began to spread through our society. And it is in her discussion of this satanism that Sontag brings to bear all her subtlety and profundity as a cultural commentator. It is as if she were signaling to certain segments of her constituency that enough was enough, and that the Nazi motif in much of today's studiously decadent pop culture was more tasteless than titillating. Even so, Sontag might have needed all her stern hectoring of Riefenstahl to get away unscathed with a passage as juicy as the following: "In pornographic literature, films, and gadgetry throughout the world, especially in the United States, England, France, Japan, Scandinavia, Holland, and Germany, the SS has become a reference of sexual adventurism. Much of the imagery of far-out sex has been placed under the sign of Nazism. More or less Nazi costumes with boots, leather, chains, Iron Crosses on gleaming torsos, swastikas, have become, along with meat hooks and heavy motorcycles, the secret and most lucrative paraphernalia of eroticism. In the sex shops, the baths, the leather bars, the brothels, people are dragging out their gear. But why? Why has Nazi Germany, which was a sexually repressive society, become erotic? How could a regime which persecuted homosexuals become a gay turn-on?"

Sontag cites also more elegant cultural symptoms of neo-Nazi decadence: books such as Mishima's *Confessions of a Mask* and *Storm of Steel*, films such as Kenneth Anger's *Scorpio Rising*, Visconti's *The Damned*, and Liliana Cavani's *The Night Porter*. Sontag finds it appropriate that Riefenstahl should be undertaking photostudies of Mick Jagger. If the essay were being written in 1978 some notice would have to be taken of the Sex Pistols for their recording of a deliberately disgusting song entitled "Belsen." And if the essay had been written in 1977 a certain amount of attention might have been devoted to the late Pier Paolo Pasolini's *Salo* and Bernardo Bertolucci's *1900*. The trend that Sontag described so perceptively in 1975 continues, and it is interesting that many of the defenders of *Salo* have fallen back on the argument that Pasolini revealed the fascist that lurked in himself and in all of us. But if we accept fascism as some form of omnipresent and eternal evil with both psychic and social properties what happens to the sacred uniqueness of the Holocaust, and the racial and ancestral culpability of the German people.

Indeed, what happens to all of Sontag's righteous rhetoric on Riefenstahl? For all her faults and clouded vision, Riefenstahl never saw the footage of the death camps when she made *Triumph of the Will.* Conversely, the Sex Pistols did not make any contributions to a regime that sent its victims to Belsen. Riefenstahl may be guilty of complicity, but not of bad taste. Of what are the Sex Pistols guilty in their incarnations of Punk taste? Perhaps only of reducing memories of Nazi atrocities to tests of youthful insensitivity.

Pasolini and Bertolucci, however, are a different matter. They are too thoughtful and too elegant to succumb to punk taste, but there is an element of confessional implication that is new to leftist cinema. For the most part, leftist filmmakers have tended to avoid any identification with sexual pathology like the plague. When a German censor complained to Brecht that one of his (Brecht's) characters in *Kuhle Wampe* very calmly removed his watch before jumping to his death, thus behaving logically rather than neurotically, Brecht marveled afterward that the censor understood the film more clearly than did the critics. Since the suicide was caused by unemployment it would have defeated the film's thesis for the character in question to display even moderate emotion, much less histrionic derangement. Marxist man could never be consigned to a case history. Lillian Hellman, whose confessions are nothing if not self-righteous, makes Jane Fonda's Miz Lillian knock an F. Scott Fitzgerald gossip out of his chair for imputing a lesbian relationship between Lillian and Julia. Again, Marx and Freud never mixed for the Old Left, and there is no nonsense in *Watch on the Rhine* about a fascist lurking even in an antifascist. Moreover, the dedicated antifascist had no time for sex of any kind until every depraved fascist was exterminated, and then, presumably, depravity itself would disappear from the world.

Salo and *1900* present a more pessimistic vision of the struggle against facism by engulfing the politics in an obsessive sexuality. The most brutal manifestations of sadism are reserved for the fascist characters, but one feels the morbid fascination of Pasolini and Bertolucci with the most monstrous behavior of their puppets. In *1900* the peasants and the aristocrats are not separated by the gulf between virtue and vice, but, rather, united in the single stream of uncontrollable desires and wistful memories. Both films are abject failures, though more for stylistic than ideological reasons. But they do represent serious, even solemn efforts to integrate the political animal with his anarchic sexuality. Bunuel has based much of the humor of his late period on the inescapable contradiction between abstract political morality and concrete sexual swinishness. Bunuel does not limit himself to the sexual behavior of his self-deceiving characters, but invades the forbidden domains of their most outrageous sexual fantasies. Bunuel, once the stormy surrealist, has mellowed in bourgeois captivity. By contrast, Pasolini and Bertolucci have registered in *Salo* and *1900* an abiding torment over the tyranny of their sex. In the end Hitler and his SS may come to incarnate all our libidinous demons, as Sontag suggests. But it is still very hard for some of us to trace the luridly speculative S & M sagas of Sade and Genet through Belsen and Buchenwald. Perhaps in the absence of any World War, and the continuing coexistence of left and right, the filmmakers may have to concern themselves more with personal morality as an end in itself, and not merely as a metaphor for the sickness of bourgeois society until the revolutionary doctor appears over the horizon. Unfortunately, no revolution yet has turned swine into saints, and the fascist allegedly in all of us can be suppressed with a mixture of decency, consideration, and good sense, but, in deference to the dramatic structure of movies, not until after a long, hard struggle.

—January 1978

Violence in Movies

THE SUBJECT of violence has been so persistently debated and so pretentiously demonstrated in recent movies that reviewers are beginning to sound more like revivalists. Unfortunately, there are always readers eager to believe that all the violence in the world has been inspired by Hollywood movies, and that if only John Wayne and Clint Eastwood could be disarmed and pacified, then all the gunfire from Bangladesh to Belfast would cease immediately. Movies have always made a splendidly superficial target for our lazier moralists. It is so much easier to ban a movie or whine about a misleading rating than to confront the social tensions that are tearing us apart. Movies are an especially inviting target for people who don't like them at all and who resent the pleasure other people take from the silver screen.

Consequently, I disapprove of the ratings games too many reviewers are playing these days. Arthur Bell, for example, wastes newsprint complaining about the alleged anomaly of *A Clockwork Orange* with an X rating and *The Cowboys* with a PG. The net effect of Bell's bellyaching is to play into the hands of the ratings people and the repressive forces behind them by inciting them to demand an X for *The Cowboys* rather than a PG for *A Clockwork Orange*. And let's face it, the advertising campaign for *A Clockwork Orange* was designed to appeal to every dirty old man in the metropolitan area. My stand has been consistent from the beginning. I am and always have been against all ratings, and particularly after Jack Valenti betrayed the original purpose of the ratings by treating X-rated movies as slimy celluloid. Not only did Valenti strengthen the hands of community busybodies in imposing newspaper and theatre boycotts on X-rated movies and even titles; he also made it necessary for the movie studios to apply pressure on the ratings system in order to survive economically. Idiocy compounded by hypocrisy. And the village elders are still clucking their tongues over the PG-rating that MGM squeezed out for *Ryan's Daughter*. But enough of this nonsense. If ratings are indeed here to stay, they deserve more a yawn than a yowl.

It is banal also to express at this late date any shock over the tendency of American censors to be harder on nudity than on blood-letting. After all, the words "moral" and "morals" have always applied almost exclusively to sexual behavior or rather to the enforced absence thereof. Silly, of course. And all these years we have been told in cultivated tones how the wondrously civilized French and Swedes were as shocked by the violence in our movies as we were by the sex in theirs. I am the first to applaud our being less uptight about grown-up European sensuality, but I am not sure that I can applaud the continuing European uptightness about anarchic American violence. Perhaps in their haste to feel guilty and inferior, too many cultivated Americans have overlooked the hidden repressions and restrictions of that picturesque European civilization they so admire. With all of America's widely publicized injustices and inequalities, there is still a larger percentage of American blacks attending college than there is of French and English youths of all races. And with all the violence and nastiness and unpleasantness in our society, there is considerably more upward (and sideways) mobility here than in any of the more civilized havens across the Atlantic. We pay a price for that mobility in violence and paranoia, and the price may already seem too high. My only point here is that the solution to one problem always creates another problem. Not that I have anything good to say about violence itself as a means to an end. It is always better to break bread with one's neighbor than to break his skull. What is at issue is the rhetoric against violence in movies, a rhetoric, particularly in the authoritarian domains of parent and child or doctor and patient, that is itself violently repressive. Let us never forget that all tyrants are censors, and that all censors seek to be tyrants.

The four movies that seem to have aroused the long-slumbering essayists on violence are Stanley Kubrick's *A Clockwork Orange*, Don Siegel's *Dirty Harry*, Mark Rydell's *The Cowboys*, and Sam Peckinpah's *Straw Dogs*. As a certified non-admirer of all four films, I have been fascinated by some of the critical polarization that has taken place, especially between the Kubrick and the Peckinpah. Whereas Vincent Canby, Judith Crist, and Rex Reed admired *A Clockwork Orange* and detested *Straw Dogs*, Pauline Kael and John Simon dismissed *Orange* and glorified *Dogs*. (I must add immediately that Miss

Kael's review of the Peckinpah is a masterpiece of auteur rationalization in that it acknowledges the conflict between the stylistic personality of the director and the moral sensibility of the critic: "I realize that it's a terrible thing to say of someone whose gifts you admire that he has made a fascist classic.")

One of the unremarked ironies in the critical debate surrounding Kubrick and Peckinpah is that although both *A Clockwork Orange* and *Straw Dogs* take place ostensibly in some version or other of England, almost all the American reviewers have treated the films as allegories of the American experience. Allegory and even analogy be damned, I say, England is England, and America is America, and no cockney punk or village yahoo can tell me otherwise. Of course, Stanley Kubrick and Sam Peckinpah are American directors, but, on this occasion, at least, I find them both dealing with material much too abstract and undeveloped for me to become sociologically implicated.

However, the last thing I want to do is to lump Kubrick and Peckinpah (and Siegel and Rydell) under the spuriously journalistic subhead of violence. Indeed, all four films under consideration are remarkably dissimilar, but the fact that I like none of them does suggest that they have something in common, or perhaps only that they lack something in common. In the past I have tended to prefer the work of Siegel and Peckinpah to that of Kubrick and Rydell, and yet I find *Dirty Harry* and *Straw Dogs* more outrageous and more offensive than *A Clockwork Orange* and *The Cowboys*. Perhaps I am more aware of a perversion of talent in the Siegel and the Peckinpah than in the Kubrick and the Rydell. Also, Siegel and Peckinpah are the kind of directors who can get to me viscerally in a way that the self-consciously arty Kubrick and Rydell never can.

For most reviewers, however, the Kubrick and the Peckinpah tend to be treated as major works, the Siegel and the Rydell as minor. For one thing, *A Clockwork Orange* and *Straw Dogs* are clearly non-genre works, whereas *Dirty Harry* is clearly labeled as an American *policier* and *The Cowboys* as a western (albeit with twists, some right out of *Oliver!*). More conspicuously, the leads for Kubrick (Malcolm McDowell) and Peckinpah (Dustin Hoffman) are as markedly non-genre types as the leads for Siegel (Clint Eastwood) and Rydell (John Wayne) are genre standbys.

If I choose to defend Wayne and Eastwood on this occasion against Miss Kael's morally inconsistent diatribes, it is not so much for their current vehicles as for their rich iconographical associations with films and directors and genres which, I feel, Miss Kael has insufficiently appreciated to this day. It is grotesque to imply, as Miss Kael has done, that no one ever made a good western until Peckinpah and Altman came along, much as I am impressed by the Messrs. Peckinpah and Altman. Similarly, I think it is unfair to brand Wayne as a screen fascist on the basis of his off-screen politics when it is Peckinpah who is the foremost fascist in this particular woodpile. Not only does Wayne not kill anybody in *The Cowboys*; he himself is killed by the viciously villainous Bruce Dern. By contrast, Dustin Hoffman kills half the male population of an English village, and smiles proudly afterward. Yet Miss Kael treats Wayne as a graver menace to the children of this republic than Hoffman. It is a puzzlement, though not so much aesthetically as morally. Miss Kael is entitled to derive more pleasure from the slaughterhouse antics of Hoffman here and of Warren Beatty in *Bonnie and Clyde* than from the more professional pulverizations and perforations accomplished by Wayne and Eastwood. But not on moral grounds. Particularly when Hoffman and Beatty clearly get their kicks (if not their orgasms) from killing whereas Wayne and Eastwood do not so much assert as confirm their virility by their violent deeds. An urban sensibility may feel more at home with actors who must overcome a neurotic reluctance even to say hello than with relatively uncomplicated mythic figures of implacability and inexorability.

Not that Wayne's career is as uncomplicated as his detractors proclaim. It has been my experience that people who think they have Wayne down pat mythically have never seen his more interesting performances. Indeed, I suspect that there are even reviewers who have never seen more than a handful of the 40 or so Wayne projects that deserve preservation over the 100 or so truly stereotyped time-killers on which he was employed. The big plot twist of Wayne being killed in *The Cowboys* struck many critics as a first, but the fact is that Wayne has died in a film at least twice before—in Cecil B. DeMille's *Reap the Wild Wind* in 1943 and in John Ford's *The Man Who Shot Liberty Valance* in 1962. Of course, it took a giant squid (a myth as well as a monster) to do Wayne dirt in the DeMille, and in those days he had lower billing than the surviving hero, Ray Milland. And in the Ford, the Duke dies of his own despair rather than from another man's wrath. Still, *The Man Who Shot Liberty Valance* is not only a film of extraordinary resonance, both spiritual and stylistic; it is also the occasion for a Wayne characterization that is completely inconsistent with the smug virility that is often attributed to his screen persona.

But I do understand the unyielding resistance to the Wayne legend among New York sophisticates. I get a great deal of it from my own students. Hence I know better than anyone the rabble-rousing temptation to dump on the Duke in this citadel of enlightenment. Also I know better than to argue with anyone on matters of chemical affinity and bone structure. The only reason I dwell on Wayne at this time is to explore some of the paradoxical attitudes toward violence on the screen. As I have pointed out on previous occasions, Wayne has seldom played the classic role of the gunfighter in the saloon shoot-out. Nor has he been noted for the phallic frenzy of his fast draw. In his most memorably murderous roles in John Ford's *Stagecoach* and Howard Hawks's *Rio Bravo*, he has used a rifle rather than a pistol, a triumph of realism over symbolism. A student reminded me recently that Wayne was not averse to smashing people in the snout with his rifle. True enough. But why does no one object when Paul Newman kicks an antagonist in the groin in *Butch Cassidy and the Sundance Kid* or fires on an enemy bearing a white truce flag in *Hombre*? I suppose partly because Newman appears in westerns only in antiestablishment roles, never in Wayne's official capacity as sheriff, marshal, or army officer. Even on the infrequent occasion when Wayne has played a badman, the plot has been so arranged as to restore his legality and legitimacy in an ordered society, most miraculously and religiously in *Three Godfathers* and *The Angel and the Badman*. By contrast, Newman pursues his rebellion against society to the point of his own destruction in both *Butch Cassidy* and *Hombre*. And by being antiestablishment, Newman is also antigenre in the sense that he plays his role from both the inside and the outside, that is, as both a character and a commentator. When he kicks his opponent in the groin, he is poking fun not only at his own ratty role but at all the elaborately chivalrous conventions of the western. Until very recently Wayne has not operated at Newman's (and Hoffman's and Beatty's) ironic distance from a genre role. But in both *True Grit* and *The Cowboys*, Wayne has come through the other side into rather startling self-parody. Still, he has remained an establishment figure, and thus anathema to vicarious radicals who would argue that a cop killing a crook (even on the screen) is repression whereas a crook killing a cop is revolution. Pauline Kael is hardly a radical, vicarious or otherwise, but her preference for the anarchic outlaw personalities of Beatty, Hoffman, Newman, and, I suppose, even Mc-Dowell over the law-and-order personalities of Wayne and Eastwood seems to be based on the less incriminating issue of originality versus banality. We have been watching the cops catch and/or kill the crooks ever since *The Great Train Robbery*. Why not let the crooks have some fun for a change even after the last fade-out? It sounds reasonable enough, particularly after we have chafed for so long against an intransigently idiotic censorship that was completely untrue to life as we knew it. Unlike Miss Kael, however, I do not feel we have to choose ideologically or aesthetically between Wayne and Eastwood on one side of law-and-order canyon and Beatty, Hoffman, Newman, et al., on the other. I can enjoy the antics of both factions without committing myself to either position. But I can never entirely ignore the moral issues involved in any manifestation of violence, and frankly I fail to see how Miss Kael can be deceived by the fake populism of *Bonnie and Clyde* when she is so vigilant against the glossy Manicheanism of *The Cowboys*. Nor can I understand why the lyrical prolongation of human slaughter in slow motion in both *Bonnie and Clyde* and *Straw Dogs* (not to mention *The Wild Bunch*) is treated by Miss Kael as the stylistic epiphany of the ages. Indeed, Sam Peckinpah has gotten more mileage out of slow-motion catsup-squirting than better directors have gotten out of pumping life (rather than death) on the screen.

II

When all the rhetoric against violence in the movies has subsided, each of us will still retain a different threshold of outrage. Some years ago a Lincoln Center black-tie, stuffed-shirt audience cheered the demolition of a café-full of unbilled French men, women, and children by a revolutionary bomb squad in *The Battle of Algiers*. Somewhere behind my own stuffed shirt, I found the audience reaction hatefully obscene. They were cheering the deaths of allegorical unpersons, the same kinds of unpersons who died in Buchenwald and Bangladesh, though under somewhat different auspices. An unperson is a creature whose murder causes exultation without any complicating feelings of pain, loss, or waste. The whole point of Pontecorvo's staging is that the bombing is mercilessly indiscriminate because the revolution must be ruthless. And how often have we been fed that line before? All right, you say you believe in indiscriminate violence. Then squeeze Robert Redford, Paul Newman, Jane Fonda, Jeanne Moreau, Catherine Deneuve, Marcello Mastroianni, Laurence Olivier, Vanessa Redgrave, Jean-Paul Belmondo, Peter Finch, George C. Scott, and Diana Rigg into a crowded café in Algiers. Then let the bomb go off five minutes after the picture starts, and show all our cameo stars as shattered corpses. It's not the same thing? Well then, close your eyes, and imagine that your wife or husband, your parents and children, your friends and relations, even Sol Hurok, are in that crowded cafe ready to be blown up. Is it still the same scene? Is it still an occasion for cheering? I think not.

Mind you, I am talking about movies, not real revolutions—that is to say, about art rather than politics, about the refinements of the spectacle rather than the raw stuff of the reality. Still, *The Battle of Algiers* reeked of Realpolitik as it went about convincing its chosen audience of the revolutionary doctrine (endorsed by both Lenin and Laird) that the good guys were always entitled to blow up the bad guys.

Northrop Frye provides us with an especially relevant insight into the *Iliad* in his *Anatomy of Criticism*: "It is hardly possible to overestimate the importance for Western literature of the *Iliad*'s demonstration that the fall of an enemy, no less than of a friend or leader, is tragic and not comic."

In this context it strikes me that the movies I have preferred in the bang-bang genres have been movies in which the sympathy gap between the hero and the villain either narrowed considerably or disappeared entirely. That is one of the reasons I have always found Hitchcock's films so rewarding as moral adventures. Think of Hitchcock's villains (with all their idiosyncratic twitches) intercepting his nervous heroes at that point in moral space where guilt and evil spills out over all the characters and the audience. And when have we ever cheered the death of a Hitchcockian villain? Indeed, it is by pouring so much of himself into his villains that Hitchcock has transcended his "suspense" genre with a moral psychology of Conradian intensity.

By contrast, try to recall a Peckinpah villain. Strother Martin, perhaps, in *The Ballad of Cable Hogue,* but only on the wee-beastie level of a desert rat. But we don't have to go as high as Hitchcock to make this sort of distinction. On more marginal levels, the relative quality of the villains gives *Shane* the edge over *High Noon, True Grit* over *The Cowboys, Madigan* over *Dirty Harry, The Maltese Falcon* over *Key Largo, Casablanca* over *Passage to Marseilles, Comanche Station* over *Decision at Sundown,* and so on. Note that I have compared films which otherwise have a great deal in common. Why then is the stature of the villain of such importance? First of all because all bang-bang genres pay a high price in credibility for the contrivance of confrontation. In movies, especially, the documentary reflex of the medium suggests a scattering of incidents far more uncoordinated than the bang-bang genre can permit. The only way the hero-villain collision can redeem itself from self-parody is for the hero to recognize some part of himself in the villain. Without this recognition factor, the climactic confrontation is reduced to mere rhetoric. Good triumphs over evil in the most obvious manner imaginable. However, when the recognition factor is present, hero and villain are poetically fused into a single spark of self-contemplation to which the violence is directed simply as a form of moral resolution. The recognition factor is especially crucial to the sublime three-way collision, confrontation, and ricochet between Charles Bronson, Henry Fonda, and Jason Robards, Jr., in Sergio Leone's *Once Upon a Time in the West.*

Of course, there are many otherwise admirable westerns in which the villains lack even minimal moral shading. I am thinking of John Ford's *My Darling Clementine* and *Wagonmaster* and, especially, *The Man Who Shot Liberty Valance* with that cartoonish trio of malefactors—Lee Marvin, Strother Martin, and Lee Van Cleef. In the Hawksian trilogy of *Rio Bravo, El Dorado,* and *Rio Lobo,* only Christopher George in *El Dorado* comes close to qualifying for the recognition factor in villains. In these instances, Ford and Hawks do not concentrate so much on the confrontations between hero and villain as on the feelings of camaraderie and community generated by the pressure of danger and evil on small clusters of proud, lonely spirits. In the best of Ford and Hawks, violence serves as an impetus to social cohesion.

Unfortunately, there are no comparable compensations in either *Dirty Harry* or *The Cowboys*. Andy Robinson's omnivorously psychopathic killer in *Dirty Harry* and Bruce Dern's Uriah Heepish rustler in *The Cowboys* are conceived and executed (literally and figuratively) as vermin on the body politic. Hence, the recognition factor is nil. The villains weren't much in *Coogan's Bluff* either, but at least the Eastwood character was spiritually transformed by his experience. In *Dirty Harry* there is only the confirmation of a psychologically constricting misanthropy. As for *The Cowboys*, many people profess to be shocked by the corruption of children into bloody avengers. Some schoolmarmish types are especially outraged by John Wayne's shock treatment to cure a sniveling child's stuttering. What a sniveling child needs obviously is years and years of psychiatric guidance, and not a cuss-out session with Wayne. My own sniveling childhood was undoubtedly affected by a complex interplay between the masculine myths of action movies and the feminizing influence of the schoolmarms, but not entirely. There were many feminizing myths in the movies to which I responded deeply, and many schoolmarms tended to cultivate the Jackie Cooperish butchness in some boys at the expense of the Freddie Bartholomewish saccharinity in others. Either way, it is silly to suggest that anyone has the foggiest idea of what makes a child tick, least of all the paid technocrats in the child-control industries.

Although I would hesitate to regard any child as either akin to the angels or a lord of the flies, I think that children (especially in bunches) are all too capable of killing if given the proper equipment. All the violently egocentric impulses are there; all that is usually lacking is the training in efficient extermination. What bothers me in *The Cowboys* is not so much that the sweet tots kill the outlaws, but that their killing presumably leaves no mark on them and no mark on us. Nonetheless, I find *The Cowboys*, for all its glossiness and giddiness (and even the felicitously Roscoe Lee Browneish fantasies about race relations in the Old West) less corrupt and corrupting than Louis Malle's much admired spree with incest in *Murmur of the Heart*. Critics who profess to be concerned about the moral welfare of the little boys in *The Cowboys* do not seem to have concerned themselves equally with what will happen to Malle's French teenage Oedipus in a few years when he grasps the full implications of his seduction of his mother. It is not such a ha-ha matter as M. Malle would have us believe. Not even in the merry upper-class world of indolence and insolence and enervating self-indulgence from which Malle himself can never entirely escape. Does that mean that murder even in a socially justifiable context is more moral than incest? Of course not. It is simply that *The Cowboys* treats the aftermath as a "down" whereas *Murmur of the Heart* laughs itself into a "high." In this respect, if in no other, *The Cowboys* honors the dignity of its genre.

When we get to *A Clockwork Orange* and *Straw Dogs*, the genre guidelines break down completely. Both films work very hard to condition the casual moviegoer to a very narrow view of life from which all good will and intelligence have been banished. The temptation among critics to take the bait by invoking the contemporary jargon of stylization, distancing, alienation, and anomie is undeniably strong, but it is my view at least that the Kubrick caper succeeds only in being lifeless, and the Peckinpah bloodbath manages to be both unbelievable and unsatisfying. In neither film is there the slightest vestige of genuine otherness beyond the directorial surrogates incarnated in Malcolm McDowell and Dustin Hoffman. If I prefer *Straw Dogs* ever so slightly, it is because I find Peckinpah's relentless savagery more compelling than Kubrick's inexhaustible derision. Perhaps it is only on the lowest level of entertainment that Peckinpah's snarl is more enjoyable than Kubrick's smirk, but both *Straw Dogs* and *A Clockwork Orange* may be much closer to this lowest level than most of their high-flown notices would indicate. There is something hurried and unfinished about both works that suggests that the directors were winging it as often as they were willing it. *Straw Dogs*, especially, gives the impression of having been made up as it went along. One can believe the rumors that Dustin Hoffman arrived on the set to find David Zelag Goodman and Peckinpah still working on the script. All the niceties of plot dynamism and character motivation are lacking. Why is the meek mathematician Dustin Hoffman married to such a bitchy, anti-intellectual town tease as sexpot Susan George? How could they have lived together under the same roof for more than a single night? Why does she expect him to prove his manhood against a horde of local handymen and hangers-on, all bigger than he is? But for that matter why does our addled academic bring his bride back to a small village where she has been passed around from man to man in her premarital past? And why does he go hunting grouse so as to become one of the boys after the "boys" have displayed their contempt for him by lynching his wife's cat in the bedroom closet? Why also do all the murderous, lecherous louts in the village dutifully attend the church social?

Why, why, why, Peckinpah's defenders will mimic back at his detractors. That's an old Hollywood script conference word, and it has no place in today's brave new world. It can be argued (though not by me) that Peckinpah and Goodman have eschewed plausible motivation for the sake of a metaphorical expression of primordial evil, and indeed Peckinpah's art is nothing if not primordial. It can be argued also that the film's celebrated double rape generates an undeniably erotic effect by a combination of sado-masochistic role-playing and macho fantasizing about that centerfold female sex machine whose battery never runs down day or night. A bit of Russ Meyer with Montesquieu thrown in for the guilt-ridden literati can go a long way in a film by a supposedly serious director. Even here, however, Peckinpah seems less devious than delirious. Hence, the violence in *Straw Dogs* seems to well up from within him as so much undigested clinical material. All the psychic violence of a hothead movie director at war with the blockheads in the industry is transmuted metaphorically into the malignant menace and physical brutality of *Straw Dogs*.

Perhaps the time has come to stop saying that Peckinpah is showing the violence in us. Certainly *Straw Dogs* doesn't make me feel the violence in me so much as the violence in Peckinpah. With Peckinpah we have violence for its own sake, and thus there can be no catharsis as there is in Fritz Lang's *The Big Heat* and Phil Karlson's *The Brothers Rico*. Dustin Hoffman's academic antihero is drawn into the vortex of violence almost in spite of himself. He fights not to avenge his wife's rape or his own humiliation, but rather on the most dubiously abstract grounds of medieval sanctuary. And as he fights, he does not embody the spritual regeneration of Buster Keaton in *College* and *Battling Butler*. There is nothing inside Peckinpah's protagonist which arouses him, but rather the external stimulus of a house full of corpses. Strangely, it is not the courage to fight that certifies his virility, but simply the fact of having killed. Indeed, it is clear once more that Peckinpah prolongs the hot process of killing (via slow motion) because he cannot confront the chilling implications of death. Ultimately, *Straw Dogs* encourages the worst in us by glorifying the worst in Peckinpah. *Ride the High Country* and *The Ballad of Cable Hogue* prove the existence of a mellower (though earlier) Peckinpah in whom the quieter virtues are never entirely submerged in a sea of blood. The issue with Peckinpah (and Kubrick) is not violence itself, but the artistic uses to which it is put. *Straw Dogs* happens to be Peckinpah's *Titus Andronicus*, entertaining enough but not particularly edifying anywhere above the belly button. By contrast, *A Clockwork Orange* is an underdeveloped essay on itself.

—February 1972

The Politics of Pornography

THE RECENT incursions of hard-core pornographic movies into the Bloomingdale Belt have terrified some of the citizenry, and titillated the rest. One never knows in these matters whether real estate values are more sacred than moral principles. Hence, though the West Side had been abandoned for years to the dregs of the devil, the East Side was still expected to uphold its standards as the last bastion of privilege in our increasingly insolvent city. Then right at the beginning of the Christmas season no fewer than five sex films slithered into theatres within a two-block radius from the shopping crossroads of Third Avenue and 59th Street. Even the titles of the movies seemed relatively respectable in the manner of cultural climbers: *The Story of O, Exhibition, The Naughty Victorians, Sensations, The Loves of Joanna.* The good, gray *Times* rose to the bait with a meditative essay by Walter Goodman (the *New York Times*, Section 2, November 23, 1975). The tone of Goodman's approach is captured in the clever head for his article: "The New Porno Movies: From X to Zzzzzzzzz." Goodman is bored by these samples of pornography: that much is clear. Nonetheless, the mere fact of the article lends legitimacy to a hitherto despised genre. Not surprisingly, the theatre in which *The Loves of Joanna* is playing runs a big blow-up of Goodman's ruminations in front of the box office. The fat is in the fire. In order to thrive, porn needs not praise, but only the most grudging toleration. This I have always given in the past in the name of libertarianism and in the spirit of libertinism. Not that I am that much of a libertine myself, but I do believe that libertines should have as many rights as the rest of us. And, anyway, no one is forcing me to patronize a spectacle which either bores or offends me. Still, I do have a responsibility to my readers insofar as the truthful recording of my reactions is concerned. I must therefore report that I have reached the point of diminishing returns with hard-core pornography. It not only bores me; it seems to be retarding the erotic evolution of the sex film. Yet, many critics (particularly on *Variety*) have been waging a devious campaign to

128

make hard-core pornography seem more "truthful" and more "authentic" than soft-core or simulated pornography. Consequently, soft-core movies are treated with less seriousness than hard-core movies, and are judged more severely. Even Goodman has given the distributors of *The Loves of Joanna* a useful blurb with this currently fashionable dialectical distinction: "Unlike *O*, which is soft at the core, *Joanna* is the real thing."

Unfortunately, the *Times* editors do not allow their writers to reprint such crucial dialogue passages as the following ritualized exchange from *Joanna*: He: "You're a cunt and a cocksucker, say it." She: "I'm a cunt and a cocksucker." One does not have to be in the forefront of the Women's Movement to be depressed by the crude masochism expressed and exalted in this exchange. That the girl delivers her line with nasal ineptitude only adds another layer of mediocrity to the masochism. But, so who listens to the dialogue, the pornophiles may proclaim. Ah, but the dialogue very accurately describes the visual obsessions of hard-core porn: Cocks and cunts, male and female genitalia, and not in passing, and not in context, but interminably, massively. Indeed, disgust is a function of duration. Of the genitalia there is not flashing, but flooding. As I sit in the porn palace minute after minute in front of lingering close-ups of gigantic genitalia from another planet on which gynecologists are the only known inhabitants, I note that the predominantly male audience is so deathly quiet that one can hear a penis drop. As my mind strays from the sleazy spectacle, I wonder if we have permanently traded in the kind of movie in which one would say "this is where I came in" for the kind of movie in which one will say "this is where I came." What else are critics talking about when they use the term "turn on" in this context? And should the term be used only for hard-core pornography, where it so often does not apply? Why not apply the term to Bunuel and Bergman and even Bresson for *Belle de Jour* and *The Silence* and *Au Hasard Balthazar*? Why not go oo-la-la over the sex passages in *Last Tango* and *Swept Away* instead of prattling away about alienation, role playing, and the class struggle? Why not fight to return eroticism to the mainstream of cinema instead of segregating it in the swamps of hard-core porn? Of course, the proper role of the critic is to describe rather than to prescribe. The problem with porn, however, is that it has not been made sufficiently accountable to aesthetic judgment. There is no body of knowledge on the subject even though there are more sex films—hard and soft—coming out every week than there are nonsex films. The disreputable reviewers tend to rave about every piece of porn while the respectable reviewers tend to ignore the subject altogether until their editors breathe down their neck for the occasional essay on the subject. And no one knows really how many people sneak off to the porn pits without telling anyone. Surveys of the market indicate that prime viewing times are weekday (especially Monday) mornings and early afternoons with attendance tapering off in the evenings and on weekends, the exact opposite of the pattern in more legitimate forms of entertainment. Porn is thus still a male preserve for the most part, and male needs and fantasies are still the prime concern of porn moviemakers. A grotesque news story carried on the AP wire to the *New York Post* of December 6, 1975, confirms the clinical preeminence of the male in these matters: "Dr. Harris Rubin [at Southern Illinois University] plans to pay adult male volunteers $20 a session to smoke government supplied dope and watch erotic films while a ringlike transducer attached to their genitals monitors physical reactions. He hopes to learn whether the drug enhances or inhibits sexual activity. The National Institute of Drug Abuse, an agency of the Department of Health, Education, and Welfare, is to supply both the money and the marijauna. Rubin has said volunteers will be people who already use marijuana and will be paid to participate. No tests will be conducted on women because there is no way to measure their responses, Rubin said."

As further confirmation of the male orientation of pornography there is the curious fact that whereas there is a large subgenre of homosexual hard-core there are no films concerned exclusively with lesbian relationships. Instead, lesbian encounters are treated as spicy variations and supplementations to the basic heterosexual couplings. By contrast, homosexual couplings seldom appear in the standard porno scenarios. That male viewers find all-female spectacles so arousing should indicate to the purveyors of porn that tenderness and foreplay are not turn-offs to the raincoat brigade.

From the five sex films now more or less in the public eye at their new, chic East Side addresses it is possible to detect certain tendencies in the genre. All the films are in color, which is now mandatory for posh porn. Four of the five films indulge extensively in sadomasochistic revels with whips, bonds, chains, and faint, unconvincing squeals of pain, though none actually for help. There are no longer any traces of the alibis for sex films in the late fifties and early sixties when we were treated to sermons on the evils of the white-slave trade, the need for sex education, and the healthful, wholesome properties of nudism. Gone, too, apparently are the lascivious group-grope-grapple encounter sessions of the late sixties. But with a lessening of hypocrisy has come the loss of the erotic élan of violated innocence. Pornography is moving more and more to the stylization of its gestures, to the documentation and celebration of a sexual subculture given over to an endless series of climaxes without build-ups. In the early days of the sex films it was possible occasionally to believe in the untutored truth of an expression. Quite often there was genuine feeling in the very inexpertness of the performances. There were attempts, however feeble, to reproduce some of the more sordid conditions of real life: like what a girl really has to put up with on her first date, or what it really feels like to be raped by a brutal stranger. For example, the costuming was casually authentic. Girls looked like girls, not like hookers auditioning for a Bob Fosse musical. Ever since *Deep Throat* and perhaps even before, the official underwear for porn actresses is not panty-hose, but the garter-belt-and-stockings. Most women don't wear garter-belts anymore, and the few stores that stock them do so mostly for transvestites. Even Victorian garters are making a comeback in porn if nowhere else. My own theory is that garter-belts are an expression of the longings of the middle-aged males in the audience for all those unconsummated struggles, real and imagined, in the back seat of the car. It may be also that the garter-belt is a code for the bisexual chic which seems to be implied in the hypersexuality of contemporary porn. After all, when people say that this movie is a turn-on or that that movie is a turn-on, they are usually talking more about quantity than about quality. In this respect, *The Naughty Victorians* has an edge on its competitors simply in the economy of its transitions. Four women are abused by a rakish professor in the carnal arts, and they are in turn revenged by one of the professor's African students in the first instance of sodomy employed as a vaudeville blackout. The women are very plain and undistinguished by movie standards, and the mechanical gyrations with bonds and pulleys become tedious after a time, but the familiar tunes of Sir Arthur Sullivan give an aural gloss to the proceedings. The very modesty of this movie keeps one from being completely outraged, but I cannot honestly recommend it even to hardened connoisseurs of porn.

Nor can I recommend the other sex movies in the Bloomingdale Belt. Still, there are distinctions to be made. Corrine Clery as O in Just Jaeckin's over-glamorized adaptation of the underground classic, *The Story of O*, is infinitely more attractive than any of the women I have seen in American hard-core movies lately. With the exception of Marilyn Chambers and Barbara Bourdon, no American hard-core performer has ever come close to equaling the erotic electricity of such soft-core sirens as Peggy Church in Mark Haggard's *The All American Girl*, a neglected classic of arousal, and Gilda Texter in a little soft-core throwaway entitled *Runaways*. If we are talking about authentic turn-ons, it is time that critics stopped referring euphemistically to the filthy industrial documentaries posing as fantasies, and thus misleading audiences into paying through the nose for eroticism, and getting engineering instead. It seems increasingly unlikely that any intelligent artists in the directing, writing, or performing categories are ever going to participate in hard-core with any degree of creativity. It may therefore be possible to encourage the erotic in cinema only by rejecting the explicit. I never thought I'd reach this point of limited libertarianism, but I have. What has particularly disturbed me is my belief that many of my critical colleagues tolerate hard-core porn simply because they condescend to cinematic eroticism in general. Hence, it is because I believe in eroticism as a potential good rather than as a necessary evil that I have taken a strong line against hard-core.

Make no mistake about it. I am still firmly on the side of Eros against Thanatos, and still committed to the legal right of all sex films to exist. I was recently reinforced in my commitment when I was told by a woman at an industry luncheon that the movie version of *Jaws* was more "moral" than the book because it had eliminated an act of adultery involving the police chief's wife from the book. Just think of it. If the girl in the opening reel fails to escape her would-be lover, and they plop down on the beach in a simulated act of sex, the movie would be dirty, and relegated to R or even X limbo. But once the girl escapes into the water, from a fate worse than you know what, and a shark comes along to devour the lower half of her body, well there you have American "morality" with a vengeance: watching people you barely know or vaguely dislike being chewed up by one kind of shark or another. The appeal of *Jaws* is thus very much the appeal of seeing your neighbor's home blown up.

In this atmosphere I am slightly sickened by the report in *Variety* of the reported surfacing of a distributor of an alleged "snuff" film in which four actresses may or may not have been actually murdered during the filming of their porno performances. If indeed it does exist, it is an outgrowth more of violence than of eroticism, and is thus closer to Thanatos than to Eros. And even the threat of its existence seems to strengthen the case for simulation over "authenticity." Is the case for hard-core sex over soft-core sex any stronger than the case for hard-core murder over soft-core?

In my disenchantment with the current porn scene, I do not wish to foreclose future discussions of the subject. Porn is a vast, provocative field of inquiry, but one in which most of the official experts seem to be culturally compromised by their neglect of the cinematic mainstream. Porn is something of a menace to the industry in that it is so cheap and easy that it can demoralize craft and professionalism altogether. Its relatively low profit margin can wreak havoc with traditional patterns of production, distribution, and exhibition. The cinema, and even the city, can be in the process of dying while porn is thriving like some virulent botulism. And although the Women's Movement seems to be on the defensive at the moment, its strong feelings against porn should make us all take stock of the situation. The fact remains that we are all free to choose our entertainment and edification and from time to time there do seem to be stirrings of ambition and remorse in the caverns of carnality.

Finally, if you happen to have developed a passion for porn, don't avoid the West Side simply on the say-so of the *Times*. In fact, the most interesting new premise for a hard-core movie has turned up at the venerable World Theatre on West 49th Street. This French movie is called *Pussy Talks* (*Le Sexe qui parle*) and can best be described as a synthesis of *Deep Throat* and *The Exorcist*. It even provides a camera point of view ostensibly from the inside of the vagina. This whimsical tendency of pornography strikes me as completely sterile, but it seems that the French, with their Beaux Arts reflexes and psychological sentimentality, may be developing an edge on the American pornographers in the matter of audience appeal. Also, they still seem to believe in *cherchez la femme* as the key to the sex film. Curiously, we critics may turn out to have more power to set standards than we ever thought possible. But it remains a dangerous subject for which ordinary candor requires a confessional bravado. How much easier it is to play to the galleries with a supercilious sneer and a veritable cornucopia of double entendres.

—July 1973

Cock-Tale Parties
on the East Side

SCORPIO would never have made the connection if he had not been partying all week up and down the Far East Side Gold Coast where, as it so happens, *Last Tango in Paris* and *Deep Throat* are playing in scandalous proximity to each other. First, there was the much maligned Mailer party which Scorpio would not have missed for the world. Why else had Scorpio ventured forth from the comfortable womb of Brooklyn and Queens up to his nefarious cliffside perch in Manhattan if not to be jostled at convocations of fame and fashion, nobility and notoriety? But even in the assemblage summoned to pay tribute (literally and figuratively) to the first half-century of Aquarius himself, the spotlight shone most brightly not on Aquarius nor even on the movie stars in attendance, but on Bernardo Bertolucci, the media marvel of the moment. Indeed, only Marlon Brando in his all too solid flesh could have upstaged Bernardo on that night of nights. And so Scorpio began unconsciously to forge a chain of associations out of his besotted confrontations with the more lurid elements of his social and professional life. "Oh, you're a film critic," one elegant hostess after another would discover with visible delight. "What do you think of *Last Tango* and *Deep Throat?* And after a time, an exasperated Scorpio would counter the recurring question with a question of his own: "What did *you* think of *Last Tango* and *Deep Throat?*" Scorpio was sick and tired and disgusted. Why didn't anyone want to talk about *The Discreet Charm of the Bourgeoisie* or *Travels With My Aunt?* Scorpio would even have welcomed an occasional digression to *Cries and Whispers*. But no, it was all *Last Tango* and *Deep Throat* and *Last Tango* and *Deep Throat* and *Last Tango* and *Deep Throat*. Not that Scorpio insisted on talking about movies. He wouldn't have minded a discussion of Lionel Trilling's *Sincerity and Authenticity* or the devaluation of the dollar. But both the savants and the stockbrokers seemed obsessed by *Last Tango* and *Deep*

Throat not so much for information as for incantation. It was as if something primal or even primeval were lurking under all the locker-room banter. Scorpio began to be aware of the stirrings of a collective unconscious in the suddenly liberated East Side soirees. This collective unconscious had very little to do with the art of the cinema, but a great deal to do with the demystification of the penis, and the missing link was a young performer billed in the credits of *Deep Throat* as Harry Reems.

Who is Harry Reems? To put it as bluntly as possible, he is one of many men who has put his penis into Linda Lovelace's massive mouth and down her cavernous throat. This is all essentially that *Deep Throat* is about, and Linda Lovelace has emerged as a campy media celebrity of sorts simply by capitalizing on a kind of Yma Sumac eccentricity to become the Martha Raye of hard-core porn. If *Deep Throat* had remained on the 99-percent-male-raincoat circuit, it would have been of scant sociological concern. But thanks to Lindsay's litigiousness, and the infinite susceptibility of the Manhattan-based media, *Deep Throat* was legitimized as a socio-cultural event, and even the good gray *Times* (which still cannot bring itself to print a word Marlon Brando enunciates distinctly in *Last Tango in Paris*) took *Deep Throat* seriously enough to commission an article on it for the prestigious Sunday Magazine section. Of course, no one had any way of knowing that two otherwise only marginally related media events would have exploded at almost the same time and in the same general vicinity. And only the most superficially sensational film historians would ever lump together Bernardo Bertolucci and Gerard Damiano (the unsung auteur of *Deep Throat* and the somewhat superior *Meat Ball*, in which the aforementioned Harry Reems plays a more central role than that of one of the spear-thrusters in *Deep Throat*). Nonetheless, if the same audiences had not been exposed simultaneously to the stylish but elliptical eroticism of *Last Tango* and the corny but explicit pornography of *Deep Throat*, there would probably have been fewer murmurs of disappointment about Brando's relative reticence in *Last Tango*. Relative, that is, to the spectacular sexual gymnastics of the deliberately unheralded Harry Reems. That is to say that if the International Olympic Committee authorizes copulation as an athletic activity at the 1976 Montreal meeting, Harry Reems has to be the winter-book favorite as the U.S. entry not only for the prowess of his penis, but also for his commendably mock-comic modesty about his shockingly superior endowment. Suddenly moviegoers of both sexes have encountered through Reems the visual reality of what up to now has been merely the safely sheathed symbol of Marlon Brando's pseudo-sensitive stud's swagger, Burt Reynold's coy centerfold swagger, and Norman Mailer's ballsy literary swagger. It is as if the swordsmen of old were ranked not by their skill in dueling, but rather by the stylishness of their scabbards. What makes Reems completely disconcerting as a potential sex symbol (even to an instant myth-maker like Scorpio) is his superb performance of sexual swordplay without any trace of sexual swagger. Here Damiano and Reems must have sensed intuitively that the preponderantly male audience that traditionally patronized porn would have been alienated by any sign of sexual complacency in a well-endowed male. Hence, the dreadful dizzy-doctor-dialect routines to which *Deep Throat* descends for its escape-valve "humor." What Damiano and Reems could not have foreseen was that large numbers of women would find themselves culturally licensed to attend their first public porno spectacle ever. And what absolutely no one could have foreseen was that Brando (and even Mailer) would become topically linked with a relative nonentity like Reems. Scorpio noted ironically that Marlon Brando's incarnation of Stanley Kowalski was once described as a "walking penis" in Elia Kazan's published directorial notes on *A Streetcar Named Desire* and that Norman Mailer told a piddling penis joke over the public address system on the occasion of his 50th birthday.

But times had moved on, and the ruthless realism of the motion picture medium suddenly cast into doubt the plastic credentials of that ostentatious machismo which had mesmerized us all for so long. Scorpio was almost relieved that the long suspense was over, and that the revelation of that most vestigial of all appendages of the romantic ego turned out to be such a trifling anticlimax. Officially, Scorpio fervently hoped that the Harry Reems episode would enable men and women to join hands at long last in a shared humanity. But Scorpio would be much less than a male if he did not worry about how much longer the female of the species would continue to smile with generous inscrutability at the disparity between the swagger and the swordplay in the macho male. And can she any longer be kept down with mere rhetoric now that she's seen Harry Reems?

—February 1973

Porn Versus Puritanism

I

THE FIVE-FOUR Supreme Court Decision on Obscenity has depressed me all week, but I am reassured by a psychiatrist at the AMA convention that, according to the *Times*, "the manic phase of the milder forms of manic-depression may be a positive energizer that drives some of the most creative and productive over-achievers in current society." In these terms, the seventies promise to be years of positive energizers indeed as we prepare to refight all the battles we thought we won in the sixties. The neanderthals will be storming out of the forest, their stone axes at the ready. The Right-to-Life zealots will extend their crusade against Liberty and the Pursuit of Happiness, and all over America the worshippers of Thanatos will rejoice over this latest setback to ever elusive Eros. And, once more, the movies are going to be made the scapegoats for all the ills of society. Indeed, what is especially depressing is the feeble response to this decision by supposedly enlightened individuals and institutions.

Let's begin with David Brinkley, pundit at large on NBC, and his instant analysis of the decision. I don't have the text of his calming rhetoric, but he seemed more enraged by the profits of the pornographers than by the Supreme Court Decision itself. They charge $7 or $8, he complained, and there is no reason that the court should do their marketing for them. If people in the community don't want a product, they don't have to buy it, Brinkley argued. The same thing should apply to movies and books. What Brinkley overlooked in his instant analysis was the legal doctrine of restraint of trade. If people in Hanging Tree, Mississippi, don't like caviar, they assuredly have the right not to buy it as long as they don't deny the right of eccentric gourmets in their midst to have caviar stocked on the shelves of the local grocery. Brinkley might argue that movies like *Deep Throat* are not the artistic equivalents of caviar, but the same principle applies to corn mush or to the processed hay so profusely advertised as breakfast food on Brinkley's medium. Indeed, pornographers have done infinitely less harm to the American people than have all the legalized dope peddlers with their alleged cold, headache, depression, and indigestion remedies. Brinkley makes a large part of his living from mercantile interests devious enough to make pornographers seem comparatively straightforward. Besides, what makes Brinkley or any other rationalizer of repression think that once the censors have been reactivated they will be content to swoop down on *Deep Throat* and spare *Last Tango in Paris* or even *Blume in Love*. Are the people of Hanging Tree, Mississippi, ready for "sport-fucking" on the sound-track, however witty its context? Even the editorial board of the *New York Times* doesn't seem quite ready for such license on its pristine pages. After deliberating for four days, the *Times* took a very measured stand against the decision in its editorial pages, but with sufficient qualifications to indicate that it will not be deterred from its campaign to "clean up" Times Square. (Walter Kerr may have given the show away when he recently wrote to the effect that the Great White Way was no longer particularly great nor particulary white.)

Herbert Mitgang, a member of the editorial board of the *Times*, wrote a column on April 9, 1973, unconsciously suggesting the thin line many liberals would like to tread between liberty and license. He was ostensibly criticizing CBS for not showing David Rabe's *Sticks and Bones*: "The philosophical question for creators and audiences and readers long preceded this particular play. They remain: Can people be considered intelligent, instinctively aware if not sophisticated, and always educable? Putting it another way: Is frontal nudity as bold as a frontal assault upon the mind?"

Mitgang did not specify which CBS affiliates preferred the boldness of frontal nudity to the boldness of a frontal assault on the mind, but an incident on another network a few weeks later belied his contrived dialectic. It seems that certain affiliate stations balked at televising a mild Ingmar Bergman teledrama (directed by Alex Segal) in which adultery is suggested by an expanse of bedroom bareback no more extensive than one might encounter at one of Tricia Nixon's beach parties. And what did the television affiliates screen to replace the lustful spectacle? Why, nothing less than Stanley Kubrick's supposedly subversive *Dr. Strangelove*. Hence, it is fallacious to assume that an assault against pornography or even eroticism need inevitably escalate into an aggression against political and intellectual expression. Nor is there an ideological correlation between right and left on one side, and Thanatos and Eros on the other. Nixon and Brezhnev, Franco and Castro, the Pope and Mao, march hand in hand to suppress the libidinous longings of their subjects, for the greater glory of God, Marx, Lenin, and the Gross National Product.

Perhaps the most outrageous reaction to the Court decision was recorded in Russell Baker's column in the *Times* of June 26, 1973. After hailing the death of pornography for ending an "embarrassment" to his family, Baker concludes with a burst of Panglossian passivity: "It is possible that serious writing and films, on the other hand, will suffer from the Supreme Court's invitation for local district attorneys to aggrandize themselves by becoming public protectors of morals. On the other hand, there is some evidence that the hostility of reactionary and repressive governments may produce high art, as the Soviet state tyranny has recently produced a few superb Russian novels. This may be because survival of the human spirit is a better theme than the mechanics of procreation."

Some great novels also came out of the holocaust of the Nazi death camps. Perhaps another world war would be equally useful in inspiring the creation of high art. Unfortunately, Russell Baker's syndicated columnist smugness is a conspicuous example of a middle-aged nastiness directed at movies of all kinds. No one forces Baker to drag his wife and kids to Times Square. There are approximately 150 movies a week on television, and a wide, wide world outside full of all sorts of recreational activities. Why then are affluent suburbanites like Baker and Mitgang so obsessed by "pornographic squalor" (Baker) or "frontal nudity" (Mitgang)? Could it be that they feel cheated because the movies of their own adolescence and young adulthood were hobbled by ridiculous taboos whereas the movies of today make even Norman Mailer seem quaintly mid-Victorian?

I can understand a certain degree of skepticism about the evangelical zeal with which certain mediocre minds promote Eros as the elixir of life. (This skepticism has been known hitherto in high legal circles as the Ralph-Ginzburg-is-snotty syndrome.) I must say that the dirty-minded, mean-spirited text with which the editors of *Screw* adorned their alleged sneak-shots of Jackie Onassis turned me off from that publication for life. Still, I can defend to the death their right to stay on newsstands beyond the reach of the local D.A. or any other official of state. That they are there is enough for me to feel a little more free than I would if they weren't. And I am proud to be part of a society sophisticated enough to accept their existence and go on about its business. I can't honestly claim that hard-core pornography has taken the art of cinema to new heights. All the same I like its being around where I can drop in on it when I so desire. In a supercilious antimovie piece in *The Voice* of June 14 ("up early, changed underwear, went to dirty movie"), joel oppenheimer (as he archly mehitabelizes himself) confessed both a "notorious aversion to movies of any sort" and a "no-doubt reactionary feeling that blue movies are best enjoyed in basements or living rooms." I may note in passing that I cannot understand why someone with a notorious aversion to movies of any kind considers himself sublimely qualified to write about movies. Of course, Freud has provided a precedent of sorts by asserting that he was moved more by literature and sculpture than by painting, and yet then almost contradicted himself with a brilliant psychoartistic analysis of Leonardo da Vinci. But Freud's analysis was motivated by admiration rather than aversion. Also, Freud was apologetic about his lack of interest in music. By contrast, movie-haters like Oppenheimer are culturally proud of their blind spot. Their hatred of movies is actually supposed to give their evaluations of movies an added authority. Oppenheimer even trots out the most banal jargon of the movie-reviewing trade with laboriously ironic casualness—"pleasant, technically well-made, dramatically awful"—thanks, joel baby, don't call us, we'll call you. Deep down, Oppenheimer considers himself morally superior to any spectacle on the screen. Why else would he describe "voyeurism" as "perhaps the most perverted of sexual acts"? Again, we are treated to the unacknowledged middle-aged nostalgia for stag films "best enjoyed in basements or living rooms." Bullshit. Perhaps the full-blooded stags of the American Legion or assorted fire departments saw the legendary footage of Candy Barr, but on the few occasions I crowded in with a gaggle of giggly high school and college kids all I saw was the same old dim couplings of sullen fugitives from another era. And it was never cool to admit that one was turned on by the spectacle, and it never happened when you wanted it to happen, but only when other people set it up, sort of always Saturday night, but never Monday morning, which is the biggest time for porn-house attendance in New York. Besides, I'm willing to bet that few stags of yesteryear attended as many tribal sessions in basements or garages as legends of the "good old days" would suggest. Of course, there were the beautiful stags who were making it with real girls or real boys, but Narcissus was never much of a moviegoer. Then there were the rich stags like the Kennedys with real starlets to play with in the family's swimming pool in Palm Beach. They don't need compassionate spectacles to relieve them of their dire wants and needs. I speak still for all the poor stags in the world who didn't want to undergo any elaborate tribal rituals before venturing one on one with their forbidden fantasies. I suspect that a good many anti-porn-movie pieces are written in fits of postcoital remorse. The medium has massaged the writer, and the writer turns around and bad-mouths the masseuse. Vince Canby has done his job by warning his readers that there are no mystical breakthroughs in the porn palaces, but mere warnings don't keep people from exercising the pleasure principle, and then instead of blaming themselves for being intermittently horny, they blame the movies for not being permanently magical.

Meanwhile, back at the ranch, the Motion Picture Association of America has found itself with egg all over its collective face. After arguing for years that the imbecilic interference of Dr. Stern was necessary to prevent an orgy of local censorship, the MPAA finds itself confronted with potential vigilantes from coast to coast. Whereas the book and magazine publishers pledged to fight this vigilantism, the MPAA deferred comment until it could figure out where and how it could surrender. Unfortunately, the MPAA has been flying the white flag for so long that some near-sighted Puritans have mistaken it for a pair of girl's panties. All of Stern's snooping and snipping have been to no avail. The occult moral distinctions by which the fondling of a breast cost a movie a restrictive R whereas chopping the breast off with an axe earned the movie a permissive PG may all have been in vain. Of course, in matters of censorship and blacklisting and moral and political courage of any kind, the motion picture and television industries have always been monumental towers of Jello. They have to be protected from their own aggressive cowardice, their own craven will to surrender, their own pitiful desire to dishonor themselves, if only to placate the tiniest and most isolated bastion of bigotry.

II

In case you were too busy celebrating the Glorious Fourth to read the *New York Times* all the way through, the following is the text of a chilling item on the bottom of page 40:

The Georgia Supreme Court has upheld the pornography conviction of an Albany man based on a June 21 decision of the United States Supreme Court saying that local community standards rather than national standards may be considered.

The 4-3 decision upheld the conviction of Billy Jenkins, a theater operator convicted of violating Georgia's obscenity law by showing the movie *Carnal Knowledge.*

Under the movie industry's guide to distributors, *Carnal Knowledge* is rated R, meaning that minors 18 and under should be admitted only with a parent or guardian.

Jenkins was charged with violating the state's law that describes obscenity as material that "considered as a whole, applying community standards," appeals mostly "to a shameful or morbid interest in nudity, sex, or excretion, and is utterly without redeeming social value."

Dissenters in yesterday's ruling were led by Justice William Gunter, who said the ruling "drastically narrows the concept of the First Amendment as applied to the performing arts in Georgia and local communities in Georgia."

The United States Supreme Court decided that local judges are not bound to a national standard on obscenity cases

Despite this opening salvo from the sin-killers, no one is quite sure at this point in time, if I may use Watergate legalese, what the ultimate import of the Supreme Court decision on obscenity will be. However, nothing is to be gained by relating a defense of R-rated, X-rated, and just plain unspeakable movies to a defense of such venerably and toothlessly licentious works of the literary imagination as *Ulysses* or *Lady Chatterley's Lover.* This dreary debating trick is an example of grinding down the monuments of the last war to fight the next one. Also, there is a lingering double standard in the comparative vulnerability of books and movies to community pressure. Book-burning is still regarded as a no-no with Nazi overtones, but movie-banning does not seem nearly so sinister. Long after Joyce and Lawrence had been absolved of obscenity on the printed page, relatively mild film adaptations of their works experienced censorship troubles.

By today's standards, Marc Allegret's genteel version of *Lady Chatterley's Lover* with Danielle Darrieux would have deserved a PG. Still, the New York blue-noses of that pre-rating era thought otherwise. As for Joseph Strick's reverential and visually repressed adaptation of *Ulysses,* no less a personage than the head of the Cannes Film Festival supervised the obliteration of offensive French sub-titles. For that matter, even the supposed landmark judicial decision on *Ulysses* did not sanction eroticism, but instead allowed *Ulysses* absolution on the grounds that it was more "emetic" than "erotic." Indeed, the *Ulysses* decision sanctions antieroticism under the cover of wholesome "socially redeeming values" which are invidiously infiltrated by the impurities of an extraneous eroticism. But why cannot eroticism itself be regarded as socially redeeming, and why cannot a strip-tease, that most solemn ceremony of the flesh, be regarded as a form of social therapy for the sexually repressed and traumatized? For certain males of Philip Roth's generation and my own, the late Rose La Rose left Saint Teresa in the dust, ecstasy and all.

The problem with most libertarian defenses of film is their apocalyptic assumption that something worse may happen tomorrow if the silly cinema isn't protected today. However, the Supreme Court decision is far more likely to affect movies than books, and is infinitely more likely to affect sexual spectacles of all kinds than even the most subversive political ideas. In fact, the first fallout from the decision was a legal move in San Francisco to ban bottomless—as opposed to merely topless—dancers in night clubs. (See Roland Barthes on the mythic significance of the jeweled G-string.) Is it conceivable that our Founding Fathers meant to protect bottomless dancing and its ultimate body language with the First Amendment to the Constitution? Or should the question be rephrased from Why? to Why Not? By this shift of emphasis, is it conceivable that bottomless dancers can be considered a threat to the Republic?

Here we enter a maze of facts and rumors, in which what is true becomes indistinguishable from what people think is true. We hear that hard-core porn movies are breaking box-office records, and we hear almost simultaneously that many pornographers are going out of business because of declining demand. Meanwhile, a supposedly liberating lifestyle movie like *Here Comes Everybody* with much nudity and verbal frankness flops badly at the box office. *I Am Curious Yellow* made a mint, but *I Am Curious Blue* didn't make a nickel. And in Georgia they're not yet ready for *Carnal Knowledge*, and in Hanging Tree, Mississippi, they're probably not yet ready for *The Graduate* or for some of the vile language in *Love Story*. Bullshit, indeed! Some psychologists contend that hard-core porn reduces rape in the streets, others that rape increases in direct proportion to the permissiveness on the screen, and still others that porn on the screen merely takes masturbation out of the bathroom and into the social arena. With no more knowledge than the next idiosyncratic voyeur sitting two seats away from me, I would recall in this context Lionel Trilling's perceptive rationale for the first Kinsey Reports as the means of rescuing citizens from their individual islands of sexual guilt by floating them on a sea of statistics to the mainland of self-acceptance.

It is my personal feeling that hard-core porn came too hard and too fast. And it was probably the publicity breakthrough for *Deep Throat* that set the stage for the Supreme Court decision. I would have gladly settled for a few more years of simulated soft-core experimentation. Even so, recent soft-core entertainments like *The All American Girl* (thoughtfully dedicated to Joseph Sarno) and *The Cheerleaders* strike me as infinitely more erotic and less derisive than *Deep Throat* and *The Devil in Miss Jones*. The soft-core starlets happen to be younger, prettier, shapelier, and just plain nicer than the rather worn-out hard-core superstarlets. It seems that by moving from simulation to certification, the sex film took that last fatal step from fantasy to documentary. I remember a conversation last year with Ken Gaul, the organizer of the New York Erotic Film Festival. I told him that Sam Peckinpah's rape scene with Susan George in *Straw Dogs* was more erotic in its dynamic sado-masochism than anything I had seen on the porn circuit. Gaul scoffed: "They don't show anything actually happening." Later I read a newpaper interview in which he was quoted as saying that he had tried to show more elliptically erotic films at the festival, but that these films had been hooted down by the audience, which clamored for the hard stuff. That reportedly clamorous audience didn't sound like the deathly quiet porn assemblages I had encountered in the course of my misspent life. It sounded instead like the last dregs of the camp crowd howling their derisive chants of self-hatred.

Of course, even hard-core porn could conceivably find its Griffith or Eisenstein in the next five or ten years. Soft-core flicks have already found their Lumière (Sarno) and Melies (Meyer) and Ingram (Metzger), but somehow the oral-genital gymnastics of Osco and Damiano seem regressive by comparison. And what will happen to "performers" like Marilyn Chambers, the girl on the Ivory Snow soap package, who switched careers and images in mid-smile to make her hard-core debut in *Behind the Green Door*, an intermittently intriguing saga of satanic corruption with a surprisingly formal attitude toward its material? I ask because I do not know anymore.

Movies have never been particularly free. Censorship is but one of their problems. The high cost of production (compared to other art forms), the restrictions of distribution, and the barbarities of exhibition have been additional handicaps. But the medium is endowed with an inherent facility for rendering lifelike illusions with dream-like intensity. And it doesn't take genius or even talent to ignite the moviegoer's imagination, if only for an instant, with the most exquisite imagery. Some of the most hauntingly beautiful moments in the movies are sheer accidents, and it seems unfair somehow to the toilers in the other arts. Hence, the exasperation many intellectuals feel toward a medium with a raging and unprogrammed unconscious, especially today when this same medium is so fiercely fragmented, and so romantically dissociated from any semblance of social responsibility.

Pauline Kael shrewdly cultivates the most primitive antimovie and antimodern fantasies in her readers with one of her patently absurd conspiracy theories:

> After half a century in which movies were indeed a medium that linked people, and gave us, for good and ill, common experiences, we get this public-relations "suddenly" stuff when the bulk of American movies are being aimed directly at the young audience and are sold to it on the basis that it's different from all previous audiences. In its small way, the pitch is as deliberately calculated as the teenage magazine ad (the two are even dotted the same way). By the time the media men, with the teachers at their heels, have finished indoctrinating school kids to be the film generation, that "core language"—whatever it is—may be the only language they've got left. The joker in this stacked deck is that school kids and college students go to movies less frequently than earlier generations did. Although students are saturated from watching television at home (which may be a major factor in why they expect to be passively entertained at school and turn off when they aren't), movies are being pushed in the school systems because the number of paid movie admissions per year is about a fourth of what it used to be. Movie companies are trying to develop new customers, like the tobacco companies when they sent free cartons to the soldiers in the second world war, to get them hooked on cigarettes. (*Deeper Into Movies*, page 146)

It is strange enough for a highly regarded professional film critic to describe the moviegoing habit as a probable cause of cultural cancer. It is stranger still to suggest that film courses have been sneaked into high schools and colleges by those same old, nameless media monsters. THEM! Quite the contrary. What is left of the film industry has been cashing in on the rising academic interest in the cinema. Film rentals go up every year, especially for the fashionable classics like *Citizen Kane* and *Potemkin* and *Persona*. I wish to go on record right here that I would love to be corrupted by free films for my students from any source.

However, the major thrust of Miss Kael's argument is propelled by the assumption that kids are being taken away from their precious books by the mesmerizing media, as if kids of any previous age spent all their days and nights reading the classics. I have been teaching film-related courses for seven years, and it has been my experience that the best students in film are also the best-read in the other humanistic disciplines. Film does not reject the other arts; it embraces them. Film is a window on the world and it is everyone's concern when it is threatened as it is now by the current crop of know-nothings and see-nothings. I wish I could count on the sincere concern of all intellectuals, but I strongly suspect that more than a few nonmovie types are at least subconsciously relieved by the Supreme Court Decision. Well and good. We moviemanes will fight on—alone if need be.

—July 1973

Semiotics and Cinema

I WAS INVITED (and paid) to attend a seminar on "Film and the University" at the City University Graduate Center right near the heart of Times Square from July 15 through July 18, 1975. The meeting was organized by Gerald Mast, Associate Professor of English at Richmond College, CUNY; and Marshall Cohen, Professor of Philosophy, City University Graduate School and Richmond College. By a not so strange coincidence there was a preponderance of professors of Philosophy and English represented at the conference, and hardly anyone from the field of Fine Arts. All in all, there were 32 presentations of varying length (from long to extra-long) and formality (from ad libs to book chapters.) On the first morning of the meeting I noticed an earnest young woman furiously taking notes from people during the preconference coffee session in the lounge. I later learned that this woman was Lucinda Franks, and that she had disappeared shortly after the session began. Her account of the proceedings in the *New York Times* of Wednesday, July 16, contained the following two paragraphs:

> Some of the phrases that rang through talks by Professor Stanley Cavell of Harvard University and Leo Braudy and Andrew Sarris of Columbia University seemed to fulfill Professor Sesonske's prophecy of the cocoon of "impenetrable jargon" that would be spun around the academic study of film.
>
> In discussing two films that will be viewed and analyzed in detail by the conferees—the 1930s comedy, *Bringing Up Baby,* and a Soviet revolutionary art film, *The Man With the Movie Camera*—such phrases as "evidentiary detail," "epistimological [sic] problems" and the "semiotics of film" appeared like paint spattering a clear window.

Aside from misspelling "epistemological," a word that I have trouble pronouncing in private, much less speaking in public, Lucinda Franks has completely misrepresented the tone and spirit of the first day of the conference. Professor Stanley Cavell has actually written quite clearly on the need to discuss film (and philosophy) without jargon. Leo Braudy warned of the dangers inherent in the doctrinal tyranny of semiotics (the relatively new offshoot of linguistics concerned with systems of signs in the arts and artifacts around us). As for myself, I began my ad-lib remarks with a joke about Dean Martin, talked extensively about Cary Grant and Katharine Hepburn, and noted, in passing, that our major objective at the conference was to avoid becoming figures in a New Yorker cartoon. If anything, my presentation was considered too informal for the august halls of academe, and the joint was packed with aspiring semioticians. To put a point to it, I have never in my life employed the phrases "evidentiary detail" and "epistemological problems." If I have ever mentioned the terms "semiotics of film," it was to warn of its pitfalls. Hence, I consider myself in my role as a gainfully employed journalist to have been slandered by Miss Frank's sloppy, irresponsible, and uninformed brand of coverage.

Of course, the *Times* is under no obligation to publish the proceedings of a panel here, there, or anywhere. Many of my colleagues on *The Voice* are paranoid on the subject of the *Times*, and I understand that many people on the *Times* are paranoid on the subject of *The Voice*. I refuse to get too deeply involved in the politics of publications. I have friends on the *Times* and I have enemies on the *Times*. I have friends on the *New Yorker* and I have enemies on the *New Yorker*. I have friends on *The Voice* and I have enemies on *The Voice*. Boy, do I have enemies on *The Voice*! And as it happens, I have never known a publication that was so far beyond redemption that it could not regain its soul by commissioning an article from me. The *Times*, however, presents a special problem because it is read so literally and so religiously, and I use both terms advisedly. Tens of thousands of people believe everything they read in the *Times* as gospel. We New Yorkers are the most naive and provincial people in the world to put so much faith, not in princes and priests, but in a mere publication.

The trouble with Lucinda Franks is that she has built her article around a New-Yorker-cartoon preconception of college professors as crocks and bores and windbags of the worst kind. Then she adds a mildewed argument that movies are too much fun to be analyzed in Academe. Her article thus practically writes itself. By hanging around the conference she would have run the risk of being confused by mere facts. She would have had to take into account conflicts and complexities far beyond the scope of her assignment. The eyes of her editors would have glazed over in boredom as she tried to explain how the semiologists were trying to take over film education from the auteurists, who had taken it over in their turn from the sociological technologists. This overly thoughtful, overly theoretical article would then have been bumped from the *Times* for a relatively straightforward piece on Pakistani cuisine.

What then did happen at the seminar on "Film and the University"? I am not entirely sure because I did not attend all the sessions, and I do not want to make Miss Franks's mistake of pretending in print to have witnessed events at which I was not present. But I do wish to make at this time a few observations inspired by the specific remarks, reactions, and ambience of the conference under discussion.

Professors can no more be typed as to temperament than can journalists. Some professors are stand-up comedians while others are crashing bores, but if I had to pick a trend I would have to say that it is toward the stand-up comedian. When the kids took over higher education in the '60s, the axiom for academic tenure switched from Publish or Perish to Entertain or Exit. More than half the speakers I heard seemed to be auditioning for Las Vegas nightclubs, and the timing of most of the gags was razor-sharp. Professor Umberto Eco of the University of Bologna was a particular favorite with his finely honed dialect humor. He argued at one point to great effect that semiologists did not take the fun out of movies any more than gynecologists took the fun out of sex. The audience roared before he could even finish making his parallel. But I wonder. Has not the gynecological camera viewpoint of hard-core movies taken all the eroticism out of screened sex? And is not semiology inherently hostile to the extraordinary allusiveness of film? There are very profound ideological implications involved in these supposedly esoteric areas. Thus, the fact that most of my journalistic colleagues know little and care less about the so-called science of semiology does not lessen the appeal of this new discipline to a hard core of dedicated disciples, who are making incursions into many universities and scholarly journals. In the latter days of the conference there were snorts of derision at the notion of pluralism or eclecticism in the study of film. Not that the semiologists had it all their own way. They had great difficulty in defining where they were at the moment. Their possible affinity with the alchemists of old was brought up both by them and by their opponents. One gifted heckler suggested that the semiologists (like the alchemists) could not turn dross into gold, but perhaps they could shine up the dross. For myself, I want to keep an open mind on semiology until I find out more about what it is doing. The semiologists at the conference seemed to have repudiated the works of Christian Metz and Peter Wollen. Professor Gilbert Harman of Princeton presented a masterly demystification of semiology, and I was not converted by the rebuttals of Professor Seymour Chatman of Berkeley and Professor Dudley Andrew of Iowa. But I could feel in the audience a voluptuous tremor at the notion of a closed system which could solve all the problems of analysis once and for all. As Professor Andrew put it, semiology would enable us to liberate the cinema from the tyranny of the auteur. Down with the artist! Long live the semiologist!

Professor Andrew can at least be commended for not walking around the conference on cat's feet. He laid it on the line: semiology is the wave of the future. In contrast, the other semiologists seemed intent on winning friends and influencing people by exuding modesty and tentativeness. Indeed, some of my best friends are semiologists, but when they begin drawing charts with such headings as sign and signal, index and icon, system and syntagm, I begin groaning under the enormous weight of the methodological machinery. Semiology is much too cumbersome for any criticism which has the slightest aspiration to belles lettres. And there is nothing new about the modesty and tentativeness of semiologists. Back in 1964 Roland Barthes wrote in *Elements of Semiology*:

> Now it is far from certain that in the social life of today there are to be found any extensive systems of signs outside human language. Semiology has so far concerned itself with codes of no more than slight interest, such as the Highway Code; the moment we go on to systems where the sociological significance is more than superficial, we are once more confronted with language.

By the same token, semiology seemed to have very little to offer to cinema in 1975, which is not to say that individual semiologists are entirely lacking in insights into cinema, but these are the insights one would expect from concerned intellectuals in any discipline. I am sure that there are biologists and astronomers who can come up with interesting ideas about *Bringing Up Baby* and *The Man With the*

Movie Camera. But film scholars are not therefore obliged to master the discipline of biology and astronomy even though every bit of knowledge helps enrich the texture of the humanities.

Ultimately it is not semiology itself that is the problem, but rather the tendency of many intellectuals to lean on it too heavily as a cultural crutch. Worse still, the semiologist's addiction to charts and diagrams at the expense of flowing prose threatens to bureaucratize culture into mechanical molds. Not much harm can be done to menus, but movies are something else again. And there are totalitarian tendencies in semiology when it is allowed to become the dominant or exclusive discipline. As Barthes noted in 1964:

> The aim of semiological research is to reconstitute the functioning of the systems of significations other than language in accordance with the process typical of any structuralist activity, which is to build a *simulacrum* of the objects under observation. To undertake this research, it is necessary frankly to accept from the beginning (and especially at the beginning) a limiting principle. This principle, which once more we owe to linguistics, is the principle of relevance: it is decided to describe the facts which have been gathered *from one point of view only*, and consequently to keep, from the heterogenous mass of these facts, only the features associated with this point of view, to the exclusion of any others (these features are said to be *relevant*).

After all it was the school of Logical Positivism and Linguistic Analysis which eliminated religion and metaphysics from philosophy. The Behaviorists suppressed the unconscious, and virtually banned Freud from serious study. Similarly, the semiologist's obsession with relevance to an arbitrary structure imposed on the work of art tends to conflict with the traditionally elitist notion of the artist as creator. The semiologist does not seek to understand the meaning of the artist, but instead he strives to extract from the work of art the elements which properly belong to the society at large. This is the distinction which semiologists and structuralists have made between *la langue* and *la parole*, between language and discourse, between communication and expression, between the community and the individual. Barthes suggests that there is a dialectical tension between these various manifestations of the many and the one. But actually Barthes and his colleagues are on the side of the many. Thus, what is original in a work of art is sacrificed to what is conventional. Nuances of style, in particular, are anathema to the semiologist. Of course, every book and play and movie is very delicately balanced between language and discourse, between communication and expression, between the audience and the artist. And it is possible that we have gone so far in sanctifying the artist's individuality that even his insanity is idealized. All through the ages the world has been full of untalented people simpering about their artistic sensitivity, but perhaps never more so than right now when the mere affectations of artistry have been known to earn huge foundation grants. Even so, film criticism has been rescued only very recently from its sociological straitjacket, and it seems premature to abandon the artist when we have only just discovered him up there on the screen, particularly Hollywood's silver screen. But it must be remembered that even the greatest writers can only select words from a language which has already been accepted by their readers; the writers cannot create the language in which they forage. Similarly, directors, however gifted, are burdened with givens.

The key political scene in *Nashville* is not the assassination scene, but the striptease scene featuring Gwen Welles. Very little attention has been devoted in print to this exquisitely realized sequence because no one seems able to cope with the tantalizing complexity of the attitudes involved. Vincent Canby of the *Times* gave the scene an offhandedly derisive reading by suggesting that the Gwen Welles character was so untalented that she couldn't even strip properly. Now a semiologist could argue that Robert Altman did not invent the striptease as a social ritual in America. Indeed, the striptease is one of the most gleaming pearls of American Puritanism. Barthes himself has written eloquently of the jeweled G-string as one of the most glittering artifacts of Capitalist Culture in its transmutation of sexual mystery into monetary symbol.

But the striptease in *Nashville* is completely unconventional as it piles ambiguities upon ambiguities upon ambiguities. Altman makes it quite clear that the Gwen Welles character has no singing talent even in terms of the modest musical demands of Altman's tone-deaf *Nashville*. But she has no real vocation as a stripteaser either. To put it bluntly, her breasts are too small. Earlier we have seen her putting on falsies to pad out her figure. A derisive touch to be sure, but there is something so grimly determined in the girl, and something so respectfully distant in the director's attitude toward her that the audience can never release a roar of contemptuous laughter. When she appears at the stag nightclub where the town's fat cats are gathered for a political fund-raising smoker, the entire scene is bathed in a hellish red, and everyone is implicated in this inferno together. The men are rowdy, but not in an individually lustful manner. Altman does not cut from one sweating face to another, nor does he isolate Gwen Welles as if she were a Joan of Arc on the stake of the strip-tease. At first, she tries to get by on her singing, but the audience makes it impossible for her to continue. Even the heckling, however, is more frivolous than brutal. The men want her to strip, but they are more concerned with the camaraderie of watching a striptease than in the striptease itself. Indeed, they look at each other as much as they look at her. This is a very perceptive and original staging of this kind of scene. The Gwen Welles character protests to the political front man who hired her that she is a singer, not a stripper. But when he promises her a spot on national television, a promise he later keeps, she agrees to strip. We thus begin with the erotic *frisson* of a transaction and a violation. There is pride in her performance, but not the professional pride of Lola Albright's stripper in *A Cold Wind in August*, nor Natalie Wood's ugly-duckling-turned-stripped-swan pride in *Gypsy*, nor Joanne Woodward's existential pride in *The Stripper*, nor Patricia Owens' sexually liberating pride in *Hell to Eternity*.

Ironically, the screen taboos against nudity in the early '60s were so strong that all the strips ended prematurely, but the idea of the striptease was still erotically powerful enough to generate excitement. Gwen Welles does not so much strip as undress. Within her privileged space in the same frame with her ritualistically raucous audience she is working out a private decision she has made to advance her career. When she flings out her falsies at the audience, her gesture is neither contemptuous nor despairing, and the stags cheer it routinely. Since she is not dressed for stripping from a standing position, she nearly stumbles when she tries to take off her panties, and (miraculous nuance of personal style) Altman's camera stumbles with her and temporarily obscures part of her performance. Hence, the overwhelming impression of clumsiness in the performance, but the girl's total frontal nudity is still breathtaking in this context. We have suddenly sneaked into the hall with the stags. Altman does not cut away abruptly from the ultimate revelation, but neither does he linger. He does not cut in to the girl's face to separate it spiritually from the shamed body. She remains a whole person, her pride intact in the presence of her tormentors. We are all trapped together, Altman seems to be saying, and, stylistically at least, he does not take a cheap shot at the figures in his frame. That is why so much second-guessing thematic analysis of *Nashville* is inadequate as an explanation of the saving graces of Altman's stylistic nuances. The semiologist might interpret this sequence in terms of how audiences traditionally interpret the spectacle of the striptease. The stylistic auteurist is more concerned with the director's attitude toward the spectacle than to the spectacle itself. For myself, I shall stick with stylistic auteurism.

But how many people really care about semiology? Eight years ago I tried to place an article in *The Voice* on the subject from a Parisian correspondent, but I was told that the topic was too esoteric for *Voice* readers. Semiology has its roots in the linguistic theories of Saussure and in the structuralist anthropology of Levi-Strauss. Its political bias is Marxist and antibourgeois. In film it strives for an esthetic Esperanto by emphasizing pattern over variation. Since I find most of its jargon impenetrable, I have not followed it into its innermost linguistic lairs, but have instead waited for it to emerge from its theoretical thicket with insights into the cinema. I have dutifully read Barthes on Garbo, Wollen on Eisenstein, and Metz on *Adieu, Philippine.* I have struggled through *Tel Quel* and *Cinethique* and the revamped *Cahiers du Cinema.* I have toiled through Derrida, Lacan, Foucault, and have found to my amazement that Freud has been converted to Marxism and Structuralism. Nonsense, I keep telling myself. But that was what most of my contemporaries and colleagues said about stylistic auteurism at the time I was preaching *that* gospel in America. Am I then simply the victim of a generation gap? Not entirely. Listening to the semiologists at the conference, I suddenly realized how much romantic individualism remains in my makeup. When I supported *Cahiers du Cinema,* its gifted young critics were looking forward to making movies. Their Maoist-structuralist successors look forward to making Revolutions, and, as Jean-Luc Godard has demonstrated so dismally, the most personal, the most lyrical art is expendable in the name of Revolution. I was told at the Conference that a professor at one branch of City University is training his open admissions students by assigning readings in Parisian structuralism as a course in cinema. Auteurism is denounced as a colonial ploy, and the students are exhorted to begin a revolution in the streets after completing the curriculum. I have no objection to Revolution 1-2 or

Structuralism 1-2 being taught at City University, but I have strong misgivings about courses in Revolution being mislabeled as courses in Cinema.

The problem in the present situation is that the more dangerous botulisms of semiology will thrive in the vacuum created by journalistic know-nothingness about all film theories. If all academic disciplines are declared to be inimical to film, then the most absolute discipline will seem to possess the most intellectual authority. I think that film journalists should take more of an interest in the state of film scholarship. With a foot in each sector, I find myself being considered too formal for the journalists, and too flippant for the academics. But this is the problem with film as well. It belongs to everybody, but its tone cannot be fixed by anybody. As I said at the conference, methodology is no substitute for history. Thus, I would have liked to have seen more art historians and fewer philosophers at the conference.

There was even a time during the conference when I actually played hooky by sneaking down 42nd Street to catch a screening of Gilles Pontecorvo's *Burn* with a politically, racially, and sexually masochistic performance by Brando. Times Square sure ain't what it used to be, I thought, as I ducked lit cigarette butts flung from the balcony, but, still, I felt it was appropriate that I should duck a conference on film by going to the movies. I have been teaching movie appreciation for ten years, and the atavistic "fun" of moviegoing hasn't left me. So why all the fuss about talking and writing seriously about something one loves?

Arthur Schlesinger, Jr., arrived at the conference to deliver an attack on *Bringing Up Baby*, and he stayed to listen to a very lengthy exegesis on Hawksian symbolism by William Rothman of New York University. I was very stimulated by Rothman's paper. It was audaciously and uncompromisingly auteurist in a way that I am not so much any more. Rothman took chances as he plunged into a great many films, and his arguments were not neatly wrapped up with rhetorical flourishes. But Rothman kept me thinking about movies as established experiences rather than as hypothetical structures. The truth is that a great many people in the conference did not want to talk about movies at all, but rather about the academic machinery required to take over film departments in their universities.

I disagreed with Professor Schlesinger's attitude toward *Bringing Up Baby* and toward screwball comedy in general. I thought he over-rated the satiric criteria, for example. Unfortunately, there was no time to pursue our differences beyond a few furtive whispers. What I admired in his arguments was his historical perspective. I felt in his presentation the contours of the past. By contrast, philosophy people tend to flatten out pastness when they talk about cinema. In their view it is as if cinema were always on the verge of being born (ontology) and we must begin to define its essence before we are engulfed by its existence. For my part, I am already engulfed by the cinema. Its past inhabits our present as movies from all periods stream through our consciousness. One has only to flip through a few pages of *Gravity's Rainbow* or *Ragtime* to realize the extent to which cinema is repaying its debt to literature. Indeed, it is too late to argue whether movies should be taught or not. They are already an indispensable part of our cultural heritage.

Curiously, a popular entertainment like *Bringing Up Baby* seemed more revelatory to the conferees than did an official Soviet avant-garde classic like Dziga Vertov's *The Man With the Movie Camera*. Not only was the Hawks more "fun" than the Vertov; there seemed to be much more to say about it. There were more levels to it as well. Score a point for the American narrative cinema over the Russian avant-garde. Dwight Macdonald, grumpy iconoclast that he is, enlivened the panel on *The Man With the Movie Camera* by suggesting that Vertov's theoretical writings on film were more interesting than his films themselves. Macdonald's academic manners left something to be desired as he came on like Monty Woolley in *The Man Who Came to Dinner*. Vlada Petric, Luce Professor of Film Studies at Harvard, was outraged by the short shrift Macdonald gave to Petric's very detailed formal analysis of the Vertov, and for a time personal insults flew back and forth. I respect Petric as a film scholar, and I sympathized with his vulnerability in his role as the rigorous analyst of a film being debunked by a very erudite classical humanist like Macdonald. Still, I couldn't help agreeing with Macdonald's skepticism about the exaggerated claims made for *The Man With the Movie Camera*, a film with the minor charm of dedicated self-consciousness, but hardly a conceptual breakthrough to the universal language Vertov proposed in his writings.

I was told that at the very last session there was a feminist resolution on the exclusion of women from the panels. (Twenty-seven men, no women.) But the resolution was ruled out of order due to the absence of a quorum.

After all was said and done, I was glad that I had attended. I didn't get many definitive answers, but I did pick up some interesting questions. The seminar was well worth doing, and at times it was even fun. The mind, like the heart, has its own reasons.

—August 1975

My Uncle Antoine

CLAUDE JUTRA'S *My Uncle Antoine* is the kind of film for which I would like to write a review full of the hyperbolic hysteria which can get the most uninspired critic free but priceless publicity in the entertainment pages of the *New York Times*. Mind you, I am not pointing an accusing finger. I get more than my share of abuse from lofty personages on the quarterlies and semiannuals for indulging in rush-to-see-it rhetoric. But I don't know any other way to get people to see a film I think is worth supporting at the box office. Unlike a critic of my acquaintance, I'd rather induce people to see a meritorious movie than condemn them afterward for having passed up the opportunity. Hence, hyperbole is to the practicing film critic what demagogic conciseness is to even the noblest candidate in the Presidential primary. On the existential plane of have-you-seen-any-good-movies-lately, hyperbole is the critic's method of rousing the rabble. Unfortunately (for the picture I like), I lack the ability of many of my colleagues to rise to new summits every week. I am afflicted with memories of too many good movies from the past ever to believe that any single new movie can completely erase that past. And that is what hype is all about: Out with the old and in with the new; folks, you ain't seen nuttin' yet; step right up, get away from me with that memory machine, Bud, you're bothering me, and stop pestering those people standing on line for *The Godfather*.

Why then can't I get into the spirit of things and describe *My Uncle Antoine* as a heart-warming humdinger and the greatest film I've seen since February? Partly because I think I would be betraying the complex sensibility and exquisite self-awareness at the heart of the film by praising it mindlessly. From his first film, *A Tout Prendre*, Jutra had struck me as a typically tortured French Canadian filmmaker lost somewhere between Norman McLaren's playful drawing board and Jean Rouch's ponderous ethnography. Back in 1963 at my first Montreal Film Festival, everything seemed to be a goulash of *Mon Pays* and the *nouvelle vague*, and we all seemed to be waiting literally and figuratively for Godard. The atmosphere at the Hotel Windsor was heady in the cerebral rather than the champagne sense. I had never seen so many earnestly intellectual people hovering around film. And Jutra was the hero of the hour for a film in which his search for his own identity (and indeed his own sexuality) was intercut with a meditation on the ultimate fate of all French Canadians. Somehow the film never caught on commercially even in Montreal, much less New York, and least of all in English Canada. I wrote favorably on the film in these pages, but my mind didn't dwell on Jutra. A talent? Yes. A force? No. Over the years I saw a variety of Canadian films ranging from the throbbing rawness of Larry Kent to the tiresome refinement of Paul Almond. Don Owen had a brief vogue, but, otherwise, most Canadian filmmakers remained the creatures of festivals, the mosaics of museums. Actually, few Americans have any serious interest in Canada beyond the winter wonderland level. And I certainly don't pretend to be any sort of an authority on Canada. People in Montreal tell me that Jutra is not entirely accurate in his depiction of the milieu. I have no way of evaluating the charge, least of all in my ancestral bones. My point of view, like that of most Americans, is that of a nearby outsider. Nonetheless, I do have certain very strong feelings about the film.

First of all, I feel more than mere nostalgia in this saga of a young boy growing up in the back country of Quebec at a moment in history when a race and a class is beginning to stir up fissures in the glacier of oppression. To his credit, Jutra does not romanticize these stirrings as Widerberg did in *Adalen 31*. Hence the Jutra zooms, unfairly criticized, I think, by one critic. For Jutra, the zoom is not a restrictive or manipulative device, but merely a means of expressing the difference in size and emotional focus between the huge waves of individual memory and the small ripples of continental history. Nor is it particularly useful to compare Jutra's view of childhood with Truffaut's in *The Four Hundred Blows*. Truffaut filmed in the first person, Jutra in an elaborate mixture of first, second, and third. (Actually it is author and scenarist Clement Perron's childhood that is the subject of *My Uncle Antoine*, and not Jutra's.) Also, Truffaut's view of society is anarchically, even crankily individualistic, and this view tends to charm moviegoers who feel their own ineffable individualities are insufficiently appreciated. By contrast, Jutra gets inside the otherness of stock characters by showing them in their most privileged privacy.

Subtlety and obliqueness are difficult virtues to publicize, and I know that there is a tendency now to suspect elliptical artists of not having had anything to leave out in the first place. Indeed, I suspect and deplore supposedly tasteful ellipses as much as anyone. But *My Uncle Antoine*, I submit, may be the exception that proves the rule. For example, the apparently obligatory scene of the migrant worker finding his son's coffin on the snowy trail is elided by Jutra not out of coyness, but out of a profound respect for the dignity, privacy, and mystery of that awesome moment. It is much better that we see only the aftermath of that shattering encounter so that we can move backward not only to the moment itself but to all the moments before strung out in cruel clusters of icy history. Unlike the pretty movie version of *One Day in the Life of Ivan Denisovich* with its idyllically photographed snowscapes, *My Uncle Antoine* expresses a horror and hatred of winter in the lungs and souls of its characters. Thus not the least of the distinctions of *My Uncle Antoine* is that it chooses not to describe Canadian experiences in universal terms, but rather to describe universal experiences in Canadian terms. Ultimately, Jutra does not tell us everything we want to know, but what he does tell us he tells with such intelligence and conviction that we yearn to know more. I was moved. What more can I say? See it.

—April 1972

Marilyn, by Norman Mailer

NORMAN MAILER'S book on Marilyn Monroe is shaping up as the book industry's most scandalous event since the Clifford Irving hoax with Howard Hughes. As it happens, *Marilyn* is largely a critique and cannibalization of earlier writings on the subject, and much of the controversy seems to have arisen from Mailer's belittling of his predecessors as if they were his research assistants. It would certainly be too tedious for anyone but a lawyer or a judge to compare Mailer's copy word-for-word with the full texts of Fred Lawrence Guiles's *Norma Jean* and Maurice Zolotow's *Marilyn Monroe*, the two most-quoted sources for the book in question. It would be even more tedious to accuse Mailer of sins to which he has confessed freely in a series of self-scourging interviews with the media magistrates of CBS, *Time* Magazine, and *The New York Times*. In this very lurid context, confession may be as good for sales as for the soul.

But what may have been lost sight of in all the confusion is that Mailer has manfully transformed a tackily commissioned coffee-table project into a personal crisis. We have been told that Mailer received a $50,000 advance from a photographer named Schiller to write a 10,000-word "preface" for a picture book on Marilyn Monroe. If all that had mattered in Mailer's mind had been the hard cash he needed to support two homes, five wives, and seven children through double-digit inflation, he could have ground out a 10,000-word "meditation" on Marilyn Monroe in his sleep, and then spent his waking hours toiling on that white whale of a novel his more tiresome admirers keep demanding from him. But it would never do for a writer of Mailer's magnitude to be dropped lightly on a coffee table, to be demeaned by the literati as the glib librettist for the visual music of a horde of lens-hounds. By expanding the 10,000-word preface into a 90,000-word "novel biography," Mailer now lands on the coffee table with a heavy thud, but he has become the master of his own book, and Marilyn Monroe, in death and in dreams, has become his mistress, a moonlike mystery to be penetrated by his literary astronaut's projectile.

Since there is no writer maler than Mailer, the cultural coupling of two sex symbols, one a prisoner of sex and the other a hostage to Hollywood fortune, makes a certain amount of mythic sense. The built-in publicity value alone is beyond measure, and Mailer's professional talent is virtually beyond dispute. To say, therefore, that Mailer's latest venture is more readable than admirable, and that it displays more charisma than character, or charity, or even courtesy, is to say that it is the least we might have expected under the circumstances.

Of course, Mailer is an old hand at confounding his critics by confusing their categories. What is Mailer's "novel biography," after all, but the New Journalism transported to those outer limits of perception where the lies of art whore around with the lies of gossip. If Tom Wolfe with his invisible white suits and his chastely uncommitted persona embodies the voyeuristic branch of the New Journalism, Mailer with his mauled machismo thrust upward and outward is New Journalism's most extended exhibitionist branch, veritably its Lenny Bruce of letters. The problem here is that movies and movie stars are more fitting subjects for voyeurs than for exhibitionists. As the glaring illumination of New York City's skyline obliterates the luster of the Milky Way, so does Mailer's own superstar status dim the flickering glow of Marilyn's milky screen incarnation. And being a man closer to politics than to poetics, he is obsessed more by the Machiavellian processes of power and publicity than by the magical idiosyncrasies of her image. The book is therefore richer in intrigue than in insight as the Marilyn we all knew dissolves in a mist of fresh metaphors and stale anecdotes, the latter mostly borrowed and mostly blue.

In the midst of all these commercial considerations is the ever-elusive ghost of Marilyn Monroe, who died of an overdose of sleeping pills during a lost August weekend in 1962. She had been born Norma Jean Mortenson on June 1, 1926, not far from where she was to be eventually incarnated and ultimately entombed as the American sex goddess of her era. Her mother actually lived for a time in Hollywood and worked at the processing laboratories of Consolidated Film Industries. The identity of her father always remained a speculative question, and Norma Jean ran the gamut of orphanages, foster homes, madness in the family, and the savage, rootless religiosity, then as now, of southern California. However, Mailer's effort to drag in Richard Nixon's boyhood in Whittier as a broken-mirror reflection of Norma Jean's girlhood seems to be strictly a post-Watergate conceit to make the book more relevant. At times Mailer conveys the impression that everything west of Elaine's is malignantly Middle American and that anything Far West is especially far out. This kind of presumptuous New York provincialism has more to do with Mailer's own disorientation from the nonintellectual middle class than with the life story of a pretty girl who wanted to get into the movies.

At 18 Norma Jean marries James Dougherty, whose story now is that his bride was a virgin on her wedding night. Ergo, virgo. Mailer chooses to believe everything Dougherty says because this relative nobody is such a humble, cooperative witness, such a fountain of information for the otherwise parched biographer. By contrast, Maurice Zolotow and the late Ben Hecht are not to be trusted. They are in the myth-making business along with Mailer, and they have already covered most of the terrain. Mailer seeks to dislodge them by suggesting that their anecdotes on Marilyn are too symmetrically ironic, too conveniently psychoanalytical. Mailer recounts their anecdotes just the same, but he is too much into tarot cards, word games, karma, and the afterlife to play Freud with Freudian fan-magazine material. Still, Aquarius refuses to liberate himself from the Robbins-Susann drugstore rack formulas for fictionalized biography. Instead of pinning down the beautiful butterfly of Marilyn Monroe, he crawls back to the cocoon from which Norma Jean Mortenson wriggled like a carnal caterpillar to womanhood and stardom.

But, irony of ironies, it is now Norma Jean Mortenson who is the fabricated myth and Marilyn Monroe who is the authentic reality. For Norma Jean to become Marilyn, she must discard Dougherty and take up with a succession of producers, photographers, and agents. She will engage make-up men and masseurs for her body and her mind; she will marry and divorce two worthy consorts—Joe DiMaggio of Yankee Stadium, Fisherman's Wharf, Toots Shor's, and then Arthur Miller of Brooklyn Heights, Connecticut, Karl Marx, Reform Judaism, and *Death of a Salesman*. From the crowd to the crucible to the grave, and in between some 30 movie appearances, thousands of photos, millions of words of publicity copy and reported affairs with Marlon Brando, Frank Sinatra, and Yves Montand, to mention only the most newsy. Indeed, the most striking picture in the book is Bruce Davidson's harshly lit three-way confrontation of Simone Signoret and Marilyn Monroe with Montand, his back to us and presumably to the wall as well. Mailer is singularly unkind to most of the men in Marilyn's life. Montand he dismisses as a pushy Italian peasant (right out of an Arthur Miller play about the little people) who merely uses Marilyn to get some needed Hollywood notoriety; Miller he ridicules for the pontifical pipe with which Miller hopes to puff his way into becoming the first Jewish pope; DiMaggio degenerates into an ethnic joke as an over-the-hill-athlete-turned-saloonkeeper, and Sinatra is rather conventionally maligned as a Mafia singer right out of the pages of *The Godfather*.

It is to Mailer's credit that he at least goes through the motions of discussing Marilyn's movies as artifacts apart from her sex life. He claims to have screened 24 of 30 movies, but that's precisely the trouble. He's had to catch up on movies the authentic Monrovians caught at the time they came out. Hence, there is no historical resonance or iconographical perspective in Mailer's account of Marilyn's career. After all, it isn't as if Marilyn were the first sexy blonde Hollywood had ever seen, or the last. Fox, the studio that first found Marilyn and finally cast her aside, was noted for its blonde succession, from torchy Alice Faye to tip-tappy Betty Grable, and from Betty Grable to June Haver (through their sibling act in *The Dolly Sisters*), but poor June couldn't cut the mustard and betook herself to a nunnery. Way back in the thirties of course, there was the classically bawdy blondeness of Jean Harlow and Mae West, and also soulful Carole Lombard, snazzy Ginger Rogers, snappy Joan Blondell and sloe-eyed Ann Sothern. Even the bosom build-up wasn't new. Forget about Jane Russell's publicity H-bomb in *The Outlaw*. Lana Turner as doomed jailbait in *They Won't Forget* (1937) enters and exits in a sweater which helped pull the wool over the eyes of the proletariat during the Depression.

The dumb-Dora blonde who can't type, or act, or say anything intelligent but oh-watch-her-hips-and-other-protuberances (essentially the ethos for the eye-popping walk-ons Marilyn did in *Monkey Business, All About Eve, The Asphalt Jungle, Love Happy*) happened to be a staple of comic strips, movies, and television. Barbara Nichols,

Marie Wilson, Joi Lansing, and Dagmar were around at about the same time doing the blonde archetype bit. Kim Stanley executed the definitive Method interpretation of Marilyn in Paddy Chayevsky's *The Goddess*, and Lola Albright crossed the erotic frontier of film in *Cold Wind in August*. Jayne Mansfield became the first prominent Monroe imitator, but went so far into harsh, Westian self-parody that she marked the beginning of the camp female impersonation of the Warhol era. Through the sixties and seventies, camera magic endowed Stella Stevens with some of Marilyn's fleshy phosphorescence, and Tuesday Weld with some of her luminous nymphet's soul. Which is not to say that there could ever be another Marilyn, but her ineffable uniqueness hardly qualifies her as Mailer's "Napoleon" of the medium, a conqueror with no need of a context. She had severe limitations as an actress, particularly with her voice, which, fortunately, we don't have to endure in a picture book.

It just so happens, however, that Marilyn was in the business of talking pictures. Yet she could never do any of the wise-cracking Lombard, Rogers, Arthur, Harlow, West roles of the thirties. She was all marshmallow, with perpetually moistened, quivering lips, and males of a certain sensibility in search of sexual redemption worshipped her for her divine compliance with their fantasies, but most women despised her for throwing the game to the boys in the locker room without making a fight of it. Nowadays, of course, feminist myth-makers try to transform her into a Joan of Arc who died because of the sins of men, but Marilyn was really done in by the women who stayed away in droves. That is why Fox was paying her only $100,000 for her last movie while Elizabeth Taylor was raking in a cool million from the same studio.

Mailer underrates Marilyn's more interesting cult movies like *River of No Return* and *Don't Bother to Knock* and even *Niagara*, while overpraising her laboriously chic performances in *Bus Stop* and *The Misfits*. Worse still, Mailer either ignores or demeans the contributions of other players to her most successful movies, particularly in *Some Like It Hot*, a Billy Wilder classic of transvestism which Mailer describes bizarrely as a Marilyn Monroe comedy with support from Jack Lemmon, Tony Curtis, and the late Joe E. Brown, when it is precisely the other way around. Marilyn is winsome and winning, and gives her part something extra. But even her biggest scene, in which she seduces the supposedly impotent Tony Curtis, would have made audiences uncomfortable if it had not been intercut with the Last Tango in Drag of Jack Lemmon and Joe E. Brown, with one wild rose between them to switch from mouth to mouth.

As for Mailer's "theory" that Marilyn was murdered by a right-wing conspiracy to embarrass Bobby Kennedy, even the author finds it hard to believe. Indeed, it is somewhat disingenuous of Mailer to catalogue all her pills, sores, wrinkles, abortions, and tubular pregnancies, to describe all the scars of her soul and all the muddle of her mind, to drag us through all her bitchy days and lonely nights, and then tell us with a straight face that this 36-year-old sex goddess on suspension from her studio in hostile Hollywood had everything to live for. Perhaps she sensed intuitively that her most devout admirers would never forgive her for getting old (*vide* the sad, lonely death just recently of Veronica Lake). Perhaps also, she could look into the future to see the blowsy screen image of Diana Dors in middle age. At the end she needed friends more than she needed worshippers, and she didn't really have enough of either. In the East, the elitists were savoring Jeanne Moreau in *Jules and Jim* and Emmanuèle Riva in *Hiroshima, Mon Amour* and Jean Seberg in *Breathless* and Monica Vitti in *L'Avventura* and Bibi and Harriet Andersson in the Bergman films. In the West, the Fox and the other species of studio were dying before her eyes. Look at the last pictures of Marilyn in the book, and you will see her gazing very gallantly at the angel of death.

His Picture in the Papers:
A Speculation on Celebrity in America, Based on the Life of Douglas Fairbanks, Sr.

THERE IS something inescapably morbid about Richard Schickel's meditation on the life and good times of the late Douglas Fairbanks, the Elder, perhaps the most completely self-created and self-propelled of all the media meteors launched from Hollywood. By now we have become overfamiliar with the gloomy mottoes of the gravitational moralists: What Rises Must Fall; What Shines Must Fade; The Path of Publicity Leads But to the Grave. Hollywood celebrities are subjected to double jeopardy in the Courthouse of Cant, first for being merely human, and second for being culturally unworthy of the adulation heaped upon them. Schickel is at least not guilty of this kind of snobbery toward his subject. He likes movies; he likes old movies; he even likes American movies. Still, his vantage point is difficult to locate in that he seems to take off from movies rather than sink into them. The result is a curiously cerebral celebration of the visceral.

Indeed, the very beginning of the book constitutes a literary leap of sorts:

> To see him at work—even now, over 30 years after his premature death, a half century, more or less, since he made his finest films—is to sense, as if for the first time, the full possibilities of a certain kind of movement in the movies. The stunts have been imitated and parodied, and so has the screen personality, which was an improbable combination of the laughing cavalier and the dashing democrat. But no one has quite recaptured the freshness, the sense of perpetually innocent, perpetually adolescent narcissism that Douglas Fairbanks brought to the screen.

The key phrase in the preceding passage is, of course, "perpetually innocent, perpetually adolescent narcissism." What a strangely stunted quality to wax nostalgic about! And make no mistake about it; Schickel has defined Fairbanks's lasting screen image with deadly accuracy. The relentless grin, the oppressive conviviality, the interminable facetiousness, the passion for practical jokes make of the

Fairbanks persona everything Ring Lardner hated in "Haircut." Or so it seems today in retrospect and in retrospectives in which Fairbanks functions merely as a minor footnote to the careers of Allan Dwan and Raoul Walsh. In his own time, Fairbanks was admired by such perceptive critics as Alistair Cooke, Vachel Lindsay, and Robert Sherwood; and Schickel quotes these and other critics copiously to give his subject some historical resonance. But Schickel himself is never able to suggest a great deal of personal affection for his subject, only a vague longing for the kind of time in which Fairbanks flourished: "Watching him, indeed, one feels as one does watching an old comedy by Keaton or Chaplin; that somehow we have lost the knack, not to mention the spirit, for what they did, and that the loss is permanent."

Schickel's linking of Fairbanks with Keaton and Chaplin seems aesthetically ill-advised. Whereas Keaton's athleticism and Chaplin's narcissism bear a superficial resemblance to the kinetic image of the running, jumping, and never-standing-still Fairbanks, the Keaton and Chaplin films come down to us today as reflective art, unlike the Fairbanks films, which have faded into exhibitionistic artifacts. In the cinema of Keaton and Chaplin, the muse was their mistress; in the cinema of Fairbanks his ego was his master, and not even the ego of his psychic depths, but rather the ego of his social facade. One sympathizes (even if Schickel does not) with D.W. Griffith's gruff dismissal of Fairbanks's gymnastic histrionics. It seems that it was Griffith's idea that Fairbanks should seek employment with Mack Sennett. But if Fairbanks was too broad a clown for Griffith's delicate brush strokes with intimate performances, he (Fairbanks) was too much the snob to associate himself with the low-life milieu of the Sennett ethos. He wanted his picture not merely in the papers with the other hoi polloi, but also in the rotogravure of the society section.

To his credit, Fairbanks never magnified himself in his own mind. Schickel quotes Chaplin, no less, on Fairbanks's self-deprecation: "He often said that Mary Pickford and I had genius, while he had only a small talent." Actually, Fairbanks might have been more interesting today if he had displayed some of the pretentious grandiosity of Griffith and Stroheim and Ingram and DeMille. His was not a life or career of impulsive folly, but rather of prudent calculation. Hence, as high and as often as he leaped, he never soared. And his goals—success, celebrity, status, prominence—seem today more earthbound than ever.

Even his royal union with Mary Pickford seemed to have proceeded more as an affair of state than as an affair of the heart. And in
Pickfair, their cozy palace in Beverly Hills, they reigned over Hollywood with ridiculous regality even after age and talkies had overtak-
en their careers. Yet, they were both so terribly transparent in their
rise and fall that they provided a lingering spectacle of social and
emotional aspirations for millions of Americans. They could have
been characters in a Sinclair Lewis novel of the very *nouveau*, but
somehow they were completely passé before anyone had had a
chance to figure out what they had been up to all those years on the
crowded lawns of Pickfair. No one could have been angry with them.
Despite their founding of United Artists with Griffith and Chaplin,
they were never movie moguls in the malignant sense, and their personal publicity was never converted into power or influence. And
toward the end of their joint reign, they both turned out to be more
vulnerable and pathetic than anyone could have imagined at their
peak.

Schickel is well-suited as a writer and as a thinker to trace the
trajectory of Fairbanks's life from obscurity to eminence to oblivion.
The stylistic line of his writing is melodic rather than harmonic, with
the result that he extends more than he penetrates, an approach that
is not entirely inappropriate for a Disney (in Schickel's *The Disney
Version*) or a Fairbanks. Many of Schickel's best insights tend to
spring unforced from his information. Indeed, an entire book could
be written on Schickel's description of the darker side of Fairbanks's
youthful spirit:

> In fact, *The Gaucho* was the clearest public evidence yet that Fairbanks had spared not a
> moment's planning for that most inevitable of contingencies, age. He was completely identified
> with a screen character who had no capacity built in him to age. This character was rather like Peter
> Pan; his appeal was based on eternal youth. But he was not, of course, a literary construct, one
> which could be fleshed out anew by a different player for each succeeding generation. He was
> Doug and Doug was him. And Doug, alas, was only a man, and a man is condemned to grow old.

If the preceding passage is never fully developed to provide a
theory of movie myths, one must concede nonetheless that only a
writer as intelligent and as perceptive as Schickel would have provided the philosophical premise for the inquiry. It is the fate of all
movie stars to have their flesh torn by the camera from their faces to
fashion permanent masks. But no movie star in history ever impris-

oned himself so completely behind his own mask as did Douglas Fairbanks, Sr. In the end even his mask deserted him as the jolly hiding place from his own mortality.

Schickel has freely proclaimed elsewhere his great debt to the late Parker Tyler in the very speculative realm of psychosocial analysis. Still, there is an oddly original inner wrangle in Schickel's own personality. With a consciousness of American roots beneath a European flowering, Schickel escapes both the easy optimism of the provincial, and the facile pessimism of the expatriate. His view of Fairbanks and Pickford is therefore pardoxically one of pitiless compassion. Schickel's own voice is a public voice in the process of alerting without alarming the citizens of this republic as they go about their daily religious rites of building up and tearing down their sacred celebrities.

—August 1974

Your Show of Shows Revisited

THE FUNNIEST MOVIE in 1973 may well turn out to be a collection of old kinescopes entitled *Ten From Your Show of Shows*. Who would have imagined that ancient television would turn out to be so much more fun than modern cinema? Unfortunately, audiences haven't yet been cued in to the volume of laughter the show deserves. I suppose they're waiting for some prestigious critic to call the show a "break-through" of some sort or other. But it's already too late for a *Time* or *Newsweek* cover for Sid Caesar, Imogene Coca, Carl Reiner, Howard Morris, and their merry crew. They remain enshrined back in the supposedly humorless years of the Eisenhower and McCarthy '50s when so many humorless essays were being written about the de-cline of humor and satire in America.

So many of us would laugh our heads off on Saturday night through *Your Show of Shows*, but by Monday morning we would be nodding in agreement at some gloom-and-doom pronouncement in the public prints on the sad state of humor in our repressed republic. The gloom and doom were dispensed in regular dosages by James Thurber, E. B. White, Malcolm Muggeridge, Marya Mannes, John Crosby, and other eminent takers of the public pulse. Where, we were asked again and again, was America's Aristophanes, Moliere, Voltaire, Beaumarchais, and Swift? On occasions, we were even asked to mourn the absence or inactivity of such supposedly tren-chant satirists as Mark Twain, Will Rogers, and Fred Allen. No matter. By Saturday night we would be rolling off our collective couches in the national living room only to forget by Monday morning the art and craftsmanship we had been privileged to witness.

Of the ten skits in the current selection I would say that only three—the take-off on *This Is Your Life*, *Bertha the Sewing Machine Girl*, and *The Bavarian Clock*—rank anywhere near the top of the Caesar-Coca-Reiner-Morris repertory. *Big Business* and *The Music Evening* are middle-range sketches with great moments while *From Here to Obscurity*, *Breaking the News*, *The Prussian Doorman*, *The*

Interview with the Viennese Space Expert, and *The Movie Theatre* are closer to the bottom than to the top of the vast reservoir of revue material from *Your Show of Shows.*

Even so, there are more deserved belly-laughs in the single Caesar-Morris-Reiner demolition of *This Is Your Life* than in the total oeuvre of Woody Allen. And yet I dare say that the humor-exhumers of the future will decide on the basis of printed artifacts that Woody Allen deserves an entire chapter whereas Sid Caesar deserves at most a footnote, Hence, though 20 movies on the order of *Ten From Your Show of Shows* could be assembled without dropping down to the dregsier sketches from the show, there does not seem ever to have been the slightest interest in writing a book on this show-biz phenomenon.

If indeed there is such a book I stand corrected, but I've never heard of it. I've never encountered a decent essay on the subject. When I happened to mention Sid Caesar on my WBAI radio program some years ago, people congratulated me for my emotional loyalty to an obscure pleasure from the past. As I recall, the only reference I have ever made to *Your Show of Shows* in print occurs tangentially (and parenthetically) in a review of a book on the Judy Garland television show (*The Other Side of the Rainbow,* by Mel Torme):

> The recent history of the medium is replete with instances of sophisticated shows being swamped in Trendex terms by cornpone attractions.
>
> It probably all began when Lawrence Welk drove the *Show of Shows* off the video screen even as Sid Caesar, Carl Reiner, Howard Morris, and an army of professionals were doing scathing satires on the folksy amateurishness of the Welk Show.

The same question therefore comes back to haunt so many of us: why have we been so ungrateful and forgetful over the years to a group of people (and let us not forget producer Max Liebman and writers Mel Tolkin, Lucille Kallen, Mel Brooks, Tony Webster, Caesar, and many others) who have given us so much exquisite entertainment in spite of the minimal cultural encouragement provided by the medium itself and those who profess to meditate on it? But before we consider this question of our own perplexing ingratitude, we must attempt to recapture the atmosphere in which *Your Show of Shows* originally materialized.

The first big comedy star of television was Milton Berle, in many ways the stylistic antithesis of Sid Caesar. It would be startling today to rerun the ole Berle shows simply to check off the innumerable times Uncle Miltie made his grand opening entrance in drag, and how often he indulged in pinky-twiddling, powder-puffing routines out of the gay grotesqueries of the Borscht Circuit. He was low-down, vulgar, dirty, boisterous, obvious, and outrageous, and the kiddies loved him even more than they loved Pinky Lee with the latter's lisping juvenilia. Berle established the comic tradition on television of an insolent unprofessionalism by which the comedian was rewarded by the audience with bigger laughs for going up in his lines than for delivering them correctly. This tradition was later extended and perfected by Jackie Gleason, Red Skelton, and Dean Martin.

Sid Caesar was different, one might even say dialectically different. He appeared at the beginning of each show in his bathrobe to announce the various acts with dull humility. His manner and dress seemed to say: I am not a stand-up comedian with a glib line of patter, but rather a most humble artist or even an artisan trying to entertain you with bits and pieces of comic legerdemain. Of course, the 'umble pie routine didn't come off what with all the grandiose fanfare preceding it, and with all the abrasively pushy personality sketches which usually followed the character comedian bathrobe bit.

Truth to tell, Sid Caesar lacked the ineffable beauty and divine charm of the greatest comedians. He had first emerged from under the very large shadow of Danny Kaye, and their early airplane-movie routines were strikingly similar, but whereas Kaye started out in his Sylvia Fine period as a beguiling blend of Harpo Marx and Noel Coward, Caesar was a roughneck by comparison. He could function properly only in an atmosphere of perpetual parody. There was nothing really "straight" about him, whereas Kaye could sing and dance with sufficient charm and dexterity to beguile even the Russian Tea Room out of its slow, surly service.

Also, Kaye was the verbal dervish par excellence, whereas Caesar had a voice problem in the off-putting realm between the perpetual rasp and the frequent cough. (Of course, I am speaking of the demonic Danny Kaye who kowtowed to nobody in those early days before the Queen Mother and UNICEF turned him into a dull, public institution.)

Still, Caesar's voice—rasp, cough, and all—was very finely tuned to the cadences (though not to the textures) of parody. In *From Here to Obscurity*, Caesar takes on a composite part that is half Montgomery Clift (the trumpet part) and half Burt Lancaster (the love scene on the surf-soaked beach), and he doesn't really evoke either actor.

Indeed, Frank Gorshin can do a better imitation of Burt Lancaster in his (Gorshin's) sleep. What Caesar successfully parodies is not any particular performer, but rather the clumsy mechanism of middle-brow allegory with low-life characters.

Actually, Caesar and Coca were far more devastating in their take-offs and put-downs of *A Streetcar Named Desire* and *A Place in the Sun*, two skits not in the current series. Even so, Caesar did not so much evoke Marlon Brando as expose Stanley Kowalski, and Coca did not so much express Shelley Winters as excruciate the shrewish wife-to-be in the rowboat on the lake. Thus, *Your Show of Shows* was unique in going beyond the surface of performances to the substance of characterizations in its show-biz satires.

Nonetheless, the most precious moment in *From Here to Obscurity* is connected less with the satiric sensibility of the enterprise than with its "live" professionalism. The moment I speak of is the moment in which Imogene Coca breaks up as she watches Caesar's shrewdly sappy expression of surprise as a bucket of water splashes over his timing of the scene. But rather than exploit her breaking up for the easy laugh of amateurish-audience identification, she covers the breaking up by turning her face from the audience while seeming to nuzzle Caesar's shoulder.

Every week for six or seven years, a group of talented performers would undergo the most stringent demands of both theatre and cinema. That is to say that they were locked up in both the inexorable time machine of the theatre, and in the cold-fish-eye objectivity of the camera lens. Their opening nights were thus not only their closing nights, but also their eternal incarnations. And as much as they might have been appreciated by their live audience, they knew that their ultimate fate depended on a vague, amorphous mass of viewers with whom they could communicate only through an electronic image. Performers in the theatre can have an occasional bad night without jeopardizing their reputation. Performers in the cinema (and now canned television) can do as many takes as they need to become letter-perfect. But the very real charm and excitement of early live television B.T. (Before Tape) consisted of the suspenseful possibility of human error by even the most professional performers. Hence, no recapitulation of *Your Show of Shows* can fully reproduce the exquisitely wrought emotional tension of the original experience. And no revival can ever bring back the full force of the earlier laughter.

Although the current selection from *Your Show of Shows* is not ideal by absolute standards, I am not sure that I would like even the best skits to be assembled in this fashion. Ultimately, *Your Show of Shows* does not belong on the movie screen, but on the video screen and not just the comedy sketches, but the whole show.

As it is, the laughs come too close together, without the pleasing interruptions of the snazzy dancing of the Hamilton Trio, the singing of a personable tenor named Bill Hayes and his female operatic counterpart, Marguerite Piazza, a veddy, veddy stylized twosome called Mata and Hari (a bit of a drag, I always felt, and too close to the burlesque ballets of Imogene Coca), the ever ebullient Billy Williams Quartet, and, more often than not, a guest star from the silver screen. If none of the major networks want to pick up the show, why doesn't the Educational Network pick it up in the name of early and middle fifties nostalgia and social history? Or is there an unconscious fear of demonstrating that the much-maligned fifties were infinitely more entertaining than the hyped-up seventies?

Of course, *Your Show of Shows* never sought to fulfill the tendentious rhetoric of the more solemn soothsayers of the Republic. There was none of the pseudosignificant topicality of the proto-talk-show-type comedians like Mort Sahl, Steve Allen, and even the relatively expurgated Lenny Bruce of the television medium.

Although most of the writers and performers of *Your Show of Shows* might be said to have partaken of a distinctively Jewish sensibility in their satiric orientation, they were nonetheless completely immersed in the ambience of popular culture. What makes *Bertha the Sewing Machine Girl* truly magical is not merely the lurid precision of the eye-rolling and lip-speaking "pantomine" of the silent screen, but the emotional energy that Caesar, Coca, Reiner, and Morris expend on the enduring vitality and sincerity of that ancient form of dramatic expression. This then is the source of their stylistic conviction as satirists: a loving complicity with their mass audience on the inherent absurdity of all dramatic formulas and melodramatic mechanisms.

To return to the Jewishness of *Your Show of Shows*, it was still light years away from the more modish late '50s absurdism and alleged anti-Semitism of the unexpurgated Bruce, the Omnibus-oriented Nichols and May, and the *Voice*'s very own Jules Feiffer. The difference between a Sid Caesar skit and a Nichols and May skit was not only a difference in period, but also in class consciousness. With Caesar, a fundamentally popular common sense was appealed to with every bellow of outrage. With Nichols and May, an elitist *frisson* of intellectual and cultural superiority was cultivated at the expense of our most sacred cows. This was the beginning of the civil war between the Jewish intellectuals and the Jewish philistines, and also the beginning of an era of cultural affluence and alienation, and of increasing fragmentation of audience sensibilities.

Thus, in a sense, *Your Show of Shows* was more a hangover from the socially united forties than an expression of the socially divided fifties. Caesar and Company steered clear of politics and any trace of sick humor. Ethnic jokes were verboten unless they had been filtered through a secondary cultural source. Hence, Italians could be caricatured only in a parody of neorealism. Germans of the Blue-Max Prussian-Yiddish School of dialects were okay. But the Black-Shirted SS Men of such later entertainments as *Stalag 17* and *Hogan's Heroes* remained alien to the circumscribed comic vision of *Your Show of Shows*.

The clinical orientation of most of the slapstick humor tended to be oral rather than anal. *Big Business*, for example, depends for most of its humor on the debunking notion that food is more important to a hungry executive than even the fate of his firm. Curiously, the basic joke in *Big Business* is redone with off-key ennui in the meeting of the media people in *The Candidate*. Then or now, it isn't that much of a comic idea on the drawing board, but who can ever forget Howard Morris's flapping his pickle with diabolically phallic force right in Caesar's drooling face. The plastic precision with which this incredibly intricate sight gag is executed takes us into the highest reaches of humor and archetypal imagery. And to watch Howard Morris's clinging to Sid Caesar like an overly affectionate orangutan in *This Is Your Life* is to feel a primal laughter gurgling out once more from the depths of one's intestines.

Louis Kronenberger recently requested a moratorium on the use of the words "subsume," "epiphany," and "persona." I'll try to accommodate him on the first two, but I'll have to borrow "persona" one last time to try to explain why Sid Caesar has never retained a loyalty among his laughing followers comparable to that accorded to Chaplin, Keaton, Lloyd, Langdon, the Marx Brothers, W. C. Fields, and Laurel and Hardy. What they and most comedians have, and what Caesar did not, is a persona.

With the persona-performer, we can't remember after a time which gag was in which picture, and we mercifully forget all the lapses and *longueurs.* We remember only that Jack Benny was stingy, that Jackie Gleason preferred ouzo to water in the office cooler, that W. C. Fields disliked women and children, that Groucho enjoyed playing the cad, that Hardy was eternally exasperated with Laurel.

A more severely limited comedian like Jimmy Durante seemed to earn the gratitude of his admirers simply by having survived to entertain them with the same old jokes and routines. Ultimately, therefore, the strongest link between the lasting comedians and their admirers is one more of ritualistic love than of renewable laughter.

Caesar in his bathrobe of the anonymous craftsman did not ask for our love, only for our respect and admiration. What little did filter through about his "true" personality seemed to accord with the imperial cast of his name. There were rumors of his tyrannical temperament, and rumblings about his video "divorce" from Imogene Coca. And he very often played bosses and bullies, but, just as often, he played against type as the hapless schlemiel of *The Movie Theatre* and *The Bavarian Clock,* thus shrewdly indulging the audience's subconscious desire to see him dampened and virtually dismembered.

In terms of media poetics, he was anti-McLuhanist to the core, of high rather than low definition, and ultra-professional in every bone of his body. Indeed, he seemed somehow to thrive on the insane stopwatch pressure of live television where pure energy was at a premium, and where the rough edges of a performance could be blasted away with sheer gusto. He was considerably less effective on the stage and screen, where a further refinement of his talents was required and never forthcoming.

Unfortunately, the current series fails to do full justice to Imogene Coca and Carl Reiner as invaluable mercenaries in Caesar's imperial army. Imogene Coca's supper-club subtlety was one of the earliest casualties of ad agency decisions to equal so-called "national" taste rather than elevate it. Whereas Lucille Ball triumphantly incarnated the West-Coast nitwit housewife with more things than thoughts on her mind, Imogene Coca seemed to be powered by the cosmopolitan neon of New York as she floated throgh boozy mantraps, one eye beckoning and the other blotto.

As a failed femme fatale, as a hiccupping Helen Morgan with more of a whine than a catch in her voice, or as a Pavlova sinking gradually from a swan's glide to a duck's waddle, Imogene Coca represented a culture secure enough in its sensibility to laugh at some of the convulsions of art appreciation at any cost. Over the long TV haul, however, Caesar and Coca did not make a compatible couple with their strenuous idiosyncracies. Certainly, they were no match for the witless authenticity of Lucy and Desi as a wildly Pirandellian pair of performers, or of the joyless gutter sentimentality of the Kramden couple impersonated by Jackie Gleason and Audrey Meadows.

In addition, Lucille Ball was one of the most beautiful women ever to take pratfalls in any medium, and this may help explain Caesar's desperate decision to revamp his own image by taking on Nanette Fabray and Janet Blair as video wives after disposing of Imogene Coca. Despite the comeliness and talent of the newcomers, the "marriages" never really worked. Instead, Caesar seemed broader and more raucous than ever before, now that Coca's slyly provocative stylization was no longer available to relieve him of some of the comic responsibility.

By contrast, Carl Reiner was always Sid Caesar's indispensable right-hand man, his genial fool, and his willing foil. In their years together, Reiner joined the select company of sterling straight men— George Burns, Bud Abbott, Dean Martin—who eventually eclipse the top banana in the eyes and ears of the connoisseurs. I remember at the time we were always nudging each other over Reiner's catatonic comedy style lurking around the edge of Caesar's hysteria.

Toward the end, I was laughing more at Reiner than at Caesar, and I am reminded particularly of Reiner send-ups of James Mason's emceeing a drama series on television, and of Mike Wallace's inquisitorial techniques on *Hot Seat*. But by then it was too late. The cost-per-thousands boys and the ratings rajahs and the sponsor's wives and the demographic samplers had taken over television, and the

noble experiment with live, sophisticated entertainers was termi-
nated. Even the survival of *Your Show of Shows* on kinescope is an
accident of television history. The studio kinescopes have long since
been destroyed. Only Max Liebman's personal copies have survived
to remind us of a fantastic episode in the history of popular entertainment.

—March 1973

Sixties Cinema:
Zoomshots, Jumpcuts, Freeze Frames, and Girls, Girls, Girls!

NOW THAT we have supposedly summed up the twenties, the thirties, the forties, and the fifties, what of the sixties? What trends do we perceive? What new directions were taken?

It's all nonsense, of course. Decades never divide as dramatically as journalists would have us believe. The twenties were not composed entirely of *bons mots* exchanged between Ernest Hemingway and F. Scott Fitzgerald in the presence of Gertrude Stein. Nor were the thirties all bread lines and dance marathons. Nor were the forties all gallantry, idealism and here's-looking-at-you-kid. And the fifties were not just ducktails, chino jackets and Method mumbling.

Movies are especially difficult to tie up into ten-year bundles simply because there are so many of them. To do only a sketchy survey of the cinema of the sixties would require mentioning 2,000 or 3,000 movie titles. To do less, one risks the wrath of the random moviegoer who thinks that *The Tingler* is so much the most preposterously premised horror movie ever made that it deserves a place in history for that reason alone. (I myself still hold out for the climax of *The Fly*, which Vincent Price and Herbert Marshall had to play in an Antonioni lookaway two-shot for fear of breaking up if they had to look at each other while they were reading their lines.)

As it happens, I came of age as a film critic in the sixties. Although I had published pieces in esoteric film periodicals beginning in 1955, it was not until my first review in the *Village Voice* (in August 1960) that I first made contact with masses of outraged readers. My offense? I praised Alfred Hitchcock's *Psycho* in highbrow terms, indeed in *Cahiers du Cinema politique des auteurs* (later, "auteurist") terms. For weeks afterwards there came angry letters, demanding my head and my job. (Actually, I was not getting paid at the time for my reviews, but I valued a personal byline as the currency of immortality.)

Later in the sixties I was attacked for liking other Hitchcock films—by Dwight Macdonald in *Esquire* for my championing of *The Birds*, and by Richard Gilman in the very *Voice* itself for my defense of *Topaz*. Still, the notion of Alfred Hitchcock as a serious artist was not nearly as unfashionable by the end of the sixties as it had been in the beginning of the decade. Among other things, influential studies of Hitchcock by Robin Wood and François Truffaut had helped turn the tide. (Indeed, Wood liked *Marnie* much more than I did, and *Torn Curtain* much less, and so by the end of the sixties even the hard-core Hitchcockians felt confident enough of the change in critical climate to disagree publicly on nuances of their enthusiasm.)

I begin with Hitchcock because his rising reputation through the decade is symptomatic of an altered perspective on the movies. Once upon a time if a movie called *Oh Brother, Where Art Thou?* came out on the same day as a movie called *Bang, Bang, You're Dead*, the first-string reviewer would cover *Oh Brother, Where Art Thou?* and the second-stringer would cover *Bang, Bang, You're Dead*. Nowadays it is more likely to be the other way around. Indeed, flicks have become so much more fashionable than fillums that I find myself almost apologizing for movies (usually foreign) made under arty auspices.

Back in 1960, however, Hollywood movies were at their lowest ebb as far as the culturally fashionable commentators were concerned, and, conversely, the art film was at its apex. In 1960 Ingmar Bergman had finally fluttered out of the cultists' cocoon and into the Sunday supplements. I had done my own obligatory exegesis on *The Seventh Seal* at the end of the fifties and had been tagged by movie press agents on the projection room circuit as "one of those Ingmar Bergman freaks." After spending a year in Paris to savor the nonlinguistic mysteries of *mise-en-scene*, and my rediscovery of the American Cinema, I begin to blow hot and cold on Bergman, though his particular brand of surface mystification was not so much *Oh Brother, Where Art Thou?* (sobbing social consciousness) as *Oh Father, Where Art Thou?* (misty metaphysics).

In the realm of *espresso esoterica*, Bergman was buttressed in the sixties by such *nouvelle vague* directors as Alain Resnais, François Truffaut, Jean-Luc Godard and Claude Chabrol, from Italy by Federico Fellini and Michelangelo Antonioni, and from the Spanish-speaking world by a regenerated Luis Bunuel. The films most often hailed as "turning points" in the history of the medium were Resnais' *Hiroshima Mon Amour*, Godard's *Breathless*, Antonioni's *L'Avventura*, Fellini's *8½*, Truffaut's *Jules and Jim*, and, much later in the decade, Bergman's *Persona*. In one way or another, each of these films exuded alienation and pessimism with an arty aroma which delighted the nostrils of the more sensitive moviegoers. Meanwhile, back at the ranch, the bang-bang-you're dead genre movies were systematically denigrated except when they were augmented with angst as in Arthur Penn's *Bonnie and Clyde* and Sam Peckinpah's *The Wild Bunch*.

In the spring of 1961, I went to the Cannes Film Festival for the first time, and then proceeded to spend a year in Paris. I was still very much an outsider on the international critical scene, but it was a time in which cinema seemed to be exploding in every direction. Cannes itself at festival time was a veritable hellhole of status-seeking snobbery, press-agentry, and vulgar display. Within one afternoon in front of the Carlton Hotel I was treated to the mutually cannibalistic spectacle of Sophia Loren and Gina Lollobrigida devouring and being devoured by a flock of *paparazzi* right out of Fellini's *La Dolce Vita*. One spent one's mornings hearing about parties one hadn't been invited to the night before, and one's afternoons looking out into the harbor at the yachts to which one would never ever be invited. And by the end of the festival, one ended up wiring home for more money. The biggest shock, however, was discovering how much of the world's cinema simply couldn't be sat through. In this context, Luis Bunuel's *Viridiana* was doubly welcome, coming as it did near the end of a dismal festival.

Actually, the first public screening of *Viridiana* occurred on a somnolent spring afternoon when most of the other critics were off on an outing to the Picasso Museum in Antibes. I had overslept that morning, and missed the outing, and so I had nothing else to do but look at *Viridiana*. When I emerged into the sunshine two hours later, I was in a state of delirious discovery. As I wrote later, I was astonished to discover not merely a great film, but, indeed, a really good movie. All that day I shouted Bunuel's praises to anyone who would listen. What amazed me most of all was that Bunuel had broken through into the blazing sunlight of success in what should have been the tapering-off twilight of his career. On my way that night to the evening screening of *Viridiana*, I kept hearing murmurs about "people" saying that *Viridiana* was great. For me, as an obscure critic, it was an epiphany of sorts. One person, one opinion, could make a difference or, at least, create a climate of expectation.

Of course, *Viridiana* was such a rousing entertainment in its own right that no critic or gaggle of critics could have denied it the tumultuous audience approval it so keenly deserved. But it must be remembered that Bunuel's visual style with its metaphorical montage and starkly ideological imagery looked decidedly old-fashioned in the context of the reigning *Antoniennui* of that period. Bourgeois boredom gave way in *Viridiana* to surrealist fantasy. The discreet aestheticism of Antonioni and Resnais was blown away by the indiscreet outrageousness of Bunuel.

Despite his ideological inclinations, Bunuel had more in common with Hollywood than even I realized at the time. He did not "develop" individual shots at the expense of the flow of his narrative, and he was not afraid of lurid action in his scenarios. But the most important lesson I learned as a critic from Bunuel's seemingly miraculous resurrection from the limbo of festivals and film societies was that cinema was not a matter of vogues and fashions, but rather of individual artists, each with a unique vision. Thus, Bunuel was for me the first battleground of auteurism, a policy of describing the cinema personally rather than nonpersonally.

From Cannes I went to Paris where I unexpectedly rediscovered the American Cinema of Howard Hawks and Alfred Hitchcock and John Ford and Leo McCarey and George Cukor and Gregory La Cava and Frank Borzage and so many others. Consequently, my critical sensibility began to divide into two branches, one historical—the American Cinema—and the other prophetic—the European innovators. When I returned to New York at the end of 1961, I declared in the *NY Film Bulletin* that the two most important films to open locally that year were *Breathless* and *L'Avventura*, but I placed on almost the same level John Ford's *Two Rode Together*, a James Stewart–Richard Widmark Western that had suffered the indignity of opening in Brooklyn, and Blake Edwards's *Breakfast at Tiffany's*, a stylish film that at the time displeased its scenarist George Axelrod and its author Truman Capote. *Tiffany's* was embellished also by the distinctive Henry Mancini sound of "Moon River" sung, more or less, by Audrey Hepburn, and is Mancini any less symptomatic of the sixties than the Beatles and the Stones?

I was genuinely excited also by the forceful close-ups and concisely Jacobean melodramatics of Samuel Fuller's *Underworld, USA* with Cliff Robertson and Dolores Dorn doing a dregsy duet to a fare-thee-well. And Gerd Oswald's *Brainwashed* still happens to be, among other things, the best movie ever made about chess, apart from V.F. Pudovkin's Russian short classic *Chess Fever* back in the twenties. Fuller and Oswald were directors in whom I had stylistic investments because of their expressive camera movements in their previous films. At the time I was in the midst of reevaluating the camera movments of F.W. Murnau, Kenji Mizoguchi, Max Ophuls, and Douglas Sirk, the first three having died before 1960, and the fourth having become inactive.

Thus I carried into the sixties many of my belated probes of the fifties. For me camera movement had become a form of spiritual contemplation, and thus I became overly suspicious of the gaudy gut realism of Robert Rossen and Elia Kazan. Hence, I tended to underrate both Rossen's *The Hustler* and Kazan's *Spendor in the Grass*. From the fifties, also, I had inherited Nicholas Ray (*The King of Kings*), Anthony Mann (*El Cid*), Robert Aldrich (*The Last Sunset*) and Raoul Walsh (*Marines, Let's Go*) because of their neglected off-beat masterpieces in the forties and fifties, and thus I fell into the trap of rationalizing the shortcomings of their relatively inferior 1961 offerings, if only to keep their careers alive.

For my lonely defense of Jean Renoir's *Picnic on the Grass* in 1960 and Luis Bunuel's *The Young One* in 1961, however, I feel no need to apologize. Nor do I feel that I underrated Karel Reisz's *Saturday Night and Sunday Morning*, John Huston's *The Misfits*, Billy Wilder's *One, Two, Three*, John Frankenheimer's *The Young Savages*, and Stanley Kramer's *Judgment at Nuremberg*. In case you've forgotten, the big blockbluster of 1961, critically and commercially, was *West Side Story*, a serviceable entertainment that has dated very badly. But my biggest goof of the year was completely misunderstanding what John Cassavetes was up to with *Shadows*. Again I was agitating so strongly against facile formulations of "realism," that I often reacted against a grimy kitchen sink before I had a chance to appreciate the poetry and fantasy flowing out of the faucet.

In 1962, my rediscovery of the American cinema of the thirties and forties and fifties had launched me on a crusade to resurrect the neglected American directors at all costs. Hence, I startled my regular readers in one *Village Voice* column in 1962 by ranking John Ford's *The Man Who Shot Liberty Valance* over such more fashionable foreign films as Francois Truffaut's *Jules and Jim*, Federico Fellini's *8½*, and Michelangelo Antonioni's *Eclipse*. What then seemed even to me a bit of daring perversity now seems eminently sound by any critical standards. I have no regrets.

The Man Who Shot Liberty Valance is a monumental summing up of a career and a genre. It is possibly John Ford's last great film, and its moral aesthetic rigor still awes me. By contrast, *8½*, *Jules and Jim*, and *Eclipse*, celebrate certain chic tendencies cultivated by their directors as they allow their narratives to be eroded by lyrical essays on their own feelings. But without *8½*, *Jules and Jim*, and *Eclipse*, it is doubtful that such modish films of the late sixties as *The Graduate* and *Easy Rider* would ever have come into existence, and, with them, all their disastrously derivative imitations.

The officially big film of 1962 was David Lean's *Lawrence of Arabia*, a film that combined elements of *Bridge on the River Kwai*, *Citizen Kane*, *Billy Budd*, and *Oscar Wilde* in a desert storm of elephantine ambiguities held together only by Peter O'Toole's blue-eyed *somnambule*. If I had to do it all over again, I would still pan it. And I would still prefer to the laurel-wreathed *Lawrence* such unsung flicks as Samuel Fuller's *Merrill's Marauders*, Joseph Losey's *The Concrete Jungle*, Vincente Minnelli's *Two Weeks in Another Town* and *The Four Horsemen of the Apocalypse*, Robert Aldrich's *Whatever Happened to Baby Jane?*, Otto Preminger's *Advise and Consent*, Orson Welles's *Mister Arkadin*, George Cukor's *The Chapman Report* (or at least the chromatically eloquent Claire Bloom and Jane Fonda episodes thereof), and John Cassavetes' *Too Late Blues*.

The sleeper of the year was Sam Peckinpah's *Ride the High Country*, and it passed us all by on its way to England and France for its critical vindication. Some of us had been thrown off by the fearsome turgidity of Peckinpah's first movie, *The Deadly Companions*. Then too, how many Gotham critics were culturally conditioned at the time to suspect that Joel McCrea and Randolph Scott could have been involved with an authentic work of art?

The sixties began on the falsely promising note of John F. Kennedy's accession to the presidency, but the decade achieved its prevailing mood of absurdist despair only *after* the assassination of John F. Kennedy in late 1963. It isn't that movies, here or abroad, referred to his assassination directly, but rather that all sorts of hitherto subterranean trends in the cinema burst through the surface and became both critically and commercially viable. *Dr. Strangelove*, for example, might still have been made if the disaster in Dallas had never occurred, but the sourly anarchic humor of Stanley Kubrick and Terry Southern would not have seemed nearly as appropriate to its time (1964) as it did. And journalists would not have been emboldened to demand of the cinema a new tone of irony and cynicism.

In the thirties and the forties, it had been possible to speak seriously and meaningfully of an RKO style, a Fox style, an MGM style, a Columbia style, a Paramount style, a Warners style, a Universal style, and even a Republic, Monogram, and PRC style. MGM, for example, turned out the most refined and genteel cinema with the best lab work, but it lacked the more stylish idiosyncrasies of the more ambitious Paramount and RKO products. Fox was known as the goy studio with a distinctively middle-American vulgarity embodied by Alice Faye and Betty Grable. But it was also very socially conscious in the distinctively twangy cadences of John Ford and Henry King on the directorial level, and of Darryl F. Zanuck, Nunnally Johnson, and Kenneth Macgowan on the project level. Universal had preempted the Gothic vertigo of the horror film with the stylized staircase-to-crypt camera forensics of James Whale, Tod Browning, and Edgar G. Ulmer. Warners monopolized the morbid night quality and prison pallor of its tough but sometimes merely turgid melodramas. Greer Garson and Norma Shearer were no more accidents at MGM than were James Cagney and Humphrey Bogart at Warners.

There was through the thirties and forties a distinctive studio pattern which only the strongest artistic personalities were capable of transcending. Then under the fearsome pressure of television competition in the fifties the studios fired most of their contract players and liquidated most of their production facilities. Thus, by the sixties, movies tended to be individual projects with pick-up casts and assorted technicians, and, increasingly, authentic locations for inauthentic plots. The studios became arbitrary distributors of whatever packages had been prepared by outside agents, stars, and "creative talent."

It was a decade also in which the "Film Festival" fever hit the United States with predictable reactions and counterreactions. Also, as habitual moviegoers disappeared by the millions, serious scholars of film increased by the thousands. It is a generally overlooked paradox of the famous auteurist controversy that though my debate with Pauline Kael in *Film Quarterly* attracted a great deal of attention as a squabble between two schools of thought, it served also to propel two obscure polemicists from the little film magazine backwaters into the mainstream of the critical establishment. For what Kael and Sarris had in common was a historical perspective on film that preceded any commitment to journalism or belles-lettres.

But it would not have been possible for this new historical perspective to take hold if the habits of movie audiences had not been revolutionized by the resurrection of old movies on television at the rate of approximately a hundred a week. Suddenly, it seemed, audiences were well enough educated in the history of film to follow and appreciate the most esoteric references to figures of visual and verbal style. Of course, there were the usual tendencies toward trivia and smug derision, but generally all movie reviewers began to feel an academic pressure on their profession to keep up with the growing historical awareness of the public.

Unfortunately, too many reviewers became only semiliterate in the visual vocabulary of the medium, and thus a great deal of pretentious nonsense was published on the level of the discovery made by Moliere's Monsieur Jourdain that he had been speaking prose all his life. Indeed, one New York reviewer became conspicuous toward the end of the decade by his bizarre crusade against the zoom shot.

Still, he did have a point. When we think of the most characteristic mannerisms of movies in the sixties, we think of the zooms and jump cuts and freeze frames, and each of these mannerisms evokes a mood of the time. First there is the paradox involved in the operation of the zoom and telephoto lens: Filmmakers move optically closer to their material while remaining physically distant. No longer did directors delight in riding their cranes into and away from scenes as their directorial feelings dictated. Thus, whereas Max Ophuls and Vincente Minnelli had gloried in their artistic power as they bombarded the screen with their boom shots, the new breed like Arthur Penn (*Bonnie and Clyde*) and Mike Nichols (*The Graduate*) professed to prefer less ostentatious means of presenting their material.

At about the time that Penn was shooting *The Chase* on the old Warners lot in Hollywood, he found himself on a set adjoining that in which Nichols was shooting *Who's Afraid of Virginia Woolf?* They both had a laugh at the expense of the elaborate equipment used by Wyler and Curtiz in the days of *Jezebel* and *The Letter* and *Casablanca*. This was fashionable sixties thinking in a nutshell: Let's get rid of all the expensive equipment and fall back on our liberated ideas and freedoms. Unfortunately, the movies that resulted from this "liberation" were generally colder than the movies that the old studios had ground out supposedly for the crassest considerations.

Indeed, the distinction I have noted between optical intensity and physical fastidiousness with the zoom shot marked a trend away from fiction, away from fantasy, away from myth, and toward documentary, toward the freezing of reality into satiric patterns, and toward a derisive diminution of the story film. If there were one "in" (or actually "out") shot that characterized the spirit of the sixties, it would be the telephoto turgidity of Dustin Hoffman's Benjamin running toward the camera to rescue his fair Elaine in *The Graduate*, and not seeming to be making any progress.

Of course, there was nothing absolutely new about the zoom shots, jump cuts, and freeze frames, all of which antedate the sixties. Also, there were many directors who did not choose to look modish at all. Kurosawa's *The Seven Samurai* was one of the last major movies to use the wipe as a transitional device. The wipe, very prevalent in the thirties, is a shortcut to narrative movement and represents nothing so much as the turning of a page. Similarly, the slow dissolve was very fashionable in the thirties and forties and even in the fifties both as a form of symbolic linkage between shots, and as a means of evoking the mental imagery of a novel. Yet by 1967 Joseph Losey was explaining apparently gratuitous camera movements in *Accident* in terms of the need to match color shots without employing opticals in the editing. Why? No particularly profound reason. Perhaps Losey's instinct in editing was based on nothing more substantial than the suspicion that nothing really connected anymore. This is the kind of instinct that tends to identify the sixties.

By contrast, the jump cuts that shocked audiences so much in Jean-Luc Godard's *Breathless* in the beginning of the sixties tended to make them yawn by the end of the sixties. Godard's career through the decade was a descent into apocalyptic despair for a medium that he thought was dying. By 1968 he ended a film (*Weekend*) with the title Fin Du Cinema, but, much to his discomfiture, the cinema refused to die. And the world also.

Among these "modern" techniques was the freeze frame, first popularized in Francois Truffauts's *The Four Hundred Blows* and later memorialized with loving still shots of Jeanne Moreau in *Jules and Jim*. In many ways, the freeze frame as a way of stopping a movie without really ending it was equivalent to the tendency of the rock songs of the epoch to stop without really ending. The freeze frame was used as extensively as it was in the sixties largely because many filmmkers of the period had lost a sense of a logical and meaningful end to a beginning, or perhaps a metaphysical sense of the story. This loss of conviction in beginning, middle, and end had occurred in literature and the theater much earlier, but its coming to the cinema met with a great deal of resistance nonetheless even from people who were supposedly sophisticated and modernistic about the older art forms. Truffaut got away with his self-conscious freeze frames and quotes from older films only because his juicily literary romanticism was offered to the audience as compensation. But more austere directors like Godard and Antonioni encountered hostility whenever they disappointed the audience's fantasy expectations. Godard, especially, became an albatross around my critical neck through the decade, and only recently Billy Wilder took a poke at me in *Esquire* for allegedly imagining that Godard made good movies.

When we look back on the films of the sixties, it is hard to remember that there was ever a time when a vast part of the cultural establishment did not take the Beatles seriously. But I remember vividly that as late as 1964, the year of Richard Lester's *A Hard Day's Night*, more than a few eyebrows were raised in the groves of Academe when I hailed *A Hard Day's Night* as "the *Citizen Kane* of jukebox musicals, the brilliant crystallization of such diverse cultural particles as the pop movie, rock 'n' roll, *cinema verité*, the *nouvelle vague*, free cinema, the affectedly hand-held camera, frenzied cutting, the cult of the sexless subadolescent, the semidocumentary, and studied spontaneity."

Most of the reviewers were favorably disposed toward *A Hard Day's Night*, but there was a tinge of condescension in their suspicion of the hysteria aroused by four mop-headed moaners from Liverpool who sounded more black than most black American singers. The media and the hucksters had not yet decided to acknowledge the youth market, and the Mafia-backed singers of the fifties had not yet been dislodged by a resurgence of rhythm and blues from across the ocean. It was not that I was any kind of prophet about the Beatles, nor that I became one of their professional admirers. I was relatively let down by *Help!* the following year, and despite such spectacular aural coups as their *Sgt. Pepper*, they never figured prominently in my film aesthetics after their initial coup, to which I paid tribute with these heartfelt words: "My critical theories and preconceptions are all shook up, and I am profoundly grateful to the Beatles for such a pleasurable softening of hardening aesthetic arteries."

The hardening aesthetic arteries to which I referred were visible in the deep ruts I had dug myself into as a consequence of perpetual attacks by a wide variety of philistines. I had been kept so busy defending established positions in the cinema that I had neglected the medium's miraculous capacity to renew itself in the most unexpected manner. For once, I had been able to express my enjoyment of a movie experience without dragging in all the cumbersome historicity of auteurism, and I was truly grateful.

Even so, my enthusism for the Beatles led me to overlook completely, in 1965, a more modest enterprise than the bash from the Beatles. The film was entitled *Having a Wild Weekend*, was directed by John Boorman, and featured the now extinct Dave Clark Five. At the time I was mildly amused by the film-buff phantasmagoria of the mise-en-scène, but I couldn't figure out what the film was supposed to be about. After *Point Blank* came out two years later, I began to take more interest in Boorman, and a recent revisit to *Having a Wild Weekend* confirms it as one of the more charming though chilling entertainments of the decade. Suddenly the film makes sense as a meditation on loneliness and mediocrity and the fatal inability to find adventure in the unknown. And the Dave Clark Five were perfectly cast in their extraordinarily unprepossessing way. The moral? Simply that we are still much too close to the sixties to render any definitive judgment. Also, when one talks about movies with any degree of devotion to the subject, the footnotes are often more interesting than the chapter headings.

Indeed, as time goes on, the early part of the sixties will adhere more to the late fifties, whereas the last years of the sixties will slide in with the swinging seventies. It was always thus. I don't know when the break occurred exactly in the sixties, or rather I don't want to proclaim the exact date of the break at this moment. Let us say simply that as the decade progressed its movies seemed to become more attuned (at least in part) to black ghetto audiences. (In fact, it was during the sixties that Negroes officially became blacks in literary circles.) Also, the movies of the sixties became increasingly erotic or at at least increasingly lascivious and pornographic as audiences panted their way out of the frustrated fifties and into the supposedly sated Seventies. There were also tendencies toward switching from soap opera to dope opera, and toward a belief that at long last crime could be made to pay if the caper were amusing enough and ingenious enough.

As far as black cinema was concerned, it could only go up after its pitiful showing in 1960. Even so, Philip Leacock's *Take a Giant Step* struck me as far more felicitous than Daniel Petrie's puffed-up adaptation of Lorraine Hansberry's *A Raisin in the Sun*. A preference for the little picture over the big picture? Perhaps. But also a very fervent appreciation of the performances of Ellen Holly, Ruby Dee, and Johnny Nash in *Take a Giant Step*. From abroad there was the French-Brazilian flash-hit of the 1959 Cannes Film Festival, *Black Orpheus*, with the beauteous Marpessa Dawn from the ghettos of Pittsburgh, Pennsylvania, but the context of *Black Orpheus* was too exotically tokenish to have any impact on the American scene. The point is that until very late into the sixties, black performers appeared almost exclusively in films designed by white liberal filmmakers for white liberal audiences. For the most part, these films stank of sanctimonious self-righteousness. An intelligent exception to this rule was *Nothing But a Man* in 1964, but it was not until the very late sixties that black cinema began to spill out its guts so as to reach its proper constituency. This transition is continuing well into the seventies, and it may take us all the way into 1984 to determine where it is leading us.

And what is there to say of eroticism when it is well-known that one man's aphrodisiac is another's soporific, and no one seems to know what it is exactly that turns women on? As a reasonably lecherous observer of the movie scene, I can only report on my own reactions. However, I can remember with a fair amount of objectivity that back in 1960 we were still a long way from the porno permissiveness of the later sixties and early seventies, but films were nonetheless becoming more explicit in their eroticism. Though New York was not yet topless, and nudity was not yet matter of fact, there were at least intimations of a breakthrough in Janet Leigh's mesmerizing sensuality in *Psycho*, Sophia Loren's cool voluptuousness in *Heller in Pink*

Tights, Jean Simmons' passionate susceptibility in *Elmer Gantry,* Lee Remick's thoughtful carnality in *Wild River,* and the modified strip-tease acts of Patricia Owens in *Hell to Eternity* and Joan Collins in *Seven Thieves.*

Still, none of these projections of future permissiveness could be compared with the displays of lush sensuality embodied in Louis Malle's *The Lovers* by Jeanne Moreau, and in Alain Resnais' *Hiroshima Mon Amour* by Emmanuèle Riva, and in innumerable Ingmar Bergman films by Harriet Andersson, Eva Dahlbeck, Bibi Andersson, Ingrid Thulin, and Gunnel Lindblom. Hollywood was still hamstrung by censorship, particularly when it came to exposing female flesh. And looking back now, we were truly pathetic in our celebration of "breakthroughs" achieved in movies of the middle and late Fifties as the competition with television became more desperate. Actually, some of the so-called breakthroughs of the fifties were merely throwbacks to the early thirties. To see Patricia Neal flaring her nostrils as she paraded provocatively in a black negligee (*A Face in the Crowd,* 1954) or to watch Lee Remick do a modified strip tease on television (double titillation) in the same film was merely to return to the lustful lingerie era before 1934.

But even by 1960 none of us dreamed that the day would ever come when our favorite actresses would bare their breasts on the screen as they had hitherto bared their souls. We didn't even dare hope for such a bounty from our sex goddesses. I remember when I went to Paris in 1960 I rushed off to see all those little snippets of nudity and desire that never crossed the censorious ocean to New York. On my most recent trip to Paris in 1970, I found that Parisians were unable to see all that was freely available in New York, and now whenever I wallow in the fleapits of Times Square I am aware of furtive Frenchmen wallowing alongside me as once I patronized their Pigalle.

Again, I'm not sure when it all happened, but there were all kinds of hints at the very beginning of the decade, and certainly on the script level. Hence it seemed only natural in 1960 that the more clinical aspects of the Oscar Wilde scandal should be the subject of not one but two movies: *Oscar Wilde* with Robert Morley as Oscar and Ralph Richardson as the prosecutor, and *The Trials of Oscar Wilde* with Peter Finch as Oscar and James Mason as the prosecutor. Jules Dassin's *Never On Sunday* was another tricky breakthrough of sorts as Melina Mercouri clumped to international stardom as a sentimentally musical-maternal whore. But by having the film spoken in both Greek and English, Dassin broke through the ooh-lah-lah arthouse barrier to speak naughtily to American audiences. Sexy subtitles were harmless enough but the sensation of an American (Dassin) from the Bronx saying to a woman quite simply and eloquently: "I want to sleep with you" was something else again. Revolutions have broken out with even less of a spark than that.

Anyway, things had reached such a pass by the sixties that the pseudo-sophisticated taste-makers were provided with enough ammunition to begin demolishing Doris Day's (and Stanley Shapiro's) coy double-entendre yes-yes-no-no sex comedies that crested in 1960 with *That Touch of Mink*, a concoction in which no less a personage than Cary Grant was the virgin's Crackerjack prize. Tiresome talk-show jokes about Doris Day's onscreen virginity at a relatively advanced age offscreen reached their peak also about this time, and signaled the break between the mass audiences of the Radio City Music Hall and the mandarins clustered around the espresso bars of the art houses. Later in the decade the career of Julie Andrews would be blighted by the same kind of wise-guy antisweetness routine on the fearless open-mouth programs on television watched largely by people who would rather watch television than go to movies. As Doris Day and Julie Andrews were unfairly denigrated in the sixties, so had the luminous Lillian Gish been slandered as a vapid Victorian way back in the early twenties.

In contrast to the smug put-down of Doris Day and Julie Andrews were the copious crocodile tears shed for Marilyn Monroe, who died of an overdose of sleeping pills during a lost August weekend in 1962. I note that some feminists are now attempting to canonize Marilyn as the movement's Joan of Arc. The truth is that it was the indifference and even hostility of women moviegoers that made Marilyn's movie career expendable in Hollywood. The strange thing is that even today Marilyn doesn't evoke sexual liberation so much as sexual repression. If she was anything at all, she was the poetic creation of American Puritanism, the apotheosis of every girl who ever stood on a street corner with her skirts swirling in the wind like flags of fantasy for the guilt-ridden American males standing at attention around her.

To be sure, this is an image that faded rapidly as the movies of the sixties became almost incredibly licentious to the point of a world-weary lethargy. But before the bottom fell out of even toplessness, there was still time to savor the relatively suggestive sensuality of Lola Albright in *A Cold Wind in August*, Tuesday Weld in *Soldier in the Rain* and *Lord Love a Duck*, Cyd Charisse in *Two Weeks in Another Town*, Claire Bloom in *The Chapman Report*, Stella Stevens in *Too Late Blues* and *The Nutty Professor* and *Synanon*, Ann-Margret in *Bye Bye Birdie*, Sarah Miles in *The Servant*, Jane Fonda in *Sunday in New York*, Julie Andrews (yes, Julie Andrews) in *The Americanization of Emily*, Patricia Neal and Samantha Eggar in *Psyche 59*, Samantha Eggar in *The Collector*, Julie Christie in *Billy Liar* and *Darling*, Francoise Brion in *L'Immortelle*, Sarah Miles and Vanessa Redgrave in *Blow-Up*, Tuesday Weld in *The Cincinnati Kid*, Susannah York in *Kaleidoscope* and *The Killing of Sister George*, Angie Dickinson in *Point Blank*, Sandy Dennis in *Up the Down Staircase*, Sharon Tate and Claudia Cardinale in *Don't Make Waves*, Catherine Deneuve and Genevieve Page in *Belle De Jour*, Jean Seberg in *Birds in Peru*, Shirley MacLaine in *The Bliss of Mrs. Blossom*, Billie Whitelaw in *Charlie Bubbles*, Lynn Carlin and Gena Rowlands in *Faces*, Anne Heywood in *The Fox*, Bibi Andersson in *Le Viol*, Inger Stevens in *Madigan*, Julie Christie in *Petulia*, Joan Hackett, Jessica Walter, and Shirley Knight in *The Group*, Susan George in *The Strange Affair*, Pat Quinn in *Alice's Restaurant*, Rita Moreno in *Marlowe*, Diana Rigg in *On Her Majesty's Secret Service* (Miss Rigg of *The Avengers* fame from television having earned the distinction of being the only Bond playmate of whom I ever approved), Zina Bethune in *Who's That Knocking at My Door*, and Audrey Campbell in Joe Sarno's soft-core porn in the days before the deluge.

It was in the sixties that I once asked myself to define the cinema in three words, and replied with more delirium than discretion: "Girls! Girls! Girls!" Alas, I am older and wiser now, and must balance my blatant valentines to the opposite sex with more measured comments on the decade as a whole.

It was neither the best nor the worst of decades. I had become ten years older at the end of it, and more deeply involved in my profession. I retain the conviction that the field is bigger than myself and all my colleagues put together, and that we have only begun to scratch the surface.

—November 1973

Avant-Garde Films Are
More Boring Than Ever

I SPENT two joyless evenings last week by suffering through the first two programs of the "American Avant-Garde Cinema" on display at the Museum of Modern Art. Since joylessness is part of my job, I have no valid cause for complaint. Besides, my main objective was to test the reactions of the spectators to these sustained assaults on their senses. All in all, seven evenings (May 4 to 11) have been devoted to a History of the American Avant-Garde Cinema (from 1943 to 1972), a traveling film exhibition organized by the American Federation of Arts, personally selected by John G. Hanhardt, Curator of Film and Video at the Whitney Museum of American Art, and supported by a grant from the National Endowment for the Arts. The age of foundation films is thus well upon us as the National Endowment people made it possible for free tickets to be issued for the performances— the patrons avoided even the general admission charge into the museum—and for the publication of a 176-page catalog on the exhibition.

For years people have been pestering me with questions about the American Avant-Garde Cinema, alias the Underground Film, alias the Independent Film, alias the New American Cinema, alias the Experimental film, alias the Nonnarrative Cinema, alias the Poetic Film. Whenever possible, I have walked away without giving an answer. Now I can ask accusingly of my questioners: "Where were *you* on the nights of May 4 through May 11 in the year of our Bicentennial?" Unfortunately, I am not quite as innocent of complicity with the American Avant-Garde Cinema as I would like to be. Through the I'll-do-anything-for-a-living sixties I even lectured on the subject at college campuses hither and yon. One way or another I managed to view most of the alleged classics in the genre, but I seldom wrote about them. My heart and mind were so overwhelmingly committed to the "narrative" film that it seemed to me unconscionably frivolous to flail away at a fringe subject. Also, I owed (and owe still) an enor-

196

mous debt of gratitude to Jonas Mekas for enabling me to break into print, first in *Film Culture* (1955) and then in *The Village Voice* (1960). It was a delicate situation, to say the least. Here I was a movie-movie maverick on a collision course with Mekas and his avant-garde followers. The battleground was *The Voice* itself, and there are those who believe that if *The Voice* had committed itself as whole-heartedly to the nonnarrative film as it did to the Off-Broadway theatre, the paper would have wound up granting annual Avanti awards for the cinema with as much aplomb as it displays in granting annual Obie awards for the theatre. I doubt it. As much as I admire the cultural audacity of Jerry Tallmer and his successors in the *Voice* theatre department, I believe that they would be the first to admit that they could not have put over Off-Broadway if there had not been enormous talent and even genius there in the first place. By the same token I cannot find in myself the presumption to lie awake at night feeling guilty for having single-handedly stifled the alleged genius of the American Avant-Garde Cinema. Indeed, if there had been a single avant-garde film around which *Voice* readers could have rallied wholeheartedly, I would have been the first to shift my focus. As it is, I have written with moderate approval of works by James Whitney, Andy Warhol, Ronald Tavel, Jack Smith, Kenneth Anger, Jonas and Adolfas Mekas, and, in my capacity as an editor, I have commissioned articles by people sympathetic to the movement. Live and let live has been my motto, and since most American avant-garde film artists have tended to be as poor as church mice, it seemed unduly cruel to heap abuse atop neglect. My first impulse on this occasion, therefore, was to let some "inside" writer do the usual publicity blurb on the museum program in the guise of a critical piece, but then I took a look at the incredible arrogance of the program catalog and decided that the time had come to draw the line between foundation-prose illusions and screening-room realities. For starters, I think that every foundation power person with a predilection for avant-garde cinema should be compelled to sit through the entire oeuvre of the favored artists.

Marilyn Singer's opening paragraph in her introduction to the catalog entries on individual films sets the tone for the enterprise:

For each age, for each place, for each time, there has always been an avant-garde. Hector Berlioz, a musician much maligned in his own time, relates that when Beethoven's C Minor string quartet was premiered, "After a short while, people grew restless and began whispering . . . . . Eventually, most of them got up and left, protesting aloud that it was meaningless, absurd, unbearable--the work of a madman." James Whistler's "Nocturne in Black and Gold: The Falling Rocket," today seen as a major work, was lambasted by critic John Ruskin who accused Whistler of "flinging a pot of paint into the face of the public." The public agreed. And Gertrude Stein's "A rose is a rose is a rose," one line from her many writings which strove to reexamine language, was the subject of many a cartoon, the punch line of many a joke. These and other artists were avant-garde; their work was misunderstood, mocked, even banned or destroyed; but eventually, they became familiar, acceptable, sometimes even traditional, or reactionary."

This is the familiar argument that because Beethoven was once reviled, Brakhage must now be revered. It reminds me a bit of an old Jimmy Durante routine: "They said Columbus was crazy! They said Edison was crazy! They said Louie was crazy!" Chorus: "Who's Louie?" Durante: "My uncle—he *was* crazy!"

As Dwight Macdonald has so astutely observed, audiences since the end of World War I have tended to err on the side of susceptibility rather than of skepticism. Or, at least they did until a few years ago when the mania for modernism at any cost began to subside. Minimalism and conceptual art have not carried the day. The *nouveau roman* is virtually extinct. Cage and Stockhausen are still not household words, and Grotowski is but a gurgling memory. The self-proclaimed artist is no longer being given the benefit of every doubt.

But where have been the great scandals of the American avant-garde cinema: Jack Smith's *Flaming Creatures* caused something of a fuss back in the early sixties, mainly because the hyped-up audience's erotic expectations were disappointed by the film's disconcertingly unaggressive transvestism. Andy Warhol's reductio-ad-absurdum exercises were always good for an argument or two. Unfortunately, the works of Smith, Warhol (and the very precisely perverse Gregory Markopoulos) were not available for the current program at the museum. Robert Nelson's *Bleu Shut* did cause considerable booing at the New York Festival, but only because it was inflicted on a captive audience waiting for a narrative feature film to follow this exasperating 33-minute "short" subject. In my experience, audiences almost never boo American avant-garde films, but they often walk out on the lengthier works if their content is not compelling enough. In this respect, the museum programs are monopolized almost entirely by relatively short efforts. No fewer than 34 of the 38 films run 30 minutes or under, and 15 run 10 minutes or under. The two longest films are Michael Snow's *Wavelength* at 45 minutes, and Stan Brakhage's *Anticipation of the Night* at 40 minutes. Under these circumstances, it is remarkable how many of the films achieve tedium in so short a time. For one thing, the program as a whole is singularly lacking in shock value. By contrast, the non-avant-garde cinema can look back on a long history of shocks, sensations, and scandals, beginning with Louis Lumière's *The Arrival of the Train at La Ciotat,* and continuing with the first screenings of D. W. Griffith's *Birth of a Nation,* Sergei Eisenstein's *Potemkin,* Jean Vigo's *Zéro de Conduite* (a disaster with bourgeois audiences), Jean Renoir's *The Rules of the Game* (hooting and whistling), Orson Welles's *Citizen Kane,* Max Ophul's *Lola Montès* (a debacle at the Marignan and Francais theatres in Paris on December 23, 1955), and Michelangelo Antonioni's *L'Avventura* (the tumultuous scandal of the 1960 Cannes Film Festival). The house theoreticians of the American avant-garde may argue that many of the aforementioned narrative films contained avant-garde elements. Indeed, Annette Michelson and others have suggested that there is some sort of link, however remotely dialectical, between Sergei Eisenstein and Stan Brakhage. By looking at film history through the wrong end of the telescope, the avant-gardists reduce the great bulk of film history to a sketchy overture for the presumed grand operas of Michael Snow (interminable except for *Wavelength* with its peculiar qualifications as spatial narrative) and Hollis Frampton (invariably insufferable, which constitutes a stylistic signature of sorts).

I realize, however, that it is hardly sufficient for me to declare that most American avant-garde films bore me to tears, and that most of the theoretical writing on these films strikes me as the rankest of rationalizations. My own addiction to narrative is too well known for me to pose as a disinterested observer of the nonnarrative scene. That is why I attended the first two programs: To see if there was any sizable bloc of moviegoers with whom I was out of step. The first program attracted a capacity audience. (Cecile Starr's piece on Maya Deren in the Sunday *Times* may have spurred attendance.) The audience was predominantly young, and I recognized many of my film students. After *Meshes of the Afternoon* (1943) by Maya Deren and her husband Alexander Hammid there was reasonably substantial applause. I was completely unimpressed by this clumsy rehash of Luis Bunuel's *Un Chien Andalou* and Jean Cocteau's *Blood of a Poet,* the estimable precursors of the American "trance" film. Among Deren's celebrated avant-garde strategies are the photographing of the feet of the character she plays, and then of the character's shadow. The use-

lessness of these oblique gestures establishes the avant-garde credentials of the film from the outset so that when we later see a door key
turn into a kitchen knife (or is it a kitchen knife into a door key?), we
do not dare suggest that the artist has been dipping into Penguin
Freud. The surrealistic device of placing an enclosing mirror where a
head is supposed to be works well on the first go-round, but even this
image fails to redeem the strained posturing of the entranced performers. One suddenly appreciates the conviction a Conrad Veidt
can bring to these kinds of Caligarics, for sleepwalking is not that
simple an acting exercise. You may recall that the late James Agee
panned the acting of the late Maya Deren in *Meshes of the Afternoon* even as he praised her artistic ambitions. What you may not
recall is that in the same column Agee gave short shrift to three Hollywood movies (*Three Strangers, Scarlet Street,* and *The Road to Uto-
pia*), any one of which shows more creative flair than is to be found
in the great mass of avant-garde films. Still, it must be recognized that
the avant-garde films have promoted themselves from the beginning
as an antithesis to Hollywood movies. That most avant-garde activity
originated in New York and San Francisco reflects the dialectical relationship of these two cities to Los Angeles. I have always disagreed
with the denigration of Hollywood movies, but back in 1943, when
foreign film distribution had been almost completely curtailed by the
war, and Hollywood censorship and sentimentality were running
rampant, there was an understandable hunger in New York for an
artistic alternative. By 1946, however, Italian Neorealism and British
hyperclassicism had come to the rescue of American art-house audiences, which is to say that people who did not like movies very much
were now able to find films from abroad. Hence, the natural audience
for the American avant-garde cinema was diverted to the foreign art
film in the forties and fifties, and then to the imitation-foreign Hollywood art film in the sixties and the seventies. When Amos Vogel
organized a symposium on Poetry and the Film at Cinema 16 on
October 28, 1953, with Maya Deren, Arthur Miller, Dylan Thomas,
Parker Tyler, and Willard Maas as chairman, it was significant that
both Miller and Thomas articulated an anti-avant-garde position on
film to the noisy approval of much of the audience. Certainly neither
Miller nor Thomas could have been classified as Hollywood junkies,
but they still failed to respond to Maya Deren's vision of a poetic
cinema.

Geography of the Body (1943) by Willard Maas seems more coy than derisive in 1976. It is hard to remember that back in 1953 this exercise in aestheticism was capable of arousing lascivious anticipation among the patrons of Cinema 16. Hollywood censorship was still in the saddle; *La Ronde* had been banned in New York. Nowadays *The Outlaw* gets a G rating.

In the auditorium there is perfunctory applause for *Geography of the Body*. Then, an unexpected scandal. *Early Abstractions* (1939-1957) by Harry Smith, a poor man's Norman McLaren, is projected to the blatant accompaniment of old Beatles songs, beginning with "I Want to Hold Your Hand." Growing murmurs in the audience of a ridiculous rip-off. It is impossible to concentrate on the images with the sound of the Beatles flooding the hall with random memories of other times and other places. There is not even any rudimentary synchronization between sound and image. Songs go on through reel changes, and images go on through record changes. A shambles. Ironic applause.

Fireworks by Kenneth Anger (1947) still jolts audiences with its explosively homosexual imagery. Anger was not content merely to come out of the closet; he blew up the closet with phallic firecrackers. Despite his formal deficiencies as a filmmaker, Anger displays an unusual amount of wit, humor, audacity, and redeeming vulgarity for an avant-garde filmmaker. Perhaps his back-door relationship with Hollywood saved him from the fashionable obscurantism of his colleagues. Some of Anger's simulated S&M bloodletting from his nostrils launches the first sizable wave of walkouts from the auditorium.

By contrast, Maya Deren's *A Study in Choreography for Camera* (1945) is well received for packing several "strategies" into four minutes of running time. I continue to find that her work suffers from the earnestness of being important. *Mother's Day* (1948) by James Broughton introduces the audience to the wizened whimsicality of the San Francisco school. There are some titters at first as the audience assumes that a satiric strategy is at work on the monstrousness of the American family, but as the incessant infantilism of grown-up people drags on and on, the squashed lyricism of the project seems more and more self-indulgent. It is possible that Broughton was slightly ahead of his time with his celebration of the Bitch-Mother and the Castrated Sons, but the theatre of Williams and Albee and their many imitators is now widely recognized as the chosen medium for this bit of American folklore. Still, *Mother's Day* seemed overlong at 23 minutes. My reading of the audience at the end of the evening may have projected my own weariness and boredom, but I was certainly not swept out of the auditorium by a wave of exultation. Incidentally, I have never agreed with Pauline Kael's assessment of the audience at the first New York screening of *Last Tango in Paris.* I was there that night, and I was not engulfed by a *Le Sacre du Printemps* atmosphere. There were a few walkouts and some muttering over Marlon Brando's simulated use of the high-price spread on Maria Schneider. Afterward we did not stand around in stunned silence, as Kael has suggested. Instead, we hung around to sip some free Sangria. On the whole, New York audiences are disappointingly polite and openminded when it comes to the staging of outrages. Over the years, they have been much harder on sweetness and sentimentality than on sourness and sarcasm. The worst reactions I can remember off-hand were aroused by Jacques Demy's *The Umbrellas of Cherbourg* and Agnes Varda's *Le Bonheur.* Hence, the average avant-garde film is not particularly courageous when it chooses to be sour and cynical.

The next evening I left a very promising party to continue my research. During *The Lead Shoes* (1949) by Sidney Peterson, I noticed a fading billboard of *Mighty Joe Young* with Ben Johnson prominently featured. Terry Moore was in the news lately in connection with the Howard Hughes situation, and I had completely forgotten that Ben Johnson was in the movie. It took me three or four minutes to get back on the track of Peterson's clubfooted trance film with its characteristically sordid street atmosphere. In a tone befitting a fate worse than death, the catalog provided the following cryptic information: "*The Lead Shoes* (1949) was Sidney Peterson's last independent effort before he entered the world of commercial filmmaking." By the peculiar standards of the avant-gardists any contact with the marketplace is fatal to the artist. This was certainly not true of Beethoven or Berlioz or Gertrude Stein or Pablo Picasso. Mozart died a pauper, but Brahms did not. Melville and James and Kafka did not sell as they should have, but Shakespeare and Ibsen and Shaw did. One cannot generalize in such a sweeping fashion about the art for the coterie as opposed to the art for the crowd. Also, the elitist cannot be ironic about popular art without being compelled to acknowledge that popular art can be ironic about itself.

It is interesting to recall that Jonas Mekas's original conception of the Independent Film back in the late fifties and early sixties was much broader than the current conception of the Avant-Garde Film. The Film Culture Award for 1959 went to John Cassavetes's *Shadows,* in 1960 to Robert Frank and Alfred Leslie's *Pull My Daisy* with a stunning cast headed by Allen Ginsberg and Delphine Seyrig, in 1961 to Ricky Leacock, Don Pennebaker, Robert Drew, and Al Maysles for *Primary.* None of these people would qualify as avant-gardists today in the very closed—shall we say hermetic—world of P. Adams Sitney. Since the high point of Mekas's crusades in the sixties was attained with Jack Smith's *Flaming Creatures,* the locus of the avant-garde has gradually shifted from bohemia to academe. Similarly, the dominant mode of expression in avant-garde cinema has gradually shifted from the vaguely lyrical to the vaguely pedagogical. While preaching liberation from the commercial conventions of the narrative film, the new avant-gardists are imposing rigid conventions of their own. Self-consciousness has been subordinated to medium-consciousness, and souls to sprockets.

One would think that *Bells of Atlantis* (1952) by Ian Hugo, with Anais Nin reading and performing her own prose poem "The House of Incest," would manage to evoke some mood in its 10-minute running time, particularly with Len Lye as color consultant, and with an electronic synthesizer score by Louis and Bebe Barron. The total effect for me was muddled, garbled, murky, indecisive, and indistinct.

Back in 1955 Jonas Mekas wrote of a conspiracy of homosexuality in "The Experimental Film in America," a scathing survey he later recanted. "If the man, the most frequent protagonist of America film poems, is presented as an unreal, frustrated dreamer, the woman here is usually robbed of both her true spirituality and her unashamed carnality. She is a white-dressed, unearthly, elusive symbol flowing dreamily along seashore (or sea-bottom), through bushes and upon hills (Deren, Harrington, Markopoulos, Broughton, Hugo, and so forth)."

Who would have thought that 20 years later the homosexual fantasies of the early avant-gardists would seem more accessible to audiences than would the hermetic formalism of the new avant-gardists? It is not that I wish to shed crocodile tears for the old avant-garde, but simply that I wish to report that a palace coup has taken place, and that a new set of slogans has been posted on the wall. Stan

Vanderbeek (*Science Friction*) has squeezed into the program, but just barely. George and Mike Kuchar, Warren Sonbert, Ron Rice, Carmen D'Avino, Ed Emshwiller, George Levine, David Rimmer, and Bob Downey have been excluded from the museum program and from most current avant-garde writings. The downfalls of the Kuchars and Downey, particularly, suggest that though referential cinema may be in, self-mockery is out.

In this context, Shirley Clarke's presence in the program with *Bridges-Go-Round* (1958) seems peculiar. Not only has Clarke leaped into the commercial mainstream, at least by the side-creek standards of the avant-garde; she also displays for urban edifices an enthusiasm and optimism completely at variance with the traditional weltschmertz of the avant-garde. By contrast, Stan Brakhage reduces the poignant spectacle of a doomed subway el to a very confidential aesthetic exercise. Within the four-minute running time of the film, his romantic idealization of his own "vision" manages to be intrusive. Bruce Conner's *A Movie* (1958) is often paraded as one of the comic classics of the avant-garde. One dreads to think what the comic duds must be like. Conner's irony becomes almost indescribably laborious after only 12 minutes. It strikes me that it is very difficult to be funny when you are culturally conditioned to despise your audience and most of the history of your medium. Robert Breer's *Recreation* (1956) with narration by Noel Burch is an elegant two-minute montage-collage on the quantification of an artist's mementos and materials. By its very nature, the extremely short film tends to flow backward from the screen to the canvas, from kinesis to stasis. One would think that the fine arts people would take over the job of criticism here from the film people. No such luck. When Vincent Canby asked Hilton Kramer a year or so ago if he (Kramer) wished to cover some of the more abstract film programs around town, Kramer replied succinctly: "Our philosophy is if it moves, it isn't for us."

In their seamless prose the avant-garde theoreticians lean very heavily on modernist movements in painting, sculpture, music, theatre, and literature. Yet I have found little evidence of reciprocal support for the avant-garde in film from painters, sculptors, composers, and writers of even the most modernist persuasion. There is no moral to be drawn from this situation. It is simply a fact of life. My own view is that the American avant-garde cinema has too often mimicked the radical styles of the older arts to no genuinely filmic purpose. My immediate concern, however, is with the efforts of the avant-garde theoreticians to take over the domain of film studies by distorting the teaching of film history. It is silly to make a small group of wordy pedagogues the heirs of a vital, messy, open-air, full-of-life filmmaking tradition. After all, Eisenstein wrote a very appreciative essay on John Ford's *Young Mr. Lincoln.* I have yet to read an Eisenstein essay on Maya Deren or Stan Brakhage.

Still, these are just my opinions. ("But that's just your opinion," a lady complained at one of Saul Bellow's lectures. "What do you want—my hair clippings?" Bellow replied.) The audience jury at the Museum of Modern Art on Wednesday, May 5, 1976, was still out when Stan Brakhage's 40-minute-long *Anticipation of the Night* (1958) came on as the last film on that night's program. I barely remembered the film from 1958 when the late Eugene Archer had reviewed it in the *New York Times* under the heading "Gleanings from the Cutting Room Floor." The film had bored me then. Would it bore me now? More important, would it bore the audience? I did not have too long to wait. The audience began streaming out about halfway through the film, and fully a third were gone before it ended. I sat through it all even though Brakhage's spastic camera movements tend to make me carsick. His contempt for cinematic forms in the name of a delirious subjectivity makes his films an affront to my sensibility. I have never questioned his sincerity and dedication, but I happen to believe that filmmaking involves obligations to the audience as well as privileges for the filmmaker. With Brakhage, particularly, expression has engulfed communication. As the unreconstructed Jonas Mekas said back in 1955:

> The work of Markopoulos is a particularly good example of this failure, though it can be clearly seen in Brakhage's films, whose work seems to be the best expression of all the virtues and sins of the American film poem today. The film poets, not unlike most of our contemporary writers, are so fascinated by their personal worlds that they do not feel a need to communicate nor give to their characters or stories a larger, more human scope.

I realize that my own past words can be used against me in much the same manner. Nonetheless, I am struck by the aptness of Mekas's observations during the period when he was more ecumenical and less evangelical. If I have dwelled on this subject at some length, it is because I felt that there has been a conspiracy of silence on the avant-garde for too long. My colleagues on the *Times* and the *Post* and the *News* cover individual programs of avant-garde films. Pauline Kael has made references on occasion to Bruce Baille and Jordan Belson, more, I suspect, out of loyalty to the San Francisco school than out of any deep devotion to the experimental scene. But there has been no systematic confrontation of the exaggerated claims for the avant-garde made by Jonas Mekas, Annette Michelson, and P. Adams Sitney. If they are right, the rest of us are not earning our keep as film critics and cultural commentators. My own experience tells me that Mekas, Michelson, and Sitney are wrong. The only trouble is that the narrative film is too rich and varied to be encompassed in the seamless prose of a closed system comparable to that of the avant-garde. There is no ontological reason for the continuing preeminence of the narrative film. It just growed and growed so that today it has attracted the serious attention of some of the best minds throughout the world. At best, the avant-garde cinema is an eccentric reaction to the narrative cinema. To argue that it is more is to ignore the evidence of the perennial walkouts.

—May 1976

Index